The Heart of Psychotherapy

The Heart of Psychotherapy

*A Journey into the Mind and
Office of the
Therapist
at Work*

George Weinberg

ST. MARTIN'S PRESS/NEW YORK

Library of Congress Cataloging in Publication Data

Weinberg, George H.
  The heart of psychotherapy.

  1. Psychotherapy. 2. Psychotherapists—Psychology.
3. Psychotherapist and patient. I. Title. [DNLM:
1. Psychotherapy. 2. Physician-patient relations.
3. Professional practice. WM 21 W423h]
RC480.5.W349 1984   616.89'14   83-26946
ISBN 0-312-36601-9

Thou know'st no less but all; I have unclasped
To thee the book even of my secret soul.

—Shakespeare

Contents

Acknowledgments

I am very thankful to a number of people who contributed in different ways to this book: Brian DeFiore, my editor at St. Martin's, whose comments at every stage were invaluable; Tom McCormack, who helped conceptualize the book and its shape; Peter Shaw, who contributed style suggestions. In addition, a number of psychotherapists read the text and made suggestions: David Balderston, Jean Balderston (who also suggested the title), Diane Connors, Joan Ormont, Louis Ormont, Helen McDermott, Cathy Roskam, Phil Roskam, Hank Schenker, C. A. Tripp, Lilli Vincenz, and Leslie Wile.

PART ONE

Introduction

1

The Therapist's Personality

The voice of a middle-aged woman came over the phone. She said to the therapist, "I've heard such good things about you. I'd like to schedule an appointment." A few more words of praise and after they agreed on a time, he told her his office address.

"What street is that?"

"Fifty-seventh."

"Which subway do I take to get there?"

"The Eighth Avenue stops nearby."

"Which train, do you know?"

Perhaps feeling mild annoyance, he answered, "The A train, I think." He then returned to the patient sitting across from him. He quickly forgot whatever disturbance he might have felt, and was glad to have another addition to his case load.

This therapist has all the right diplomas—an MD degree and psychiatric boards. Still, his practice is faltering, and he doesn't know why. Patients stop treatment with him, for one stated reason or another. Often the alibi is that they can't afford him, their insurance doesn't cover enough. Seldom has there been an outright complaint; he's so prestigious and remote that complaints would seem out of place. He's polite and so are his patients, but he recognizes that something is wrong. Beginners, people who have lesser degrees, and less experience, are doing better. Not just financially—they have a clientele of patients recommending others, a following.

In my office, I ask him about the woman. "What is she like?"

He glances down at his case folder. He has made elaborate notes, as physicians are taught to do so they won't overlook a crucial bit of information. "Has severe headaches," he begins. "She's the third child of four. Her father came here from Poland when he was eleven and owns a dress shop. She works in an accounting office. Was married for two years, and her second husband left her a few months ago. They have a thirteen-year-old child who lives with her. She's depressed, feels that she's not getting what she deserves at the office."

Ten more minutes of facts about her revealed less to me than did the dialogue over the phone, which he was able to recall only after I continually pressed him for details of the way they interacted.

"How did you feel about that phone call?" I asked him.

At first, he couldn't remember having reacted at all; then he recalled a moment of pique at her for asking so many unnecessary questions. He had shrugged off that reaction. He didn't like making value judgments, and it seemed premature to form an opinion about her. Whatever annoyance he felt seemed too unimportant to bother mentioning.

From this incident and how it was handled, we learn about both the patient and the therapist. It would not be wrong to speculate that the woman's obliviousness to boundaries, as shown in that phone call, might have much to do with why her life was going badly. And the therapist's decision not to react, to subdue the feelings he had at the time and forget them, had much to do with why his practice was going badly.

What personal attributes does a therapist need? There are many, and, above all, at the very top of the list and the foundation of his talent is the ability to feel, a readiness to react.

Therapists have often been ridiculed for making too much out of small events, but doing psychotherapy requires seeing essences in particulars and knowing how to use them. This therapist might have spent an hour on demographics without discovering nearly so much about the woman as he would have by choosing three or four particulars and recognizing a trend. His ignoring his own reaction amounted to throwing away precious data. It is far preferable to work with living subject matter, the stuff that happens with the therapist in the session, than with material that the patient merely reports.

In order to utilize moments, to identify and understand them, the therapist needs the ability to feel them. To gloss over such moments, to say, for instance, "Well, this is just a woman who is anxious, and who really can't upset me," is to discard the most vital stuff of which therapy is made. No matter how much craft a therapist learns, he is lost if he suppresses his power to feel ruffled, distressed, helpless, or to feel exhilarated, or even loved by a patient. The ability to react internally, and at the same time to control outward behavior, is a requisite for the therapist; the good therapist has reason to be proud of his ability to feel and to know what he's feeling.

Some people, and this includes certain therapists although not all by any means, see habitually into the grain of human exchanges. They feel it when a bank teller looks at them with ruthless impersonality while he hands them the change. They seem to experience every high and low. Life is an adventure for them, and every moment counts. When someone like this becomes a therapist, the sessions are like big dates in which everything said or done is important.

Others approach life as technicians, and as therapists that's the way they approach their patients. They seem concentrated on the bottom line, the nature of the problem and what must be done to cure the patient, as if any of this were possible without experiencing the patient continually. Included among these therapists are some who don't really sense the presence of other people. They have never trusted their own reactions, if they had them. It has always seemed to them that other people, who responded readily to personal detail, were making "snap judgments." They couldn't stand it when they were asked to remember how a thing was said. In high school, a sister would ask, "Did John say he would call me because you told him to, or did he really mean it?" How should they know? The very question infuriated them.

The therapist who can't recall any reactions to a patient may have had real feelings at the time. He extinguished his responses, or can't remember them because they seemed wrong. For instance, he disliked the patient and is afraid to say so. Supposedly he went into the field because he loves people; here a troubled soul has come to him for help, and he finds he can't stand the patient. It seems too unfair to contemplate, and he doesn't want to admit it, even to himself.

In other cases, the therapist feels incompetent, helpless with the patient. It's important to be aware of having that reaction, and to discern if perhaps the patient has induced this feeling: he makes many people feel futile. It takes courage to recognize and acknowledge to oneself this feeling of helplessness. To the person new in the field or unsure of himself, a reaction like this comes dangerously close to feelings of doubt he often has about whether he belongs in the field at all.

Therapists who are able to react, who have the courage to feel and identify what they are feeling, are almost invariably able to remember the dialogue of their sessions. In this field, passion is the key to memory. Those who react seem vital. True, they encounter difficulties, and they even, at the start of their careers, look more amateur than the deadheads, whose pasty nature may pass as professionalism. Of course, they must learn not to burden patients indiscriminately with their personal reactions. But the ability to react is a first-order requisite, and those who possess it become the more successful therapists by far. Even at the start, although they may bumble and say things they shouldn't, they communicate that life is important.

If you love gossip, you have the chance for greatness as a therapist; if you've always hated it, preferring to concentrate on "bigger things," you will probably be bored in this profession. Not that gossip is desirable; doubtless it does great harm in many cases, and discreetness in life is preferable. But the curiosity about the details of people's lives, implicit in gossip, correlates highly with just what the successful therapist needs.

What else does a therapist need? He must have intelligence. He must have courage—the strength to do what seems right without compromising in order to stay in the patient's good graces. These would be desirables for any parent. One needs the ability to care about another person enough to pursue the beneficial course even if that person is initially displeased. And like a successful parent, the therapist needs flexibility, the ability to switch from one approach to another, and the ability to romanticize another person's life. To see the patient's life as a journey, to appreciate both the shoals and the magic of it, its specialness, is an ideal.

One nominal leader in the field falls asleep repeatedly in his sessions; he is dogmatic, never apologizes. Three or four of his patients have told me about his naps, blaming themselves for being unworthy of this great man. Our patients won't always recognize our faults as such, but will ruminate about their causes, blaming themselves sometimes, which means that we are doubly on our honor, the way parents are. Since there is no higher authority in the room, the harm we do—like much of the good —may never be explicitly cited.

The therapist must have basic humaneness. This means he

must be able to admit errors, tolerate frustration, refuse to judge a patient by appearance, age, or social class. A surprising number of therapists become excited when they work with attractive young people, and become almost immobilized if a celebrity chances into their office. They can't wait to tell colleagues that they are treating a movie actor or some other prestigious person. They also are harmed by the inability to see how a materially successful life can be improved. Many suffer plain and simple envy. And they overdo their emphasis on material success when they work with people who have yet to achieve very much. These therapists do less motivated work with older people and with the handicapped and underprivileged. The good therapist must be aware of the danger of obsession with material things—namely, that one's own sense of worth is not intrinsic but is forever subject to being withdrawn from him. We prefer to think that our therapist would still like himself even after a stock-market crash.

Therapists as a group tend to intellectualize too much; they find it hard to acknowledge that much of life is primitive, that love may burst forth in unexpected places, as between homosexuals or people very different in age; they spend years trying to repair relationships where love does not exist, where it never existed, as if fixing up lines of communication, interpreting one person to another can result in anything comparable to the magic that simply appears at times. They try to interpret that magic, whether it is sexuality or sensuality, as if they were frightened of it. Tens of thousands of people have been prevailed on by therapists to try to force relationships to work, only to quit in the end, and thereafter they find the elixir of love's excitement with another person that never appeared even at best in the first relationship. True, there are people who find thrills only in novelty, but therapists must learn to feel the big occasions in people's lives, and to heighten their patients' ability to see them and to rejoice in them. There are irreducibles in life, or if not, they are near irreducibles, and where they are pleasurable, it makes more sense to seize them than to spend decades looking for them where they are not.

Many therapists have never enjoyed the effortless sense of being loved, of belonging; they have not been praised or enjoyed as much when they were children as at least certain of their patients were. One reason some people become therapists is to work out their own problems, to pursue the deep introspective search that begins in childhood, the huge questions about oneself and one's relations with others, the attempt to create for oneself what was not there as a birthright—these are valid reasons for a person to develop a love of psychology. And the desire to help others, often as a way of belonging, of being sure that others will return to them, of reaping appreciation, all have been motives that led people to become marvelous in this field. One difficulty is that they leave the person impaired where *taking* is concerned. It remains hard for the therapist to bask in praise, to enjoy what is given to him without question, to become an effortless recipient of love—in short, to relax when all is well. Tensely, the therapist questions why the patient praises him, thanks him, or gives him a Christmas present, and may join the patient if he expresses skepticism about what someone else has given to the patient. This therapist remains one, as Tennyson put it, "always roaming with a hungry heart"; it seems almost in the nature of his calling. The dangerous consequence is a failure to realize that some things are simply there, and an inclination to keep looking long after they are found.

The ideal therapist, like the ideal parent, should have a sense of extended family. Not just his relatives, but also his friends and his patients are central figures, the worthy. The waiter who brings food for his child is a central figure too. He teaches his child not to mistreat that waiter, not to consider him an inferior creature. Strangers, underprivileged people, passersby, have a respectable status in his life.

Without this sense of extended family, therapists have in subtle ways downgraded their patients. They have been too free in using diagnostic labels, for instance, thinking about their patient as an "alcoholic," or an "addict," or more recently, as "borderline." If someone told them that their mate or their child was an addict or borderline, they would consider it a profound insult. They would find not just the label hard to accept, but the fact that someone they love and into whom they poured so much effort and hope could be summed up by a single word that evokes pity or even contempt. They would feel the callousness of the label that they themselves applied as a matter of course to others. Those therapists with a sense of extended family have always been slower to use labels than others, especially since most diagnostic categories have a very dubious relationship to actual methods of treatment.

Sympathy is an obvious requirement. The therapist needs the ability to sympathize with people without concluding that they are merely victims of mistreatment. Our patients play an active role in creating—or at least, sustaining—their own problems. To exempt them entirely from any sense that they are contributing to their difficulties would be to betray them. The therapist needs the kind of sympathy that does not require perceiving his patients as helpless. Sympathy toward an utter victim is easy; to feel sympathetic toward a person who is acting in ways that harm him takes much more deliberation.

The last trait I want to mention I'd call "insistent egalitarianism." The therapist should always remain aware of the natural ascendancy that the therapeutic relationship offers him. The very nature of the relationship is that of a success talking to a failure. Imagine the contrast when the therapist, socially established and supposedly without problems, talks to a patient about the latter's sexual difficulties or inability to get a job or know what he wants out of life. Humaneness requires taking steps not to let this inherent imbalance undermine the patient.

I think most really good therapists loathe the notion of being a guru, or having disciples. The therapist should avoid strutting or name-dropping, or anything that smacks of contrast between his life and that of the patient. If comparisons obtrude themselves, he does not act diffident or hide them; it's merely that he is aware of the compromised position of the person coming to him for help. He is quick to admire the real strengths of his patients, to underscore them, bring them to the person's attention, and if the patient tends to disparage his own gifts, the therapist addresses himself to that tendency. Too much of psychotherapy in its first hundred years has stressed the problems that patients have, and diagnosis has not focused enough on people's strengths and potential.

These humane attitudes, and the openness the therapist conveys, are at the very core of the service he renders. The quality of his interaction with the patient is determined by these things, and that interaction is of paramount importance in therapy.

Are these essential attributes of the good therapist all natural gifts, or can they be acquired? Some of them are, to an extent, acquired—sympathy, a sense of extended family, egalitarianism. Others come with birth. Observers of newborn infants note differences in the very first few days of life. One infant is brighter, more social, cheerful, energetic than the next. Mothers observing differences among their own grown-up children often add with astonishment that at least some of these differences were hinted at during the first few weeks of life. It seems that there are talents, or at least preferences, for interacting with people, which if not hereditary are in evidence in very early childhood. Talents like these would naturally tend to go unobserved, especially if the parent did not share them. Exceptional sensitivity in a child might even seem like a form of neurosis.

Think for a moment about fields in which talents are commonly observed, where we expect prodigies. Three somewhat related disciplines stand out: mathematics, music, and chess. The mathematicians Gauss and Pascal, the composers Mozart and Rossini, were marvels before the age of ten, and so were many chess players, like Samuel Reschevsky. Genius can manifest itself to the world at an early age in those disciplines. Mozart did not need to hear a thousand symphonies to compose one. And there is such a clear-cut ladder of accomplishment in mathematics that when a prodigy skips five rungs, he is easily recognized. In chess, the evidence of solving problems and winning games is indisputable.

Language skills are harder to demonstrate, since, no matter how great the skill, it takes time to learn the words that serve as tools—in this regard language suggests the problem of the psychologist prodigy. Imagine a child of six or seven with a prodigious genius in psychology. He would lack both the language and the authority to convince anyone of this. I believe that tiny tots differ, for instance, in sensing when an adult is angry or insincere, or when the adult is boasting or using them for self-enhancement. The child may refuse to reply to a compliment, sensing that it is false or manipulative, and his mother, not aware of this herself, insists that he "behave." There are children who know while in their mother's arms that she would prefer to be elsewhere.

The implication is exciting. There are people with extraordinary gifts, who would make exceptional therapists, but who do not themselves recognize that they have these talents. Such gifts must be unblocked and appreciated for them to flourish. With some of the therapists I've trained, we have actually discovered together that they had unrealized gifts to pursue their chosen profession. For instance, one very sensitive woman could recall making very delicate readings of the psychological states of adults when she was a young child, most of which were borne out. Since these inferences were to the effect that she was unwanted by her mother, she preferred to dismiss them. But they continued to gnaw at her. Within a few years of her release from the need to suppress the truth, she became an immensely effective therapist and now has a large following. Growing up, she was incapable of dulling herself to reality, and her reward is that she is able to enjoy life as it is. She brings her entire personality to her work; and though the demands seem great, she has the attributes to meet them.

Psychotherapy demands a great deal from the practitioner. But in these very demands lie the gratifications that it can offer to those who do it well.

2

How People Change

How does the psychotherapist, drawing on these qualities, help people? That is to be the subject matter of this book. However, to set the stage, is it useful to sketch the evolution of thinking about psychotherapy over the last century.

We have gone through three phases of understanding of how therapy works, each based on a formulation about the origin of personality. In the earliest view, the patient is seen as essentially a victim of forces and as passive while in treatment. Each successive revision has attributed more to the patient's own choices both as forming his personality and as accomplishing personality change while in treatment.

Let's go back to the first stage. At around the turn of the century, Freud, in his theory of psychoanalysis, maintained that personality congeals in early childhood. Though some of his psychoanalytic colleagues disagreed with him on which events were crucial to personality formation—for instance, which were traumatic to the young child—psychoanalysts were unanimous in asserting that this hardening of the psyche does occur. A set of attitudes, feelings and impulses, which were mostly unconscious, become frozen in the personality. Over a lifetime, these unconscious forces continue to dictate the person's behavior. Thus psychoanalysis holds that what we do is merely symptomatic of who we are underneath.

And just as psychoanalysis held that the patient was passive in childhood when his personality formed, it sees him as passive in treatment. Psychoanalytic treatment conceives of the therapist as responsible for the cure. The psychoanalyst delves into the patient's psyche and alters it. More than once Freud likened the psychoanalyst to a surgeon and the patient to someone lying on an operating table. The patient lying on a couch reflected this passivity.

For a patient to try to change his underlying nature by altering, say, his everyday actions, would be as pointless as trying to alter the time of day by pushing around the hands of a clock.

But psychoanalysts did not have the power that Freud thought they held, and toward the end of his life he became extremely pessimistic about what his method could accomplish. He and his colleagues were not helping patients nearly as effectively as they had hoped. Many of his contemporaries, even psychoanalysts, shared his concern. They had taken on too much of the burden and had been viewing the patient as too passive.

The second development of psychotherapy was introduced by psychoanalysts themselves, who appreciated that Freud's view was too limited. Chief among them were Karen Horney, Harry Stack Sullivan, and Erich Fromm. Their ideas began taking hold in the late nineteen forties and have continued to influence the practice of psychotherapy. They began to realize that what the patient does—his everyday actions—may be more than symptomatic of his condition. They maintained that the patient's *own actions,* when a child and afterwards, influence the formation of his personality. They claimed further that the patient's everyday choices do affect his characteristic feelings and attitudes.

In particular, the *interpersonal* school of therapists argued that the way the patient treats others affects him indirectly. The patient, for instance, endears himself to others or antagonizes them. He can't help but react to their appraisals of him—he draws sustenance and self-esteem from their acceptance of him or is alienated by their disaffection. This school argued that the patient is more than a passive being, in the sense that his actions affect others whose reactions influence his personality development at every stage. His everyday actions are more than symptomatic—they affect his own self-image, though in only an indirect way.

For example, Karen Horney devised the term "vicious cycle" to describe how a patient, insecure in childhood, may worsen his own condition, and perpetuate it. At each stage of his life, he fails to make new relationships that could improve his confidence. Instead, by behavior already learned, such as bragging, distrust and stinginess, he antagonizes potential friends. They reject him. He feels the impact of their response; it further damages his self-esteem, leading him to do more of the same, and so forth. The vicious cycle between him and others sustains his already poor self-regard and may exacerbate his condition.

The interpersonal school sought to make the analytic sessions themselves beneficial encounters for the patient. (This, incidentally, entailed making certain practical changes, such as having a brighter office, asking the patient to sit up rather than lie down and the therapist's interacting with him more vigorously.) The aim was to show the patient approval, trust and warmth, despite, say, a cold or suspicious nature on his part. It was hoped that the patient would absorb the approval; he would see that his distrust was misplaced, and it would melt somewhat. Then the patient, by acting differently with other people would elicit better reactions from them, which would lift him still further. Thus a beneficial process could be set in motion.

Sometimes the method seemed to work; many times it didn't, and there remained the need to study why not. But the once-maverick belief that a patient's own acts play a part in his condition had taken hold.

A third generation of therapists is only now coming of age. They utilize many of the insights of their predecessors but see the role of the patient's behavior as far greater than even the interpersonal school realized. By everyday acts, the patient affects his own personality—poisons his own outlook or can cure it—and his own behavior affects him whether or not others respond to it, or even become aware of what he has done.

Like the earlier two schools, this third generation—which we may call *action therapy*—has its own belief about how personality forms and how therapy cures people. While acknowledging that people do tend to be consistent, as Freud asserted, its adherents deny that the individual ever actually loses the power to change himself. They disbelieve that character structure hardens in childhood or ever, and maintain that when it seems this way it is because people are rebuilding their own personality every day of their lives. Therapy must help the person see how he is renewing his own basic view of himself and life, and discover by which new choices he can create a whole new view—and in this sense, cure himself.

Action therapy is just emerging from its adolescence. Practitioners are coming to appreciate that patients profoundly affect their own sense of self by small decisions as well as big ones. Take the simplest kind of example: Keeping a resolution strengthens a person, and not simply because others come to regard him as worthy and pass along that appraisal. Or another: Distrustful acts heighten distrust and fear, and may go on renewing an early-formed pattern, even if no one else knows what the patient has done. The implications are enormous. Virtually all we have learned about psychotherapy and about personality change becomes instantly more useful to us as we understand the power that the patient himself possesses. The aim of therapy is to help the patient cure himself.

The guiding principle of action therapy is this: Every choice, small or large, reinforces the underlying feelings, attitudes and beliefs, the view of life that motivated the choice. Thus people restore their outlook—such as overdependence on their parents, fear of authorities, paranoia—by acting in ways they may have begun when they were young. Unknowingly, they keep themselves the same. This principle may seem overly simple as stated. But as will be seen, it arises in many subtle and complex forms; here I am constrained to express the principle in its briefest form. I have presented it, and discussed its implications in other books *(The Action Approach, Self Creation,* and *The Pliant Animal).*

Though few practitioners as yet have the principle clearly in mind when they work, in my experience those who help their patients most are the ones who utilize this principle. They sense that their patients must cure themselves, and their utilization of this principle organizes their whole therapeutic effort. The principle thus operates like the vanishing point of a drawing. Even when not explicit, it governs virtually every line and lends perspective to the drawing as a whole.

The purpose of therapy is to help the patient change traits. The complaint may be specific. "I have trouble earning a living," or "I can't decide whether to get married." But the purpose of therapy is never to enable the patient to make a particular decision. It's aim is always larger. In the process of developing new traits, the patient, ideally, will become able to satisfy his particular want—for instance, to make the decision. But the aim is always to change personality traits.

Every personality trait consists of three parts: the person's perspective on the world, his emotions, and behavior. Sometimes we customarily identify a difficulty the patient presents with his way of perceiving—for example, this is true with cynicism, narcissism, or "injustice collecting." In other cases, the "handle" is the emotional component—depression, "free-floating anxiety," jealousy. And sometimes it's the action component—as with the impulse disorder, compulsions, and indecisiveness. But this is always a matter of identification. In every trait the three components—perception, feeling, and action—exist together. And it is never possible for one of these components to change without the others changing too. For example, as the paranoid overcomes his chronic distrust, he feels different; he sees other people differently, and he acts differently.

We may think of the three stages of psychotherapy in the following way. Originally, psychoanalysis conceived of the perceptual and emotional part of the trait as congealed. This part of the trait possessed the person—it dictated the person's actions, which were seen as merely symptomatic. The psychoanalyst would have to alter the perceptual-emotional basis in order to free the patient to act differently. Then came some appreciation that the patient's actions could affect the perceptual-emotional part of the trait—albeit indirectly. And now we are coming to realize that, though the patient's actions may seem dictated by his feelings and perceptions, indeed his actions determine the rest of the trait.

The therapist must help the patient not only understand his feelings and perceptions, but appreciate how he is renewing them. Little by little, with the proper insights, the patient, by new choices, alters his own traits.

In the course of therapy, we help the person see the generality of his problem. Always we look for recurrent tendencies. For the person to see the trait in action in many places is to gain real comprehension of it. As patients see, "This problem is more pervasive than I thought," they are occasionally disheartened somewhat. But usually they sensed that something was more generally wrong, which is finally coming to light. And to the extent that the problem was broader than they thought, the gain is greater when it is resolved. The patient who began by lamenting that money troubles cost him several friends, ends by resolving his tendency to withhold, and feels closer to people, more relaxed with them, even where money was at no time an issue.

In training therapists, I always underscore the question, "Where else?" I ask it of them when they describe some practice or point of view held by the patient. The patient reports being unable to choose between two prospective mates. The inexperienced therapist may be content to weigh the pros and cons of the lovers and help the patient choose. The good therapist insists on having a handful of examples of something before concluding that he understands the real nature of the problem. The key question is, "What is the general difficulty and where else does it occur?"

It may turn out that the patient who has trouble choosing between mates is often unable to make decisions. He spends hours in clothing stores debating between outfits, calls friends on the phone to have simple decisions made for him, and then calls other friends to have them evaluate the advice. Thus the essential problem is not the choice of mate, but the inability to make choices. Helping this patient make one particular choice, or actually telling him what to do, is no help at all. It leaves the essential difficulty just as it was. The task of therapy is to help the patient overcome his indecisiveness.

Single answers to particular problems are not the domain of psychotherapy. Newspaper advisors and those on radio talk-shows render verdicts like that. The aim of psychotherapy is to uncover generalities, traits within the personality, and to help people evolve in such a way as to arrive at their own best answers. It takes experience for a therapist to routinely make the translation from the particular to the general, so that when a patient comes with some special question, the therapist is always thinking more broadly.

A few years ago, on a TV show, a caller told me she had a ten-year-old daughter. Her husband had gone away for good. But on the daughter's birthday, the mother told me, she would send a card to the daughter and sign the father's name. She wanted her daughter to feel that her father was still in the picture. Was she doing the right thing?

I answered no, in no uncertain terms. The girl would someday feel duped, and ask questions she should have asked much earlier. It was a fraud, and would make things harder. The mother hung up. A commercial ended the program and soon I was on the plane headed elsewhere to promote my book.

Thinking it over, I realized how insufficient my answer was. It wasn't simply the card that the mother sent once a year to her daughter that was the problem. The mother had a vision of her child as requiring a protected atmosphere, and very possibly had a problem in seeing her daughter deprived or in pain. Very possibly, guilt played a part. At any rate, I had failed to ask the question, "Where else?" Almost surely, if she distorted in this one place, she was doing something like it in many places in her life, and unwittingly would harm her daughter by the accumulation of such acts. I should have had the mother ask herself, "Where else?" and explained to her the kind of injury she had inflicted, and the degree to which she underestimated the power of the truth. In any event, I was purely and simply an advisor, and lost a possible moment of that tremendous leverage which a good psychotherapist can have.

In the rest of this book I will discuss hundreds of specific decisions the therapist faces in his practice. In describing psychotherapy, it is especially hard to move systematically from the simple to the complex; the therapist's smallest decisions may be based on deep theoretical considerations. It thus becomes important to discuss the theory of psychotherapy as we go along. We will start with decisions relating to the beginning of treatment and those likely to be more concrete, moving to more subtle and general problems of practice as the groundwork is laid.

PART TWO

Structuring Our Practice

To the last gasp, he was himself.

—Ibsen

3

The Therapist's Office

Nothing is more overrated in importance, takes up more time and unnecessary effort than concern over the psychotherapist's office. Therapists, especially those starting out in private practice, are likely to displace many of their concerns onto their office. Not that it's irrelevant: it's the most immediately visible part of their work, and patients respond to it. But patients respond to much more, and after a while, they come to judge the office by the therapist.

During the Second World War, when Britain was undergoing attack, it moved its criminal courts underground. I once saw a documentary film in which a woman shoplifter was on trial in the usual courthouse. Suddenly sirens were heard. The whole crowd—judge, bailiff, jury, bystanders, and the defendant—hurried down to an air-raid shelter and there the trial continued. Eventually, the woman pleaded guilty with an excuse, which was accepted, and she was given a suspended sentence after promising never to do it again.

Which would you prefer, a fair trial underground in a dungeon, or a biased one in a gorgeous courthouse, with wood-paneled walls and oil paintings of time-honored figures looking down? That's about the story as far as the therapist's office is concerned.

After getting my doctorate, I went to the renowned psychoanalyst Theodor Reik for his opinion about a few cases of mine. This man, for whom Freud had written his book, *The Problem of Lay Analysis,* didn't require the kind of splendor I felt I needed in those days. His office was small, dark, and in a dismal neighborhood. Of course, he had a few pictures of Freud on the wall, but I sensed they were there not so much to impress me as for the deep personal meaning they had for him.

Doubtless most beginning therapists can't afford a sumptuous office: they cannot show conspicuous evidence of success. The patient who loses respect for them won't have his doubts assuaged by evidence that they must have cured many people, and wealthy ones, in the past. Such a patient won't be overwhelmed and will bring up his doubts in less luxurious surroundings. The therapist will be on his own, which is the way it should be. Certain dermatologists who believe that a great many skin problems are psychological have argued that an overwhelming office engenders confidence and is partly curative in itself. Probably they overrate this, and it certainly isn't so for psychotherapists. What really matters for the psychotherapist never requires a lot of money.

What does count is that the office be clean, that it not be noisy, and that it be comfortable. Relatively few therapists have truly soundproof offices, which would assure the patient that someone in the waiting room will be unable to hear what is going on. I don't, and I ask my patients not to come too early for that reason. When on occasion someone does, my patients and I almost instinctively lower our voices, and perhaps in those last few minutes of such sessions, a real inhibition sets in. But this occurs rarely, and we take the bad with the good. In the same way, when traffic noises interfere, we talk louder. An occasional person complains about them, but there's nothing I can do.

Whatever the situation, the therapist should never apologize for his office, or for any choice pertaining to his professional image. This includes his clothing, the neighborhood his office is in, his furniture, a painting on the wall.

It need hardly be said that the office should be comfortable. It should contain no breakable items. And if the patient moves something, a chair or a table, there should not be the impression that the whole office is thrown into disarray. I like letting my patients put their feet up on something if they want to.

The office should be easy to find, and not in a neighborhood dangerous to come to at night or up steep flights of stairs. Its decor should match the tenor of the therapist's life; in its books and paintings it should reflect what the therapist loves. Plants are a natural for some people: they seem to symbolize growth and can lighten a room. Naturally, people vary in how ornate they want their offices to be; male therapists tend to do less with their offices than women, as they would with their homes. Certainly, for a man who doesn't live that way, it would be artificial to hire a decorator to put in highly matching elements—lamps that highlight the color of the throw rug, and so forth. The patient comes to feel the therapist in his surroundings and the harmony between the therapist and his office becomes an element in itself.

I guess we've all had the experience of dealing with a vulgar person, maybe an expert on handling money, whose every sentence seems crass. His office is imposing, and on the wall is a Picasso plate. We can almost see him buying it to jack up his fee —as if he sensed the element missing in his life and were going to add it. That Picasso plate, although it may be beautiful in itself, becomes the most vulgar part of him.

Lighting is a problem. Sharp, bright light can interfere with the freedom of fantasy, and patients vary greatly in the kind of lighting that makes them comfortable. What one patient considers comfortable may appear to another like the brightness associated with giving him the third degree. Add to that the variable of how much light comes through the window as the day progresses, and the therapist faces a real challenge.

In keeping with not producing too many active stimuli, I prefer to avoid items like paintings that would be too symbolic or noisy—those with highly detailed and expressive faces in them, for instance. On the other hand, some therapists like to use such stimuli, like items on the ink-blot test, so that the patient will associate to them. However, there should not be pictures of the therapist's mate or children in evidence. These invite questions and fantasies about his personal life. Often they are declarations that he's been successful in love, whereas the poor patient hasn't. He may be divorced or a straggler who hates himself for being an outsider. The therapist merely heightens his patient's sense of being alien by such declarations.

The early psychoanalysts were sometimes fanatical about not letting patients see one another. But the period of such purity is gone. People may come to recognize each other in the waiting room and say hello, and that's part of life. The burden of proof that it does harm is on those who contend it does.

If the therapist is going to change offices—because he's getting rich or going broke or for any other reason—he should give the patient warning. Write down the new address, and mention it early and again just before making the move. Whatever the reason, the therapist should not apologize or blame anyone for it. The patient who is being helped will go along with it. On such occasions, patients care much less than therapists think they will. I've had at least a dozen therapists tell me their worries about relocating, in which they associated the rise of their practice with some magical properties of their location. Each time, they expected much more upheaval than occurred.

Finally, I think it is better to have an office alone than to share one. Sharing is less costly and less lonely, which are real advantages. But being alone affords the patient a supreme sense of privacy; it seems to mirror the lonely voyage of his life, and it gives the therapist the possibility of real freedom and elation as he opens and closes his own doors.

4

Clothing

Speaking about clothing, Freud once likened the psychoanalyst to someone who approaches us at a gambling casino, and tells us he has a winning system. He needn't look opulent, but if he's threadbare, we can hardly be expected to believe him. Therapists reveal much more than their degree of success by their clothing. Like their patients, they declare their values and even their moods by the way they dress.

There are, of course, the obvious criteria of looking clean, neat, and comfortable. One's shoes shouldn't be decaying. But there's also the danger of looking inhibited and too buttoned up, or overly concerned with conventional success. The elegantly coiffed female therapist with never a hair out of place is declaring a value system; so is the male therapist who wears a different three-piece suit every time we see him. One wonders what their definition of success really is, and whether they will judge us adversely if we don't live up to their standard.

Among those therapists who pay clothing the most attention, who search through the latest ads, and spend a lot of time in the right stores, are many in the field without the proper credentials. Such "doctors," having a fragile hold on their professional identities, may feel the need to be among the best dressed. It's as if they felt their whole act would come apart if their clothing looked anything less than impressive.

Therapists who lay great stress on clothing tend to be conventional; they are likely to equate success with achieving social acceptance and making money. They tend to equate the patient's failure with nonacceptance in high society, even if the patient chose his own less traveled path. Poets can't afford the kind of clothing that therapists can.

Many therapists, including some good ones, insist that their patients dress formally too. Men are requested to wear a jacket and tie, and women to wear skirts instead of slacks. Supposedly, this makes patients take their sessions more seriously. If these therapists are right, their patients have a problem that ought to be dealt with and not encouraged.

An adult on his way from tennis should not have to go all the way home to change if the therapist's office is near the courts. A shower ought to be enough, in my opinion. Therapy should belong to the progress of life, be in the flow of it. Not that even the sticklers would throw a patient out if he came dressed wrongly, the way a casino would. But the patient is seen as resisting, as uncooperative, and his outfit becomes a subject for the session. Patients (who, after all, are there because something is going badly in their lives) may give in. The more conventional ones are especially subject to the feeling that "doctor knows best." I have been stunned at how seemingly independent adults conform to what seem to me utterly inappropriate dress codes.

It is true that self-love is often mirrored in how we dress. The very act of dressing well starts some people toward a good day. But for me, at least, it might be putting on a bright shirt with earth colors, and not necessarily a jacket and a tie. No symbol, no piece of clothing, has the same meaning to all people. Insistence on a uniform for therapy seems to fly in the face of this.

Some therapists maintain that they ask their patients to dress a certain way, not because they expect conformity, but because they wish to see tangibly where their patients are resisting them. The term "acting in" has been used to denote such violations during the therapy hour; it complements the term "acting out," which refers to such violations outside the hour. But there are plenty of rules that serve the process, such as the patient's getting there on time; it seems dangerous to add rules that could have very special meaning for the patient. For instance, it may be downright degrading to a person to put on an outfit because another person requires it.

Just as our hope or despair is mirrored in choice of outfit, so is our sense of freedom. Often, I think, patients who dress to please their therapists are succumbing to avoid a power struggle. The patient is paying homage to therapy, rather than to himself. Patients should come to therapy to discover themselves and not to conform to anyone else's expectations.

5

The Therapist's Fees

It might be hard for the layman to imagine how much thinking most therapists give to matters of money. There are countless decisions to be made—how much to charge, whether to have a sliding scale, how and when to raise or lower fees, how to charge (by the session or by the month), whether to send out bills, whether to charge for missed sessions, and if so, under what conditions, what to do when a patient is late in paying, how to deal with nonpayment, and whether to accept payment from someone else or to insist that adult patients pay for themselves. These all sound like strictly practical questions, but the answers have real bearing on the course that therapy takes.

The way the patient handles money manifests attitudes of his —for instance, he is grudging or appreciative, he remembers to pay when the time comes, or customarily forgets and expects the therapist to come to him, hat in hand. Like everything the patient does, such decisions affect his own subsequent outlook. The patient who cleverly whittles the therapist down may increase contempt for him, and may even invalidate his treatment by such acts.

The patient's handling of money is seldom an isolated activity. Those who mistreat the therapist by withholding payment are likely to do so in other ways too. However, their withholding money can sometimes strike very near home. The patient may evoke so much anger or disappointment that the therapist may become useless or even harmful to him. I have seen cases in which the therapist could think of little else, as his patient sat there week after week decrying injustices against him, while offering lame excuses for his not paying the therapist. The debt had accumulated over months, and the patient would sit there blithely and explain, "It was too late to get to the bank. I know you'll understand."

The therapist needs to remain very alert to his feelings of being deprived or neglected by such patients. Some patients don't want to pay because they want to see the relationship as "pure," but others, who may use this excuse, simply don't like parting with money.

It's of primary importance for the therapist to acknowledge a truth about himself: "I do this for a living." A surprising number of those in private practice still suffer from inability to possess this fact fully. Some have been able to hide from it because they worked in clinics. If the patient pleaded poverty, the therapist readily accepted the plea. When it turned out that the patient was lying and was really rich—that he had no business going to a clinic and being subsidized by others—again the therapist was not immediately involved. His salary didn't depend upon what the patient paid for his treatment. He could regard the fraud as part of the patient's problem: his desire to get something for nothing. However, when such therapists go into private practice they find themselves personally affected. In the clinic, they could see themselves as rendering a valuable service for which they were underpaid, and could conceal even from themselves that they made a living out of helping people.

The jump into private practice requires full acknowledgment of the fact that they are doing therapy not merely for the patient's sake but also to earn a living. Thus the switch to private practice brings with it a host of new concerns about money, as well as feelings that go with earning a living from people we help.

There are two main reasons why therapists find it hard to ask their patients for money. One is preconscious—many therapists with the problem can quickly recognize it, and if they free-associate around the subject of asking for money, the ideas come to mind. The problem is one of *overidentification.* They are like parents who find it hard to make the necessary demands on their children. Therapy is, after all, a helping profession. What could be worse than having someone come to you in need and then causing him to wince by asking him for money? Who wants to be seen as just like the gouging shopkeeper or landlord the patient complains about? So the therapist hides behind the illusion that he is a special kind of ally, one with limitless empathy and love, and suppresses, as best he can, his desire to be paid. To say, "I do this for a living," would puncture that illusion, which therapists may be loath to surrender.

The other reason, usually unconscious, is much more pervasive and powerful. Close examination reveals in many cases a deep sense of inadequacy on the therapist's part, a disbelief in the therapeutic method, or a sense of not having learned it properly, and at bottom, a profound disbelief in himself. The attempt to convey, "Money isn't important to me," is a guise for the real feeling, "I don't deserve to be paid." Logically, if the therapist doesn't deserve to be paid, then he doesn't deserve to take up the patient's time either, or to substitute for a real therapist who would merit both the investment of time and money. Perhaps there is reason for the therapist's misgivings. But often the feeling is irrational—the therapist deserves to be paid because he is as sensitive and well-trained, as devoted and painstaking as the patient would have a right to expect. In such a case, his not asking for money he has earned is an act that confirms his worst irrational fears about himself. The therapist's very asking for the money becomes important in confirming that he has made a real contribution.

The therapist ought to get clear the fact that his taking money is for *him,* not for the patient. There ought to be no euphemisms about it: he helps people for a living. It has been a popular belief, put into print by Karl Menninger and others, that it is good for the patient to pay a lot. A high fee makes the patient appreciate the insights he receives. This seems to me a nonsensical rationalization for charging high fees. If the patient is one of those who can't appreciate something unless he pays a lot for it, that is itself a problem that ought to be worked on. Simply accepting the problem by increasing one's fee is exploiting a kind of materialist irrationality—one that is, unfortunately, quite prevalent. I would like my patients to learn that there is a great deal to be found in the everyday, which will be available to him whether he makes top-dollar or not.

How much should we charge? The answer is obvious. There is no right amount. There are rehabilitation counselors, risking their lives in poor neighborhoods for next to nothing. And there are good neighbors, and Big Brothers, and volunteers working with the handicapped, and devoted ministers visiting homes, whose minutes are worth every dollar that ours are. There's an old joke about a businessman who goes to Florida, and on the first day nearly drowns. A heroic bystander leaps into the angry waves, risking his own life; he pulls the man out, and gives him mouth-to-mouth resuscitation. The man's breathing slowly becomes visible again. He nods to his rescuer, and then asks his desolate wife standing at his side, "What do you tip for a thing like this?"

Nor is precedent a real measure. I've seen therapists go into training and pay stupendous amounts to some bigwig in the field, so that they can increase their own fees, and feel righteous, hiding behind what the giant charges. They welcome the giant's regular increases (he's now up to two hundred dollars an hour so they can sneak up from thirty-five to fifty). They attend his master sessions only once a month, and so on balance they do well. In general, we base our fees, as other people do, on rising costs, on our needs, on what people are willing to pay us, and on what we feel we're worth. And these same criteria determine when we raise our fees.

Since some people can't afford as much as others, it doesn't seem right to charge the same fee to everyone. Freud had a special bias: he charged Americans more because he didn't like the United States. I don't believe we should have special categories of people we charge more, except for what they can afford. Nor do most people resent a sliding scale. And when a celebrity sends his chauffeur to me neither of us imagines that I will charge that person anything like the amount that the celebrity is ready to pay.

The amount per session should be set early, although I don't handle this on the phone. I need to know more. It is subject to change if the patient wins a lottery or loses his job. I simply state the amount I charge, although sometimes I ask if the amount is too steep for the person. If so, I may lower it somewhat if I feel I can be uniquely helpful to the particular person. Or, if I think I can be helpful on a less frequent basis, I might make the adjustment that way. It may be that the person can't possibly afford an amount that would make me comfortable in working with him. Then I find someone to refer him to. Conceivably, I will see someone for almost nothing, for a limited time when there are special circumstances. I reserve this for people who really can't afford therapy, who are trying hard—especially who are relied on by others, as with a woman whose husband abandoned the family. When we take on a patient and set our fee, we are contracting to offer one or a few hours a week for years, and so we must be more careful than other specialists, who can offer their services for a shorter time.

If I've been cheated—for example, the person has concealed a huge trust fund—this will surely come out. My usual approach would be to ask the patient why he didn't mention the trust fund when the fee was set. His answer will prove valuable to the rest of our work. But if I continue to feel uncomfortable with the amount he is paying, I will simply ask him for more, and we'll talk about it.

Often we decide to raise a fee, either because the patient can afford more or because the value of money is going down. The best way to do it, I have found, is simply to state the new amount, giving the patient a few months' notice to get ready. Any vehement objection will be considered, certainly talked about. But I find that if my request is reasonable, people go along with it. Moreover, I have had many patients volunteer to pay me more when their lives went better. In many cases, I have taken them up on the offer.

I have made it a practice to charge for a first session only if I am going to work with the person. I dislike intensely the experience of seeing someone, deciding that the person ought to go to someone else, and then charging the person for what feels like the experience of rejection. I preface my interviews by saying that I am busy, which is true, and probably will use the session to find the right therapist. Only when I feel that I have special abilities to help the particular patient do I work with him. Of course, at the start, more than twenty years ago, I saw anyone who would deign to come to me and talk about himself. Then the fee was secondary, since I wanted the experience and the sense of myself as a therapist. I am deeply suspicious of those beginning therapists who have long, empty days, and who turn patients down because they can't pay quite enough. Help people and they'll refer others to you.

What about a canceled session? Few therapists would charge a person for missing a session when he was in bed with pneumonia. But suppose he's out of town on work. He's off making his fortune, and it's costing the therapist income. I would charge the patient under this special condition. Many therapists have a rule, "If you give me twenty-four hours' notice, you won't have to pay me for a missed session." I recently heard of a case in which a man argued that he'd given proper notice, but the therapist rejoined that it was only twenty-three hours. He had to pay. I think the therapist did more harm than good. In this "business," the customer is not always right. But, too often therapists treat him as if he's always wrong. Even if the patient does feel put down by the demand, he may be reluctant to cross the therapist, worrying perhaps that the therapist will not work with him as eagerly or as well.

It's a worse violation when the patient simply misses his scheduled hour. He doesn't arrive and leaves no message giving the therapist warning. Nearly all therapists would charge for such an hour. They would maintain that they were sitting there, on tap, in the patient's employ, for the hour. They charge because if they don't, they'll feel abused. Presumably, they don't feel mistreated, or much less so, if they get paid for their time.

My position is different. First of all, I don't lose an hour if the person doesn't come. There's plenty to do. Secondly, as the renowned psychiatrist Frieda Fromm-Reichman pointed out, few in other professions charge people for hours they're not there. Why should we be the ones to do it? I would not charge the person who stood me up, for the very reason that I *want* to feel abused; not because I enjoy it, but because it will keep me in touch with what is happening. I would of course bring up with the patient what he did, and I always retain the option of saying, "If you do it again, I'm going to stop working with you; it isn't fair." At the very least, I have the option of taking a leave of absence. The patient may consider during that time whether he really wants to continue or not.

There are financially successful people who imagine that everyone, including their therapist, is purchasable. They don't appear for appointments, and then have a secretary call with the news that something came up and that I'll be paid for my time, not to worry. How condescending! I had the chance to be bought off for a year by an executive who expected to come for his weekly scheduled hour about one time in four. I declined to become just another member of his entourage, as that would have been useless to him.

I also believe that sometimes the person who forgot his hour is really sorry, whatever the reason. "To err is human." There's something lost if he pays for the hour. It's intangible, but includes his robbing me of the chance to forgive him. The fact that I care about a person enough to say, "It's okay, it's not your usual style, it's human," instead of "Pay me, of course," has lasting effects.

It's one thing to say, "I care," it's another to show it by caring. Patients respond very profoundly to such acts. I know that I myself would feel closer to a therapist who didn't seize the opportunity to make a few dollars from me out of my absence. By his generosity, he's told me something that I might long remember. As a therapist, we mustn't be afraid of the occasional bully who avoids sessions because he knows he doesn't have to pay for them. Those people need to be confronted anyhow, and you're in much better position to do so if you haven't pocketed their money for missed sessions. The strongest argument you can make is that you don't want just their money, you want them there, and if they want to stop working with you, they're perfectly welcome to do so.

What about patients who simply don't pay? There are therapists who go on with such patients, allowing them to build enormous debts; they pretend to keep trusting the patient long after their trust is gone; they are afraid to terminate because, then, they fear, they will lose both past and future money. The growing debt hovers over the sessions, often with the patient promising big things about to break. Eventually, therapy comes to an end, with the patient owing a small fortune.

There are collection agencies that therapists sometimes use, presumably after treatment has been terminated. Having made a mistake in judgment, or failed to help the patient function, the therapist resorts to muscle, threatening by use of an agent to ruin the person's life unless he pays. A sheriff told me of attaching a person's house for a psychiatrist, who was owed five thousand dollars. The sheriff recalled having been sent to attach a different house two years earlier for the same psychiatrist. One wonders if the psychiatrist had in mind the prospect of foreclosure when he allowed his patients to build up debts they couldn't pay.

It seems to me that any debt we permit is incurred as part of a calculated risk. We are gambling on the person's integrity; as psychologists, we ought to be better at such gambles than the average person. It has been our choice all along to see the patient while he owed us money; we could have insisted, as a condition of continuing, that he pay us every session. If we lose, we lose. It happens in every business. The hiring of an agent to coerce the person into paying us is an evasion of our own role in allowing the debt to accrue.

I prefer my patients to pay me on their last visit of the month and to keep their own records while I keep mine. I tell them either to pay me on their last visit or to tell me why they're not paying and when they will. Nearly all comply, although there are some who ask to pay every session to be sure they won't fall too far behind. I agree to this. However, it becomes an aim of therapy with these people to help them organize their lives better. I send out bills only to people who are paying for my patients —for instance, to lawyers or agents handling the money for an actor or artist. This is purely to simplify my own life. If a patient asks for a bill, as for an insurance company, of course I give him one.

I have always been fascinated by the degree to which patients are able to infer the therapist's attitude toward money. How badly does the therapist need it? Does he see the patient primarily as a source of income? Many things that therapists do, communicate to patients their real attitudes. The readiness to let people cancel when they have to, or even when they want to, is one. Therapists can argue the necessity for regularity, and the need for many sessions per week. They can cite psychoanalytic scripture, ad nauseam. But patients sense the role of money and the neediness in the therapist's life. I advise all beginning therapists to try to make some money out of something besides their practice, so that they won't communicate this neediness. Patients react to it by instinctively pulling away. Very often these patients suggest quitting—for a while, or permanently. The therapist then tells them that they're resisting, that they're coming to a major turn in their lives and running away, as usual. Perhaps there's some truth to that, but the therapist's fervency often betrays the fact that he needs those patients too much.

I've observed a curious phenomenon in the careers of many therapists while they are undertaking to build a private practice. There comes a time when their following seems secure, those fantasies of a marshall coming and putting their couch out on the street are gone. They lean back psychologically, perhaps not even recognizing the change that is taking place in them. They feel more secure. It seems at that very instant that patients sense the change. The therapist looks less needy, he's arrived. Suddenly the referrals start coming in from everywhere. Two years ago, a few new patients would have changed the therapist's economic life; now it seems that, when they're not really needed, they're arriving in droves.

I've often puzzled over this phenomenon, noted in Thomas Hood's poem, "There's Nothing Succeeds Like Success." Perhaps it occurs because the therapist has suddenly become someone whom the patient would like to be, a model; he's accomplished what the patient sees as success. But I think the real reason is that the therapist has stopped exerting a subtle tension on his patients, stopped pressuring them in response to his own personal need, which they could only feel and not consciously identify. The therapist has learned to let go.

6

The Telephone

There's only one mechanical instrument the psychotherapist uses and that's the telephone. Learning to handle it takes years. I've heard of patients deciding against a therapist on the basis of the opening call. After that initial conversation, the patient leaves a message, "Say, I've been thinking it over. I've got to go out of town. I'll call you back." However, the patient's real thought was, "You sounded out of town to me. I've decided to try someone else."

On the phone, the patient is evaluating the therapist just as much as the therapist is judging him. The patient responds to the therapist's warmth, spontaneity, immediacy in even a brief call. Does the therapist feel disturbed by being called?

There are a few general principles I consider worthwhile:

1. Every call should have a purpose, should be clear, and should end when the purpose is met.

2. Use the phone only when absolutely necessary. If at all possible, don't do therapy on the phone. Too many things can go wrong that might have been avoided in a face-to-face session.

What we say on the phone has a way of reverberating in the patient's mind, perhaps because other stimuli are absent.

Explorations can't be done in depth, reassurance may sound hollow, any hint of disengagement on our part may feel like abandonment. Nearly every therapist has had the experience of leaving a warm dinner table to return a call, of pouring his heart out, staying on the phone too long, only to be chastened by the patient and accused of not caring about him.

The main reason that therapists get into predicaments over the phone is that they imagine they can do more than is actually possible. I've heard of some who interpret dreams moments after their patients awake from them; others routinely give advice or reassurance, hardly distinguishing phone conversations from office time. There are real occasions when sessions have to be conducted over the phone. The patient has gone off to another city, for example. But therapy is hard enough in the office; it requires ample time and the chance for people to look at each other. The phone offers gulfs of silence in which each person can only fantasize what the other person is thinking. At best, the phone ought to be considered second best.

Our first conversation with a patient comes when he calls to make an appointment. He might wish to verify that I am the person he meant to call, and perhaps explain, "My friend went to you. . . ." My purpose is only to establish time and place. I suggest possible appointment times until one is right for the patient. I don't discuss my fee or credentials or my method of practice or the patient's problem or prognosis, or answer questions about particular psychiatrists or books. These questions may be legitimate, or at least understandable, from the patient's point of view. But my purpose is to be as warm as possible while saying in effect, "We can talk a lot better when you come in."

It would seem unfair not to discuss fees and then have the person find out, in my office, that he can't possibly afford what I charge. This is one reason I don't charge for the first session, which I keep brief. Certain of our rules for use of the phone are dictated by common decency. For instance, there is seldom a reason to answer a phone call during a session. Why should the patient have to tolerate an interruption that could be avoided? On those rare necessary occasions I get off the phone in a few seconds, and always apologize to the patient. One phone call is my absolute limit in a session; and if I'm expecting a call that can't be made at any other time, I might warn the patient in advance. If the caller stays on, I let him know, "I'm sorry. I'm keeping someone waiting in my office." That both explains the situation and puts the ball in his court. The person almost always hangs up at this point, but I don't hesitate to end the conversation, even if he thinks I'm being curt.

However, if I cut a person off, it would be rude to ask him to call me back. Either I don't want to talk to him, or if I do, I ought to get back to him. As therapists, it's our obligation to be direct, and not to treat people any worse when we aren't eager to hear from them than when we are. Only if the person can't be reached do I specify another time for him to call. People sense these nuances in relationships far beyond their ability to describe them in words.

Naturally, we must leave some route of access for people in need, yet we've got to protect ourselves against pointless incursions. Giving out one's home number can be costly. A single patient in one's whole practice may abuse it. The therapist not only is interrupted repeatedly, but may have a lot of unexpected questions to contend with. "Who was that who answered, your husband? He had a sexy voice. Are you married? I heard a child in the background."

On the other hand, there are patients who, if they knew they could reach us over a weekend, would deeply appreciate it, and would never abuse the privilege. This brings us to the problem of deciding when a phone call is really necessary, so that we won't be prey to patients who would merely like to hear our voice. These are usually patients who've been dependent on other people, often their parents; now they don't like to make a move without their therapists. In many instances, they're testing the therapist; they expect him to become annoyed with them, to abandon them, and they're pushing him to the limit.

"I just called to ask you a question. Do you think Bob still loves me?"

"I don't know. How come you ask?"

"We had this terrible quarrel, and he said that I make every little detail too important, and that he couldn't stand it, and I told him he didn't love me, and he walked out and slammed the door."

"It sounds awful."

"It is."

Long pause, while the patient waits for some concrete advice or prediction about the future.

"Mary, there's really not much I can say right now. I'm sorry it happened, and that you're in pain, but we'll have to wait until Monday."

"But you love me, don't you?"

"I'm with you, and I promise that we're going to work hard on this, and see what we can piece together."

"But do you love me?"

"You're pushing me to say your words, and I'm not going to say them."

At this point, as a therapist, I can feel myself fulfilling her worst expectations of me. I've been groomed to disappoint her. I'm baffled. But I can't substitute for the man who walked out on her, and I wouldn't want to, even if I could.

"Mary, I'm going to hang up, and I'll talk to you Monday."

"Don't hang up."

"Now Mary, you're trying to bully me, trying to keep me on the phone. It's not fair, and it's not a good idea. We'll solve this thing, but we're not going to solve it now."

"Okay, good-bye."

It's a calculated risk. The patient can hate you forever or quit. He can even commit suicide; I always feel a little bit lucky that none of my patients ever did. But sometimes the therapist's choice is either to become utter prey, doing the patient no good at all, or to risk inflicting pain in the service of insight. Obviously, this patient must learn to be alone, to contain struggles while confronting them, and to stop trying to solve her problems by controlling other people. Otherwise she'll go on driving people out of her life. Such patients nearly always sense that the therapist is on their side even as he confronts them. The very recognition that they are mishandling their lives and are not victims of fate is an antidote to suicide. I've had many patients look back at how demanding they were, and wonder how anyone could have stood it.

With such patients it may be necessary to discuss excessive phone calling, and get the patient to agree that he'll call only when he has a distinct purpose. When he does call, after saying hello, ask why he called. If the person rambles and doesn't answer, ask again, and again, if necessary, until you get an answer. This can help focus the person.

It's usually not hard to distinguish real emergencies from hysterical phone calls. Often we may be glad that a patient calls us. For some, the willingness to turn to another person for comfort can be a great advance. A patient who is robustly self-sufficient informs me that her mother has just been diagnosed as having cancer. My patient can't come in. This is a real emergency; if anything, she usually hesitates too much to ask for emotional succor. I would surely call this patient at least once, and perhaps a number of times, during the ordeal. And I would call any patient who was seriously ill, or in a hospital. It's not so much what I say, it's that I'm there, listening and caring.

From a patient who is too much the soldier, and doesn't believe that anyone will be with him in an emergency, who basically doesn't trust friendship or love, I might welcome his sharing bad news with me if it befell him. I've often told such people that I appreciated their calling, which I did, because I felt included, and that it was a real triumph for them to call.

Among the more difficult calls we get are those from irate or curious relatives. A husband calls, just to let me know that my patient uses a lot of cocaine. A mother calls to ask whether her son is neurotic. Another simply wants to know what's wrong with her daughter. Obviously, what our patients tell us is private, and we must tell the caller this. If our patients want these people to know something, they will tell them themselves. I try to explain the need for absolute confidentiality, since the caller may feel painfully excluded. "It might destroy my efforts to help your daughter if I discussed what she said. I understand your curiosity, but . . . I'm sorry, it just wouldn't be right."

Also we might get calls from therapists and other professionals, who imagine they need information about our patient in order to help theirs. "I'm working with the husband. Is your patient really having an affair?" Naturally, we can't tell them.

The two final problems are how to set up a system of receiving messages, and how to leave messages when necessary.

As for receiving messages, there is the choice between a telephone answering machine and a service that uses real operators. I favor the former. Too many things can go wrong with a live operator. The person may take too long to answer, be impolite, lose messages, confuse them, or become ruffled by a patient who acts difficult. The major advantages of a tape recorder are that people will leave sensitive messages on a tape recorder that they would not trust to an intermediary. "My lover's in town." "My wife just had a miscarriage." On a machine, patients can leave telephone numbers, addresses, hours, and dates, without relying on someone's writing them down correctly. Moreover, hearing the patient's voice allows us to make personal judgments about him from his tone, such as whether he sounded urgent.

A related problem is that if we answer our phone, say if

there's an extension in our home, we're apt to be taken by surprise. The patient is ready, but perhaps we've had a few drinks, or have been awakened or are occupied. The patient senses our distance and is upset. Therapists who get into trouble over the phone should pass a rule not to answer it, but to take messages and return calls. That gives them time to consider what they want to do.

When leaving a message for someone who's at work, it's preferable not to use one's title, "Doctor . . . ." That's apt to subject the person to embarrassing questions. Sometimes I leave a message for a patient at home, but only if I know who it is on the other end, his parent or mate, for instance, and have reason to believe the person is cooperative. Otherwise, it's better to call again. Messages can easily be forgotten or mistranslated when the intermediary has mixed feelings about the person's being in therapy.

It's a wonderful experience to turn on your tape recorder and hear a message from a patient that he's really doing well. "I just wanted you to know that I got the job." Or, "I performed beautifully; I'll tell you about it Wednesday." Such messages can be exhilarating.

7

Record Keeping

For me as a child, going to a New York Yankee game was the sublimest pleasure in life. It was like watching a sequence of Biblical revelations. There was one boy, whom I remember only by his nickname, "Mud-Balls," who sometimes joined us, and kept a meticulous scorecard. We turned to him when we needed to know where a particular batter had hit the ball his last time up.

But I remember him mainly as asking the questions. The crowd stood up and cheered. "What just happened?" He would look up from his scorecard. "DiMaggio went to second on a wild pitch," someone told him. "How do you write 'wild pitch?' " "W.P.," a man said in a row behind us. Again the crowd was cheering. "What happened?" Mud-Balls would ask.

Taking notes in sessions can be for the psychotherapist what scorekeeping was for this boy. As the patient's smoking or chewing gum can substitute for his reactions, note-taking can do the same for therapists. At worst, it can be a way of hiding from the relationship. It is sometimes used as busywork, along with asking a lot of irrelevant questions, by a therapist who feels lost and doesn't want his patient to know it.

Most of the really significant truths burn deep if we experience them profoundly when they occur. Intensity of experience is a key to remembering an event. Writing costs us immediacy. Most patients would rather have our attention than see us writing as fast as we can. Besides, they'd like to feel that we remember what they tell us, and we ought to—at least the important things.

Psychotherapists have come to take many fewer notes than in the past. The early psychoanalysts collected any kind of data that might prove useful. They wrote down multitudes of facts about the patient's past—when he had his tonsils out, how old his siblings were, nationalities of his relatives, where he went to school—even precise dates, like April 22nd, when the family moved from the city to the country. Any of these facts might prove pertinent. Losing tonsils might have been a trauma: children were often lied to before such operations, taken by surprise, and many felt terribly injured and distrustful when that happened. But in addition the early psychoanalysts placed a heavy emphasis on symbolism, on interpretations, and the more facts psychoanalysts had—what Alfred North Whitehead called "inert facts"—the better chance they had to make seemingly brilliant interpretations. If the number *22* appeared again in the patient's life, the analyst would be ready for it.

There was also an impulse to dazzle the patient. It was the special domain of the psychoanalyst to make seemingly magical interpretations, supposedly to build out of insignificant facts some insight that could change the patient's life. Such interpretations were often stunning, and could never be proven wrong.

Little by little, we've come to lose faith in such magical interpretations. It isn't a matter of whether they're true or not. They may have the suddenness of a lightning bolt. But they don't help the patient change as we once hoped. Since Freud's death, we've come to appreciate increasingly that single events seldom make the critical difference in people's lives. If the patient's parents lied to him about the tonsillectomy, they doubtless did many things in the same vein. His memory of being in the hospital may be worth exploring, and how he felt. But the exact date or hospital address, which he might also recall, aren't what we're after. Even if the patient misremembers these facts, we can use the experience.

Mystification is giving way to *immediacy* as the specialty of psychotherapy. Detailed note-taking may help with seemingly magical interpretations, but it unquestionably interferes with the therapist's ability to feel what his patients are doing and feeling.

What should we write down? As little as possible during an hour, whatever we want to write after it. Perhaps we might conspicuously go to a pad and pencil when a patient is about to report a dream. Many therapists jot down names. But it would be better to learn a mnemonic system and become self-reliant.

After a session, the beginning therapist may wish to write down instances of anything crucial he plans to bring to the patient's attention. What we write depends completely on our emphasis, and where we feel our memory or mastery are weak. One therapist may wish to record feelings he had in a session, to heighten his experience and memory of them. We may want to write down our therapeutic plan or what we've been able to form of one. It might be a reminder to explore some particular incident that seems loaded. Or it might be a poetic turn of phrase that we want to have on hand and present at an appropriate time.

Above all, if the therapist finds himself constantly lapsing into an activity he ought to stop, such as giving advice, he may want to write down instructions to himself: "Be quiet when you feel the impulse to give advice," or, "Note carefully what the patient is doing, if anything, that evokes my impulse to give advice." Such reminders can help us bind our own impulses and get better control of the session.

At most, a few quick jottings in a session, followed by whatever elaboration we want to add later, seems to me an ideal.

What about tape recorders? Obviously, it would be unethical to use a hidden mike, even for our own educational purposes. In the 1940s, some of the major universities built special hiding places for recorders in their guidance clinics. They were meant to help the students learn. But the more ethically minded in the field made clear how harmful this would be, and so far as I know recorders were scarcely used.

I remember the psychiatrist Leopold Bellak telling a class, "The patient might not know a recorder was on, but I would know, and that would make all the difference." It is remarkable how much patients infer about us and what we are doing. They may not surmise particulars—that we're talking about them behind their backs, or using a hidden mike, or in the process of getting a divorce—but they sense, for instance, that we're remote, or preoccupied, or untrustworthy. And sometimes they even make brilliant stabs at the reasons, and accuse us of what is true, or infer the truth in dreams, without having had real access to the facts.

The alternative is to ask the patient's permission, and if he gives it, to place the recorder smack on a table in front of him. The tape may be intended for another professional, perhaps someone supervising the therapist's work. If so, and the patient asks who will hear it, he should be told honestly. It may be useful to add that whoever hears it will keep strict confidentiality. However, the therapist may want it only for himself. If so, he should explain that it will help him to better understand not only the patient, but also what he himself is doing in the session.

I've sometimes given tape recordings to patients who want to study themselves. The person can observe characteristic ways he has of dealing with emotion, and of talking to other people. Consider the person profoundly worried about something, who lives utterly alone. Hearing a tape can provide great solace, and can sometimes substitute for repeated phone calls just to hear the therapist say the same thing over and over.

If the patient has even a hint of paranoia, any recording should be out of the question. Such a person will stifle a great deal and may imagine what he says being studied, perhaps laughed at, and used against him. Moreover, if the therapist himself is at all paranoid, he should never give a recording of a session to a patient. Instantly, the therapist will feel in the patient's power. Whether true or not, he may envision the patient playing the sessions for others, and perhaps using the recorder as part of a lawsuit if things go wrong. If there is paranoia anywhere in the picture, even the patient's direct request for permission to tape a session should always be denied.

Even at best, tape recordings have a way of inhibiting both patient and therapist. It's hard to free-associate in the presence of a recorder. And many patients who make tapes may, unconsciously, take their sessions less seriously. It's as if they decide, "I don't have to listen or feel as much now. I'll get it in the replay." The ideal is to rely a minimum on accessories and to make every hour as effective and memorable as possible.

8

How Often?

How often should we schedule the patient? Someone highly motivated, who aggressively studies his own feelings and behavior, and has very little money, beseeches me to work with him. He loved the first session, repeated some of my comments as if savoring them. At the end, he tells me, "I'm only in town once in a while. Could I schedule an hour with you from time to time? It would be fantastic."

It appears to me that I can possibly help him a great deal, even on an occasional basis. That will depend on how fast he can see what he does with women. He feels a false sense of pity for them, which he acts on. Before long, he's devastated another relationship. He ends up each time hating himself and the woman.

It's an exciting case. He picked up fast on the few small insights I gave him. And he even brought in an instance of his own to enhance what I was saying. That's a good sign. If he can only get a grip on his own neurotic motive! I already see some of the ways he's unconsciously renewing it.

But then, while he's telling me another anecdote, something occurs to me. Suppose he disappoints me, misremembers everything, doesn't try. If he were coming regularly, I could deal with such a tendency to eradicate his own insights. Indeed, my own disappointment would serve as a cue as to how he was failing. With sporadically scheduled appointments, who knows what other blockades he would put up! He might lead me a merry chase, using absence as his primary defense. One can't be sure.

"Okay, we'll try it," I tell him. "But if I don't think it's working out, we'll make some other arrangement."

How often should we see a patient? Unquestionably, the patient's willingness to come in often, and ability to pay have been determinants. But there are other factors too, and some therapists limit the number of sessions per week, just as others tend to keep pressing their patients to come in more often.

The economic factor seems indisputable, and this is nothing to be ashamed of. Psychotherapy is for some people a virtual necessity, for others it approaches being a luxury. There's always work to be done, the possibility of widening a horizon, and in this sense the number of sessions is elastic.

At the turn of the century, while psychiatrists were seeing patients in mental hospitals for a few minutes at a time, when they had the time, psychoanalysts in private practice insisted that their patients come an hour a day, at least five days a week. When Franz Alexander, a psychoanalyst in good standing, proposed brief psychotherapy with fewer sessions, he found staunch opposition. Gradually, as therapy spread to the masses, it became a three-time-a-week process in the 1940s and 1950s, and now many patients come once or twice a week. Experienced therapists will frequently see a patient every other week, and can often help a great deal that way.

On the patient's side, an important variable is motivation. Paradoxically, a highly motivated person, the very one who wants to come in more often, may be able to utilize occasional sessions. Such a person can use a good session, will daub it over his week, over his life. He'll remember it. An unmotivated patient, or a person with low energy due to depression, may virually forget therapy between sessions. We've got to see such people relatively often. Just as with friendship, there are some people whom you can see after long interludes, and within minutes it's as if there were no break. The camaraderie, the crackling excitement of the pursuit of truth, is there at once. With others, it seems a resurrection each time you start a conversation.

There's also the obvious fact that people in deep personal trouble may need a lot of sessions. Things are happening fast; there are decisions to make. These people need someone to talk to. And if they're in crisis, while it lasts, the therapist may assume the extra function of ally. Not that he need agree with the patient, but he's dependably there. The very process of personal discovery creates its own sequence of crises. While the patient is discovering that he's not the person he thought he was—for instance, that he is less kind—he may crave someone to talk to. Near the end of therapy, the need is much less. Many therapists taper off, seeing the patient less often, perhaps once a month at the very end so that the break isn't too abrupt.

The beginning therapist may need to see patients more often than after he's experienced. I would never have imagined seeing a patient every other week, or even once a week when I started. Not only wasn't it done, but besides that, I couldn't define for myself enough of what I was doing to tolerate the lapse. Even from one day to the next, the patient may present utterly different subject matter. The therapist need not return to old topics (although this is his prerogative), but should usually go with the flow, seeing what is invariant. The ability to see patterns and remember them enables the therapist to reduce the frequency of sessions and get the same job done.

We must be careful not to see certain patients too often, as for instance, the person in love with us and willing to pay for as many hours as we'll give, or anyone who puts blind faith in us and isn't doing enough work. We might only too easily foster dependence by doing too much of the work. Many patients are willing to pay us for many more sessions than they can sensibly afford. We must be on the watch for these people, so as not to participate in their self-destructive script.

Regularity of sessions is important. Once we fix a schedule with a patient, we should make every effort to keep the same hour on the same day or days. Patients get to feel it is their hour, and there is always some loss when a change is made. If a change is really necessary, I think an apology is called for. Perhaps someone else can't come at any other time, and our patient has plenty of time. Even then I would hesitate, and if there were no other solution, I would remain mindful that changing a time is undesirable. Regularity may mean more to a patient than he knows or would admit, and changes are highly disruptive—they are often reminiscent of abandonment in the past. Our loyalty is manifested in our being there for patients at the same time on the same day, and they unconsciously appreciate our predictability in their lives.

How long should a session be? I'm always suspicious of beginning therapists who dole out only 45-minute sessions when they have nothing else to do anyhow. I'd prefer the novice who has the impulse to stay too long, in his zeal to help the patient and to experience himself as a therapist. However, sessions must not be allowed to run too long. I for one find longer than an hour tiring, and although I used occasionally to comply with a request for a double session, I don't anymore.

As with fees and frequency, there are no ironclad rules for how long a session should be. The usual has been just short of sixty minutes, fifty as a rule, so as to allow the therapist to rest between patients while still scheduling patients on the hour. But the length is somewhat arbitrary. There seems no magical reason why a therapist should see a new patient every sixty minutes.

Indeed, the whole notion of an hour being sixty minutes comes straight from the ancient Babylonians, whose mathematics was founded on a number base of sixty. Brilliant with numbers though they were, they could hardly have forseen the necessities of modern therapy.

9

Language

Our language conveys a sense of us and our view of life. The very labeling of experience becomes part of the experience. The patient is "frightened" or "nervously exuberant," it's a "trial" or an "adventure"; there's a thin line between these, and a matter of definition, because every challenge has both anxiety and excitement in it. In Chinese, the symbol for "crisis" and "opportunity" is the same. We can label many items of life optimistically or morbidly. Therapists too often get away with morbidity, because so many patients come to us depressed. The therapist's input goes unnoticed. The ability to see adventures instead of dangers is a gift we ourselves need and we need to convey it through our use of language.

Our language should be free of heavy, Latinate constructions. Words like "repressed," "sublimate," and "defense-mechanism" have little or no place in sessions. So far as possible, our descriptions should be idiosyncratic to the case, whether or not in our minds we build structures using classical concepts. Indeed, lightness of language and conversational simplicity may illuminate even the dingiest corners of the patient's life.

Humor is a powerful tool affording the perspective of a

separate vantage point when looking at painful moments. A hint of exaggeration in a humorous vein can help us over rough spots. We're certainly not laughing at the patient or at people. But the patient who can laugh at himself, at his own repressive devices, for instance, can often delve with less pain than if everything is grim.

It's nearly always desirable to take language from the patient when referring to the topics he chooses to discuss. He tells us someone "browbeat" him, uses the word about two interchanges he had. We can use it too in similar contexts. The word "browbeat" may have many connotations to him, unconscious associations. In using the word, we are bringing those associations to the instant, without knowing what they are. Later we may discover more of what "browbeat" means to the person.

However, an exception to the rule of using the patient's language is when he uses vulgarity. Suppose a man says he "fucked someone over" in a business deal. We ask him to spell out what he meant, and then refer to the incident in our own words: he took brutal advantage of the person. Not that we should shy away from saying "fuck," but we may not wish to import other associations that go with the word in this context. We are not street people, or teenagers using the patient's language, and there's no sense pretending to be part of this milieu. Therefore it would be artificial and patently ridiculous of us to use his slang as if it were our daily jargon. It makes much more sense for us to be who we are. If drug addicts want to consider me an outsider because I don't know the latest language for sticking a needle into my arm, they are free to do so. In many such cases, those people need their therapist to be an outsider, and would lose respect for the therapist who borrowed their language as if he wanted to belong to their crowd.

On the other hand, we can make special use of the conciseness and evocativeness of metaphors. Some we may take from myths and from poetry, others we draw from daily events. It

would seem our most powerful metaphors come from the patient's own experiences—and especially from his dreams, where
the images are raw and very emotional. A man who was unhappily married felt extremely guilty about contemplating a divorce,
even though his wife had begun an extramarital affair soon after
the marriage. He had a dream that he went swimming, while his
wife waited on the shore. Deeper and deeper he went, and the
daylight began to disappear. Soon he found his feet covered with
mud at the bottom. Try as he might, he could not rise to the
surface. The light was now gone and so was his air. He was about
to drown when he woke up, in terror. His association to the
dream was that he would somehow "go under" during this
divorce. But could he? How could this happen? He wouldn't
literally drown. Then he became aware of an impulse to give his
wife everything. In reality, although he was talking to lawyers
about his rights, he felt tempted to give his wife not just their
house but a huge amount of his income for life, as if to say, "Take
it all, you've killed me. I won't need it anymore." He would
drown himself to atone for his guilt.

Later, the patient and I both used the image of his "drowning himself" to refer to his impulse for self-destruction. It appeared in many places where he felt similar guilt.

There is danger, however, in the indiscriminate use of metaphors; they may be counterproductive with some patients. Some
people are extremely concrete—they feel totally lost when we
bring in any association from outside the immediate realm of
their lives. What are we talking about? Others get so preoccupied with the metaphor that they lose all sense of what concerns them. One can say to them, "You act as if you're walking
on eggs," and the next thing you know, they're talking about
different kinds of eggs and lamenting the rise in price of dairy
products.

Above all, no euphemisms. When the session is over, it's
better to say, "Time's up," or "Sorry, we've got to stop," than

"I guess we covered everything." We didn't and there ought to be no embarrassment about having to stop.

Even where the patient uses euphemisms, we should not.

A man says he told his wife "what she wanted to hear"; later, she's angry when she discovers the truth. As his therapist, I wouldn't hesitate to say, for instance, "How did you feel, getting caught in an untruth?"

"You're saying I lied to her!" He might be exasperated with me.

"Did you know one thing, and deliberately tell her another?"

"Yes."

"Then that's what I'm saying. She caught you in an untruth."

Patients appreciate our confronting them. When the worst they feared is out in the open, it is seldom as bad as when they're fleeing from it. When Othello was suspicious of his wife, he pleaded with Iago, who supposedly knew whether she was unfaithful: "Give thy worst of thoughts the worst of words."

Because euphemisms are designed to hide shameful truths, they are always repressive. The very using of them reinfects the person with shame about what he is glossing over. By the way, the most influential scholar of the English language, H. W. Fowler, deplored euphemisms, preferring outright vulgarity by far.

The therapist's manner of speech proclaims him. Therapy is a place for poetic expression, and some of the most motivated therapists read poetry and collect terse, memorable language for their ideas. We are each moved by particular kinds of sayings, and we become repositories of our own forms of speech. We look for conciseness, emotionality, and force for our own sakes, so that we can deliver ourselves of truths that pain us while they stay lodged inside. As models we can help patients do the same.

10

The Patient's Cooperation

We would like our patients to arrive on time for their sessions, to leave when we say the session is over, and to pay us on time. We also would like them to tell us whatever comes to their minds, without censoring it. Ideally, the patient doesn't translate his thoughts into those that he thinks would be more acceptable to us. If he has thoughts of hating his loved ones or boss, or of wanting to strangle someone, we'd like him to tell us those thoughts. If we ask him to tell us what comes to his mind concerning some topic we introduced, we want his first thoughts and not revised versions of them. First thoughts are likely to prove more productive. If he's disappointed in us, or despises us, or has a sexual fantasy about us, we'd like him to tell us. Therapy is a place for him to express himself as he otherwise might never do. There are no penalties for truth with us. Out of his most honest moments, we shall be arriving at important insights.

And we'll also arrive at insights out of the patient's failure to meet these criteria. He'll be late, and he won't tell us the first things that come to his mind, but then later will tell us he kept these things hidden. He'll surely break the rules in many places. The early psychoanalysts put it well when they speculated that if a patient could say everything that came to his mind for a whole hour, he would be cured. Such behavior would indicate a freedom from repression and constraint that was almost unknown. As we help our patients, they become better able to say what really comes to their minds. They trust us more, and trust themselves more; they come to realize that no thought or fantasy or impulse truly disqualifies them—they develop the profoundest form of self-acceptance, and in the process learn to accept other people and see them realistically. They learn that talking about an impulse is not the same as acting on it. On the contrary, to become aware of such impulses is the best defense against acting on them. People who best master their passions are those willing to acknowledge their own destructive and self-destructive desires.

The early psychoanalysts made strict demands of their patients so far as their performance during sessions was concerned. The patient not only had to lie on a couch but with his feet together! If he separated them, the analyst might ask why. This requirement was intended to simplify the sessions, freeing the patient to concentrate completely on his thoughts and feelings. Also, psychoanalysts had made much of the fact that the patient's every act was motivated. The requirement gave small acts specific meanings that could be interpreted; the patient by his behavior expressed either conformity to a rule or resistance to it.

Most important was that physical restrictions disposed the patient to express his feelings in words, and so discover them himself. If the patient could light a cigarette when he was angry, neither he nor the therapist might realize that he was angry. If he could stroll across the room at leisure, that act might replace a sudden thought that he'd like to run away from certain obligations. The idea was to stop nonverbal behavior from substituting for the verbalization of feelings. Psychoanalysis was called "the talking cure"; in putting ideas into words, the patient learns about himself, whereas overt actions can mask understanding.

The idea that an act may substitute for the discovery of ideas seems valid to me. Although I don't have patients lie down on a couch, I do expect them not to walk around or to eat or smoke a cigarette, or even chew gum in my office.

I might make an exception with the patient who is very intense anyhow, or acutely anxious. Too much anxiety can interfere with thinking. Allowing such a person to walk around can help. However, I make no such exceptions where smoking is concerned. That rule is for me, and not just for them. Besides, it wouldn't be fair to my next patient to have him come into a room full of smoke when this one leaves.

We may not need to announce all these rules. It's time enough when the patient asks hesitantly whether he can smoke, to tell him the rule. There is, however, another requirement, which I may state early in the game. I ask the patient to say whatever comes to his mind, not to hold back feelings or ideas of any kind, and if he's caught himself doing that, to tell me at once. Not that anyone says everything that comes to mind, but the ideal is important.

Thoughts or feelings about me are especially important for him to disclose. During treatment I may bring up some topic, like a symbol in a dream, and ask him the first thing that comes to mind about it. Speed is important; it enables the person to identify thoughts that he might otherwise censor, if he had the time.

But there is one rule of therapy that I nearly always discuss with new patients, for various reasons, and that is confidentiality.

11

Confidentiality

Confidentiality must become a specialty of ours. Our patients often trust us with information they would want no one else to have. Moreover, they trust us to explore the recesses of their souls, and along with them to uncover other facts whose discovery is mortifying in its very prospect. They need confidence in our ability not to disclose such information to anyone.

Not surprisingly, most patients are slow to arrive at this state of trust. They wait a long time before being willing to reveal themselves fully. They watch us narrowly, and if we seem aghast at anything they disclose, they may worry that we will have a need to discuss it with others, and they may retreat. There's a burden on us to be absolutely above reproach. And even if we are, their establishing trust in us is in large part up to them. As therapy progresses, our patients discover and disclose more about themselves. Their very act of confiding in us engenders deeper trust. No matter that we can be absolutely counted on for discretion; in the end the patient must teach himself that we're worth trusting.

Often a patient will decide, "I'm going to be open about everything except one topic. I won't tell the therapist about my alcoholism." Or, for instance, "I won't tell the therapist about the crooked business deal I'm involved in."

Freud once elected not to treat a man in politics who had refused to reveal privileged state secrets; Freud reasoned that since no fact is independent in the psyche, the man would need to conceal much else. Whether or not we should follow Freud's lead and reject such a patient, it seems unmistakable that secrecy from the therapist has repercussions. The need to withhold a fact interferes with free association—with effortless traveling from one thought to another. The patient who is withholding something must pause repeatedly to decide whether he's coming too near to his secret. If it seems that he is, he stops, and deliberately changes direction. Even if he decides that his secret is safe, his very pause to make the decision has clipped the wings of the process.

It may not matter that the concealed fact is actually unimportant in the patient's life; his choice not to trust the therapist has reverberations. Any such choice renews distrust and causes it to spread. We must address ourselves early to any withholding, perhaps tolerating it for a while but always mindful of it. It becomes important to make the patient aware that he is withholding something, even before we insist that he reveal it.

Sometimes I take a radical approach.

Years ago, a fellow walked into my office, and told me that his last therapist, whose name he would not reveal, fell asleep during sessions. The patient seemed very overcontrolled, and as he droned on, I too felt almost overcome by somnolence. He then volunteered that he would never reveal the other therapist's name, in order to protect him. He showed a hint of animation in saying this; I got the impression from his tone that he was challenging me, engaging in a power struggle with me. He was saying, in effect, "I may be reduced to seeking your services, but there's something you can't have."

Afterward, in that same first hour, he told me about running into a man by accident just outside that therapist's office. They'd been in Paris together, while Hitler was there. Both were Jewish and they'd roamed the streets without passports or identification. There was the daily threat of their being spotted. The Nazis would march such a man into a nearby doorway and ask him to show his penis; if it was circumcised, the man was shot immediately. That was my patient's story, and even today I have no reason to doubt it.

I was being assigned the role of Nazi storm trooper. The patient wouldn't reveal all to me, either. Beneath his even-tempered exterior, his incredible monotony of tone, was a tenacious refusal to expose himself; and, I later learned, a power of rebellion that had saved his life. But this reaction to me might make my helping him impossible. These psychic connections were unclear to me at the time, but I could sense a necessity to take a strong position.

He was telling the story without emotion, and was droning on. On what felt like a whim, I asked him, "Where was it that you met the friend?"

"Oh, I can't tell you that. You might figure out who the doctor was." Now the belligerence was unmistakable.

A few more questions of mine during the hour were designed to demonstrate that in concealing the therapist's name, he would have to withhold much else from me. At the end of the session I told him I would not work with him unless he told me all, *including that therapist's name,* which I swore never to reveal. He refused and left.

But he called me back a few days later, after talking to another therapist. He agreed to tell me anything I wanted to know. In my office he gave me the actual name, which virtually never came up again.

It took years to help this man, whose macabre experience had motivated him to live a shell of a life in our free country. There was another thing he wanted to confide in me. He and his friend had been trapped once in Paris, with a pair of German police approaching them from different directions. They had seized the Nazis and he had strangled one with his bare hands. His own capacity for violence had astonished him; he still feared it and tried never to be angry. His mode of speech attested to the censorship of all emotionality. In treatment he sometimes showed signs of paranoia and talked about murdering people. Then he would return to a state of overcontrol, as if he were without any personality at all.

Slowly he released himself. He had sexual problems but with time he overcame them. As the interactional psychologists contend, the validation of another person may prove vital. A relationship with a woman, herself extremely patient, was central to his cure, but I am very proud of the work that I did with him. In retrospect, I am glad that I insisted at the outset that he confide in me. It was crucial that he trust me with his emotions. I think he felt it less of a defeat to capitulate at the outset of therapy than if he had set a precedent of secrecy.

I would not insist that every patient tell me everything that he conciously knew as a precondition to my treating him. But if the person didn't, I would repeatedly make him aware of his distrust, and study that distrust along with him. "Observe that you're building a barbed-wire fence around that segment of your life." The patient's choice to withhold should, at the very least, always be kept in the forefront of his awareness.

Therapists can do much to communicate their trustworthiness. For one thing, the therapist must never talk about other patients, past or present. To do so, even without mentioning the other person's name, will invariably inhibit the patient. Seemingly innocent comments, intended to reassure the patient, may have the opposite effect. "I was able to help a man just like you, who also was stuck on a much younger woman." The person can't help but feel that he might become a referent for some future patient "just like him." Who knows but that the next listener will be able to identify him? Even if he has no such actual thought, he may be undermined slightly.

The therapist, even when not with his patients, should try to act in ways that afford him a purity of spirit. I've heard many therapists talk about their patients at restaurants or at parties or in elevators—not by name necessarily, although sometimes even that. In so doing, the therapist devalues his patients and the whole process, devalues them to himself. The therapist makes himself less worthy, whether or not the patient knows what he has said. Even when the patient doesn't know, I believe that the effects of how the therapist treats the patient behind his back do become manifest in the hour. The possibility of a spiritual alliance is weakened; although the patient cannot articulate the loss, he does not rise to the relationship as he might.

The other side of confidentiality consists of the patient's responsibilities. These I bring up early, often in the first hour. I ask patients not to discuss their sessions with anyone, sometimes asking whether this would be difficult. If they say it would be, I investigate why. And, if a patient who has promised confidentiality breaks that promise, I certainly probe to find out why.

There are several reasons why confidentiality on the part of the patient is so important. One is that I want our sessions to reverberate in the patient's mind. His very intention behind talking about our sessions may be to silence their effect. There are people who make a travesty out of every intimate relationship by discussing it with others to get their opinions. Also, their discussing the sessions cuts down the intimacy of their relationship with the therapist, even if they don't distort the facts. And often they do distort them, or at the very least, choose a listener likely to support their position. "You! He said that about you? You never make excessive demands of people. Where did he get that idea?" The patient feels relieved of the need to think about the assertion.

The patient who discusses his therapy with loved ones or

acquaintances creates other problems. Knowing he'll repeat to them what he says in sessions, he disposes himself to censor what he says in the sessions themselves. And once he brings people in, it becomes hard to leave them out. He's given them every right to ask, "What did you say to the therapist today?"

Most patients understand at once the desirability of not talking about their sessions. This, of course, does not imply that if the person discovers something about himself in therapy, he forfeits the right to talk about it outside. It's enough that the patient doesn't discuss the therapy or quote the therapist. If the patient wants to make a point, he doesn't have to say that his therapist thought so. "Just say what you think is so. Possess it as yours."

During the course of treatment, patients may spontaneously ask me not to mention something they just said. It's as if after disclosing something they're ashamed of, they suddenly picture the world knowing about it. I always give candid assurance that I won't tell anyone, ever, what the patient tells me. The patient's request for confidentiality, even if it's the eleventh time he's asked, should never be treated lightly. It may be his anxiety talking when he repeats, "Now be sure not to mention this."

Such patients know they're repeating themselves, and they often feel a bit ridiculous making the request. They're likely to appreciate the therapist's decency in not making light of it. (His worst possible answer would be, "Who would I mention it to?" —at once twitting them for asking and implying that their main safeguard is circumstantial, and not the surety of the therapist's trustworthiness.)

Eventually such patients must learn not to keep asking. They must express trust en route to developing it. But while they suffer, the therapist's indulgence is absolutely necessary for them.

Interestingly, our insistence on strict confidentiality on the patient's part amounts to strong assurance that we ourselves are trustworthy. That we care so much about the inviolability of the hour is reassuring. I sometimes add that I won't talk about our sessions either, but usually I assume this is taken for granted.

There are, of course, limits to confidentiality. Suppose the patient confesses child abuse? The mere fact that it is a patient reporting this does not commit us to secrecy. Such patients may actually be using confession to lighten their guilt, in which case the therapist can too easily become an accomplice, in effect by allowing them to atone and resume the abuse. Threats of homicide and suicide must be evaluated individually. Is the thought of suicide a mere moment of "to be or not to be?" Or has the patient made provisions, rented a room in a plush hotel, and procured a deadly poison? Some patients cry out for us to protect them from their own worst impulses. They confide their plans to us so that we will take action. The decision is never easy, and these are the cases we should always discuss with colleagues. Fortunately, unless we specialize in such cases, we are faced with this kind of problem only rarely.

12

Privileges and Limits

As psychotherapists we have an almost unholy power during a session. We can ask our patient about any event or what it reminds him of. We can ask him how he acted in some situation, or why, and how he felt at the time. We can ask him what he thinks, or feels, about anything—including us. If he's quiet, we can ask, "What are you thinking right now?" No other professional, nor even the person's lover, has quite our privileges. A lover who fears he's losing ground might say, "A penny for your thoughts." We are permitted to hear those thoughts and to be paid at the same time. For anyone whose greatest excitement is to see the human experience unfold, there's no better occupation.

Our patient may offer interpretations. He tells what he thinks a dream means, or why he thinks someone acted a certain way. He speculates about the effect he had on a friend, or why he didn't get a job. He draws conclusions about his looks and personality. He tells us some topic is or isn't important. He may chastise us for wasting time on something that seems trivial to him but important to us. If he thinks something is important, we must heed it, give him time, convey that we heard it. Even if he

71

considers a thing trivial, it remains our privilege to ask him to enlarge on it. He has freedom in the sessions, but we have the right to inquire where we wish. He says what comes to his mind, uses his characteristic defenses, but we have the right to describe what he is doing. He may curse us, call us incompetent—or brilliant, perhaps, as a device to keep us far afield from some topic.

To us, everything he says or does in the hour is important. It is his product. It teaches us something about him. But his conclusions about himself must never preempt our thinking. His *interpretation* of a dream, even if true, we may construe as a *reaction* to the dream. His determination of a cause, of why someone acted, may be interesting, fascinating. But we retain the right to draw our own conclusions. His perception of us may be accurate, informative, but we may in the end consider it primarily a characterological reaction to us.

He has the right to present his theories to us. But we reserve the right to think of them in terms of him and his problems, to ask, "Is he saying something about himself, and if so what?" Such privileges in the session are absolutely necessary for us. We could not do our work without them.

Obviously, there are privileges we don't have. We're not there to gratify our impulses at his expense, as by flirting, or having sex with the person. Of course, these practices have few defenders. But there are subtler practices, forms of showing off, that have a long history even among seasoned practitioners. Indeed, the public has come to think of them as basic psychological devices, but they are tricks that nearly always do more harm than good.

One such trick is to tell people what they're really feeling underneath—to read their minds. It's as if to say, "You can fool yourself but you can't fool me." For instance, the patient says he loves his father, and the therapist says, "You're really afraid of him." If this were true, then the patient should be led to discover it; if false, it confuses things badly. It's always wrong to tell people what they're feeling. People have the best, the ultimate access to their own inner lives. Telling them that they're an open book is belittling.

Among its harms are that it accuses the person of being transparent. With paranoid patients, who suffer in nearly every case from fear of just this, it can be downright dangerous. The suggestible person will believe us, even if we're wrong. This technique deprives people of the chance to discover their own feelings and label them. Developing this ability is requisite to their real gain in therapy.

This means that we must never tell, or imply, to patients how they ought to feel. It's a holiday, they ought to be happy. Someone who had their best interests at heart just died; they ought to feel miserable. Patients turn to us as if we had some rulebook, as if their feelings needed to be sanctioned by precedent, by how others felt in similar circumstances. Few responsible therapists would answer the direct question, "How should I feel?" There are no "shoulds." And it is also dangerous to volunteer that any feeling a patient reports is "natural," which is to say "commonplace." This is seldom a valid way of offering reassurance; the hidden danger here is that the patient is encouraged to measure himself, his adequacy, by others.

In much the same vein, we must never rebuke patients for supposedly contradictory feelings. A man is cursing his wife. He says he's sorry he married her. "But five minutes ago, you said you loved her and were glad you married her." There is an implicit criticism here, a demand for consistency, which may well bespeak the therapist's discomfort at having to sit and hear the rush of anger. Perhaps it implies to the patient that he's failing in holding the marriage together. But, by the therapist's attempt to suppress such upsurgent anger, he betrays the patient's right to feel as he does.

The therapist who truly wants to communicate that the patient holds both feelings should make his intervention at another time, not while the anger is being expressed. At some other time, he might say, "You have two feelings toward her: anger and a deep compassion. It's important to realize this." He might even add that neither obliterates the other. This way he is underscoring the patient's right to have two or more different reactions toward the same object; he is not using one to mitigate the other.

People, as we all know in our more dispassionate moments, experience a rapid succession of feelings, in no necessarily logical order. The springs of our emotions are psychological, and any attempt to simplify by eliminating logical contradictions will inhibit, or infuriate, the patient.

More generally, we may ask, "What are you feeling?" Or, more specifically, "How did you feel when . . . ?" This helps him do the work. Usually, the person will tell us if he knows, and if he doesn't want us to know, then our anticipating him with our insight would have been useless anyhow.

Asking has many advantages, not the least of which is that we may evoke the patient's characteristic defenses. If he conceals a feeling, as by changing the subject, we come to recognize his resistances, and can bring them to his attention when necessary.

Another essentially belittling and always unnecessary trick is to tell the patient why he did something, rather than asking him. "You distrust me because I remind you of your father." If this is really true, we can help the patient discover it, by questions. How does he feel about us? If he volunteers that he distrusts us, why does he? Possibly at this juncture, he'll astonish us with a reason that we could never have guessed, one that we would have squelched with our surmise.

Spectacular strokes of interpretation foster dependency. The patient comes to expect them of us; he would feel lost without us. He comes to feel that his inner life is so complex that he could never fathom it on his own. Smaller steps, taken by the patient himself, are always better than a grand leap by us. Naturally, we have surmises. But the most we should do is to ask.

Finally, we must be careful not to set goals unilaterally for our patients. The feminist therapist might want a woman patient to be more than a housewife, for example—to pursue a career as well. The therapist who is conventional might expect his patients all to get married and "fulfill" themselves by having children, including patients with no such needs. It's one thing to release hidden aspirations; that's part of our work. But we mustn't superimpose our own aspirations onto our patients; all goals should derive from what we learn about the individual.

If the patient's chosen direction feels unacceptable to us—for instance, too revolutionary or too conservative—it may be that we should send the patient to someone else. Patients are with us to discover their own dreams and to pursue them as far as possible. Unfortunately, many patients, because they come to us with low self-esteem, are ready prey for conversions. We must never inflict our biases on them. It's up to us to respect human diversity, to bring out the grain in our material and not to paint over it. Indeed, one can almost evaluate the effectiveness of a therapist by the variety of lifestyles his patients feel comfortable in choosing.

PART THREE

Diagnosis

If we could first know where we are and whither we are tending, we could better judge what to do and how to do it.

—Lincoln

13

Diagnosis as Progressive

As psychotherapists, we make our diagnoses progressively. In the first session we listen to the patient's account of his symptoms, learn about his history, observe and experience his style with us. We compare what he says with how he says it. For instance, a man smiles when he talks about dire mishaps in his life. "So what could I do? My mother had unexpectedly died, I was only sixteen. Naturally I went to work"—all said with a smile on his face. As we experience the person, we begin searching for what causes his pain or interferes with his functioning. How does he see the world, including himself? And how did he evolve what we come to recognize as his characteristic outlook?

In subsequent sessions, we observe how he responds to our interventions. For example, we sympathize with him, and he becomes furious with us. He apparently despises intimacy—is afraid of it. What does it mean to him? It turns out, let us say, that he is afraid that we, too, may suddenly die if he draws us close to his heart. He gives us health tips and warns us about the potential hazards of the air-purifying machine in our office. Our perception of his problem is amplifying.

Slowly we pass on our knowledge to him, revealing how he

perceives us. What are his resistances, and how strong are they? Is he truly motivated to change? We learn by degrees what he wants for himself and how hard he is willing to work for it. For us as psychotherapists, a diagnosis would be a full statement of his problem, where it comes from, and how and why he holds onto it. Evolving such a diagnosis is intimately related to the process of treatment. The nearest we come to completing our diagnosis is after the last session, or in some cases years later, when an insight (perhaps derived from work with another patient) gives us still further understanding. The process of diagnosing a patient is integrally related to treatment itself. We proceed on the basis of what we know.

If our purpose were merely disposition of the patient—for instance, to decide upon whether he should be released from a hospital, or whether he should be allowed insurance coverage— we might be satisfied with the rough categories given in the official psychiatric manual. We sum up our patient as "Generalized Anxiety Disorder DSM III 300.02." We can do this kind of classification even before therapy begins. Typically, there is no need to revise this kind of statement; hospitals often recopy the diagnosis given to a patient twenty years ago. Such diagnoses are made objectively; that is their value. A first-year psychiatric student might arrive at most of them by looking at overt symptoms and ascertaining such objective facts as the patient's highest level of recent social and occupational functioning and his physical condition.

But such a notion of diagnosis will not serve us as therapists. By the time the psychiatric student finishes his residency and has been in private practice a while, he tends to use such categories only in official documents. They're static and insufficient, and in some cases alienate him from his patients. They simply don't do justice to the progressive nature of discovery and change, which is psychotherapy.

As a rule, our patient comes to us lamenting pain of some

kind, or inability to function, or both. Almost never does the patient say, "I suffer from a distortion in how I see other people," or "I have a distorted perception of myself." He may say, "People don't like me," or "I'm really not worth very much." He may be right in saying they don't like him, and ultimately we'll learn what he does that antagonizes them. But underlying his social difficulties are his biased view of himself and life.

Recognizing that there is a bias in one's perception is so unusual that if a patient were to tell us in a first session, "I tend to see threat where it isn't," we could immediately surmise that he'd been in therapy before, or at the very least was a reader of psychological literature.

In some rare cases, the patient gives no indication that there is anything wrong. He's come because the world is mistreating him, as if we could possibly intervene on his behalf. For instance, a man offers himself to us as unfortunate—try as he may, he simply can't find a woman truly loving, one not out to exploit him. Still, that he's come to us means he suspects that there is something more—that there's something he's doing, or not doing, that interferes with his forming the kind of relationship he wants. Nearly always, a few pointed questions will reveal such a suspicion.

To appreciate the progressive nature of diagnosis and how it integrates with what we do, it's important to step back, like artists from a work in progress, to see how diagnosis relates to therapy as a whole.

The patient often comes to us with a sense of helplessness regarding what he wants to change. For instance, he's depressed, feels empty inside, or is subject to fits of anger. If he sees that the problem dates back—was there when he was a child—he is especially likely to experience himself as in its grip. He has tried in different ways to shake the problem, to cure himself, but has failed. He is prone to contrast our curing him with his doing it himself—a very misleading opposition of ideas. Therapy enables a patient to cure himself.

Actually, we're going to reveal the problem to him—not just the outlook and feelings but also the behavior that is part of it. True, much of what the patient does feels quite natural to him; he acts in accordance with his outlook. But his own behavior reinforces the outlook. The patient is unconsciously renewing his personality traits by acting in ways that reinforce the underlying beliefs. Even such seemingly vacuous qualities as indifference or lack of desire to live are being kept alive by the patient's actions. It is because he has been perpetuating these attitudes that he has the ability to change himself. The essence of psychotherapy is to enable the patient to appreciate how he has been keeping himself the same—and how he can change.

Recall the discussion earlier, and the proposition that every choice restores intensity to the complex motivating ideas that give rise to it. The choice propels the person forward. A particular woman feels unacceptable to men and caters unduly to one man after the other. Such behavior perpetuates her feelings of inadequacy. Her very compliance reconvinces her that she is unworthy and that any man would be right to leave her if she spoke her mind. In each relationship, her anger eventually builds, and though she wants marriage, the prospect of spending a lifetime with a particular man seems dismal. In fury, she ends the relationship. This happens repeatedly. Her own behavior restores her belief that no man would want her if she expressed her opinions. Her own acts of compliance, begun with a demanding father, thus kept alive her picture of herself as inadequate and of men as intolerant.

Such patterns of behavior and point of view are quite often begun in the home. Diagnosis entails not only seeing the point of view motivating the behavior, but also identifying the network of behavior that restores the point of view.

Whatever the behavior, after a while it comes to seem

sensible and safe. The outlook disposes the person to feel that any alternative would be dangerous. There is always initial anxiety when going against the grain of an established pattern. The temptation is to regress to what is comfortable, and thus people are disposed to continue acting in the very ways that renew the outlook they hold.

The ultimate diagnosis should always include revealing to the patient exactly how his actions affect him. It should clarify by which of his actions he has been unconsciously perpetuating the very outlook he wants to change. The man who offered me health tips because he was afraid I would die was, by that single small habit, contributing to his fear. He was not merely manifesting the fear by that behavior, but propelling it into the future of his own psyche. His expressing concern about me contributed to his feeling that anyone he loved would die and abandon him.

It is because we go on making discoveries throughout the course of therapy that diagnosis must be progressive. There are new obstacles. Just as we imagine we're closing in on something, the patient decides to lead us on a merry chase. Recall the myth in which Jason, when he reached the kingdom that was rightfully his, was told that new labors awaited him before he could possess that kingdom. What seemed to us to be simple truths are barred by unexpected resistances, and as psychotherapists we must deal with them. The scene changes, often radically—the patient appears cooperative, we felt on our way to an easy comprehension of his difficulties—when suddenly he puts up obstacles we never expected. He becomes irrationally angry with us, or forgets what went on last time. The road unexpectedly lengthens. Like good Jasons, we must assume the new terms of the challenge, redefining our task. We may find ourselves diagnosing in the hundredth session, if there is one, just as in the first. Though we may already have helped the patient considerably, his unconscious once again yields up a new dragon.

Diagnosis thus follows the analogy once drawn about

Michelangelo's way of doing sculpture by a contemporary and fellow artist. Giorgio Vasari said that Michelangelo, looking at a piece of marble, pictured the nearest contour of it, working only on that surface until it was complete. Then he would go on to the next surface, so that the whole effect was like pulling a sailboat out of the water; one saw first its topmost portions and then lower parts of it, until it appeared that the whole boat had been pulled from the water.

14

Diagnosis from What the Patient Tells Us

Diagnosis has always been considered as much an art as a science. What gives rise to any of our impressions of people? There are incredibly subtle ways that people affect us. They touch chords in us of memory and association. We sometimes seem to arrive at our conclusions by flashes of insight. Yet as therapists it becomes our task to objectify as much as possible. That we "feel" a patient's selfishness or inadequacy is something that, by itself, can be of no use to him; we must become as expert as possible in documenting our evidence and putting that evidence into words.

One way we learn about the patient is from what he says about himself. "Whenever I go out on a date, I could scream." Often we must draw inferences from the way the person describes his life.

We look for trends in what the patient tells us. A man says that a woman jilted him a month ago. Soon afterward, he mentions that he thought he was in line for a promotion, felt sure he would get it, but it unexpectedly went to someone else, a newcomer in the office. Our patient felt terrible. Then another story of what seemed to him like ambush! There were unexpected bad breaks three times. How was it he had no idea of what was going to happen? Is he given to denying evidence against him, or at the very least to not seeing it? His problem is not merely what happens to him, but has to do with his *never anticipating* these outcomes.

It is remarkable how slow even very bright people can be at seeing trends in their lives. They get caught up in the moment and don't recognize repeating patterns. One man is constantly dismayed that people take advantage of him. As we look closely, we see that given the choice between two people—in a business deal, in friendship, or even in love—he chooses to interact with the one who already gave him reason to be suspicious. He invariably drifts toward that person and avoids the other. Does he *want* the experience of being taken advantage of? Or, perhaps he selects shoddy people, because they are in no position to condemn him for his own failings? We don't know yet, but we observe his systematic way of choosing—and of feeling.

Another man, whose life is a shambles, never seems to look back but is always telling us about some wonderful break, some golden opportunity that he's about to take advantage of. Although he's broke and in debt, he truly imagines that he will soon be rich and well-off. How this will happen varies from one month to the next. The one real constant in his life is his dream of success—which he takes to be a reality.

Still another person is forever acutely anxious about one thing—it might pertain to his job, where he imagines he blundered and is about to be fired, or to the birth of his child next month, who he is sure will have a serious birth defect. Curiously, he never has two such worries at the same time, and never none. As soon as one concern is erased, a new one arrives. These people never seem to learn from having been wrong. As their lives undergo change, their fixated beliefs remain remarkably constant.

Always we look for these constants—in our patients' feelings, ways of perceiving, philosophies, in their choices of friends, in the kinds of trouble they get into. We search for ways to describe what is unchanging about their outlook, seeing what is invariant amid the tumult of their lives. As we enlarge their own sense of what to look for, we become better able to perceive these invariable trends.

For example, a woman reports that her marriage of twelve years was unsatisfactory. She felt deprived, although her husband did whatever she asked. If on a whim she wanted him to build a stone wall in their garden, he did so on the first available weekend. Finally, as her anxiety mounted, she persuaded him to go to sex orgies with her. They became the swingers of their small town, and she constantly talked about their going, trying to persuade old friends to join in. A few couples did, but the majority thought she had lost her mind.

Not long afterward, as a result of some of her swinging experiences, she announced that she was a lesbian. Again she did her best to rally people she knew into trying her new lifestyle. Nothing could be better, she announced, than sex with a woman. Her formerly elegant clothing now gave way to deliberately unconsidered dress, and she derided married women who'd shared past interests with her as under their husbands' domination. She could no longer stand their company. In the end, she left her husband, tried to sue him for as much as she could get, but lost her case badly. In my office, she seemed extremely anxious, although she said she was doing well, running two bookstores for women only, and enjoying it. Her only problem, she said, was the acute headaches, which specialists called psychological.

Her life and appearance had changed radically at least four times. But there were motifs that didn't change. She was at every stage anxious and uncomfortable in her own skin. She sought to improve her lot not by studying herself, but by making a radical change, and then criticizing others and trying to change them, too. She would try to remedy her own acute discomfort by regulating other people's lives. Despite her different appearances, she was unmistakably the same person. Only the content of what she sought to do had really changed. The form remained the same.

While the patient tells us about his past experiences, we always look for what is constant. The experienced psychotherapist gradually enlarges his awareness of possible constants. We integrate what the person tells us with his reports of past feelings. We ask what he did in those different situations, and as he tells us we look for trends there too. Does he tend to overstay in relationships? Does he force moments to a crisis, as by rushing to the telephone or making irreversible decisions before giving himself time to collect all the pertinent information or to think?

Whatever we learn will integrate with information we obtain first hand. What he's done in the past, for instance, he is likely to do with us. If he's disappeared on people just when they thought a relationship was developing, and has never told them his misgivings, we had better be on the watch for his doing the same with us. He may already have serious reservations that he won't discuss with us. We observe his personal style in the room with us and relate what we see to the material he's telling us about. If we have trouble imagining the person in front of us behaving as he says he did, this in itself will prove meaningful. Also, we'll learn about his childhood, and this too will give us much more insight into why he feels and acts in the ways he's been describing to us.

The ability to draw abstract conclusions is crucial to making good diagnoses. Our patients are stuck in their particulars, worried at each stage of their lives about obstacles confronting them. We must learn to see beyond those obstacles while not disregarding them. Every particular has at least one general message in it, and usually more.

Each year, as new patterns, like "the borderline personality," are studied and described, our active vocabulary increases. We learn new implications of those conditions already familiar to us, and in this way also increase our capacity to discern trends. What the early psychoanalysts taught us about the narcissist has been greatly enlarged in recent years, for instance. As we study how our patients behave with us in the sessions, we amplify our understanding of them and of other people as well.

15

The Patient's Personal Style

A patient talks very fast, and seems to make a drama out of everything he says. He was one of seven children, and his early life was always a contest for attention. He expects to have little time to talk and so he hurries, just as he did back then. He feels breathless ten minutes into the hour. His style is a direct continuation of the adjustment he had to make at home.

Another is soft-spoken. He hesitates to voice even the mildest criticism of anything. If he feels he's been complaining, he quickly takes back what he said and assures us he meant no offense. He can't take criticism in any form. At home, a child who did anything wrong was kept in the doghouse for days. His father refused to speak to a child who got a poor report card. We can almost feel him trying to sneak through life so as to avoid repeating one of those terrible moments in childhood when he, or one of his siblings, did something wrong and was punished for it.

Another closes his eyes and turns his face to one side when we say something painful. We can almost see him in his highchair as an infant with his mother pushing the spoon with its distasteful ingredients toward his lips. Some patients blame themselves for everything that goes wrong; others start right out by criticizing us and expressing deep skepticism of everything we stand for. Even before entering our office, one person might peek around the corner, looking into the room, while another comes bursting in, finds a comfortable seat, and begins.

Such variations of style are likely to tell us a great deal about people's traits. More often than not, we can ascertain a considerable amount about their childhoods, and at the very least about how they felt about themselves and other people back then.

If we wanted to play the role of magician, we could say to the person who rushes his words out in a terrible flurry, "Your parents didn't give you enough time to express your ideas." But that's not our purpose. Still, from our observations of style, we form hypotheses, and might even ask such a question as, "Were your parents good listeners?" We're not surprised when the person answers, "Are you kidding! My father was always drunk so I never spoke to him, and my mother was so busy with the family and with work, it was hard to get through to her." As therapists, we can see the dovetailing between what the patient tells us about his experiences and his style of interacting.

As we get to know the person, we go on learning more about his style. He is secretive. We did not realize this. He breezes in one day, after saying nothing about his job, and tells us he's abruptly quit. Working conditions were awful; his boss was brutal. We wonder if this practice of secrecy followed by action began in the home; did he have parents who didn't care or who told him exactly what they wanted him to do, so that he dared not confide in them?

In addition, he may neglect to tell us good news. "By the way, I had my first acting job on television last Tuesday. People said I was excellent." Why didn't he tell us? Perhaps it has to do with our special relationship. But when we ask, we might find out that he didn't think we'd care. He tells us a sad story of being valedictorian in junior high school when neither of his parents bothered to go to the graduation ceremony. He apparently expected the same unresponsiveness from us. Better not to tell us than to risk more of the same disappointment.

We are now on the subject of *transference*, the carrying forth of expectations and impressions and feelings from a past person, usually a parent, to us as therapists. Transference includes not merely feeling the same ways about us, but also treating us as he did the parent or other past figure.

We make many judgments from how the patient interacts with us. If we point something out, does he whirl on us in anger, perhaps misquoting us? Does he listen patiently and seem genuinely appreciative? Does he feel attacked when we've merely asked him a question? Does he confide in us?

Very often, what we learn about the person's style comes to us first through our own feelings when in his presence. The patient has just walked out of the office. We feel terribly sad. "Why?" we ask ourselves. There's a sense that we're failing him. Are we? How could we be, it's only the second session? Apparently we have constructed an inordinately high expectation of ourselves, if we feel we're failing already. Is this feeling all too familiar to us? If it has currency in our lives, we had better study it both for our own sakes and to understand the patient better.

On the other hand, suppose we decide that the feeling is unusual for us. We study how the person, without our knowing it, may have induced that feeling in us. Reconsidering our two sessions with the patient, we see that he has done a number of things that might lead us to feel this way. He's told us that he has absolute faith in us; he knows from our reputation that we can and will help him. He looks at us, wide-eyed, as if to say, "I'm in your hands." He has recounted how his parents, his boss, and his last therapist all let him down, while assuring us he knows it will be different with us. By these devices and others, he has placed the burden of curing him directly on our shoulders, while he himself has only to wait and see. We're feeling the effects of this burden, which we took on without thinking about it. Suddenly, having identified what he's doing to us, we feel freer, lighter. Soon we'll be pointing out to him how he treats us. But even now, through our recognition, we've made a marvelous addition to our diagnosis of him, by this insight into how he interacts with other people.

As a rule, our impressions of the patient amplify our understanding of his life. We can see why he has the trouble he reports. We know that he hasn't simply run into the wrong kinds of people over and over again. But sometimes it's hard to reconcile what we feel in his presence with what others apparently feel. These cases often present surprises, and in many of them the discrepancy stems from problems of our own.

For instance, a woman seems dedicated to her therapy. She comes to sessions on time, appears appreciative, and seems to be on course. She expresses loyalty, but she reports that her friendships explode. Sooner or later she becomes vehemently angry at people she treasured and never sees them again. As her therapist, we wonder why.

One could too easily succumb to the notion, "Well, it's different with me. I'm more sensitive than the others in her life." But this vainglorious conclusion can lull us into a state of unreadiness. Our time will come.

Sure enough, one day things backfire in her life. She takes our lightest comment of reassurance and snaps at us, "I know you're saying this just to humor me." Suddenly she's in a fury and storms out of the session. Nor was her comment completely wrong. We recognize that we have felt twinges of annoyance, which we haven't acknowledged to ourselves. We were afraid that she might blow up and didn't want to incite her to fury or to risk possible damage to the relationship. Now we see clearly what we had wanted to overlook—her own role in her failures; we had colluded with her in the theory that others were to blame. When she was unfair to us, we willingly endured the annoyance, supposedly for her sake, but really for ours. We have done her a disservice by letting her go on without starting to reveal to her how she had been harming herself. Hopefully, she'll be back and we can make use of what we now appreciate fully. But if we had studied the discrepancy between our relationship with her and how she gets along with others, we would have approached the problem more directly at the start.

Contrasts between how we experience a patient and how others have apparently responded to him are always informative. From such contrasts we can enlarge our diagnoses and often discover important truths we've overlooked.

I personally favor beginning treatment by not asking numerous questions about the person's life, questions he can answer factually, for the very reason that I want his style to emerge as early as possible. He can begin talking about whatever content he wants, in whatever way he wants. If he wants to start out by telling me that the pictures on my wall are crooked, he has that right. Little by little, I will learn about the significant people in his life. If there are omissions—he mentions his mother but never his father—I can ask about what I need to know. His very choice is instructive.

As the patient's mode of perceiving us and behaving with us changes in therapy, so does his diagnosis. The relation between diagnosis and treatment is an ongoing interchange from the first session to the last.

16

Heightening Our Diagnostic Sense

We've discussed how to obtain a diagnosis from what the patient tells us about himself, knowingly or not, and from his style in the room with us. These sources reveal what is most obvious about him, such as the way he dresses, and his tone. As Oscar Wilde once put it, "Only the shallow refuse to judge by appearances. The secret of life is in the visible, not the invisible." Psychology, in trying to distinguish itself from the body of knowledge that might be acquired by the laity, has overstressed the invisible, and has sometimes overlooked the obvious.

Every therapist develops his own set of questions, which he answers for himself about his patient, whether or not he need actually ask them of the patient. In large part, these questions reflect our own conceptions of health. Is the person engaged in a long-standing love relationship? How well does he function at work? Does he get along with fellow employees? Has he kept friends over a long period of time? Of his own sex? Of the opposite sex? Of different ages, or only younger? Or only older? What does he value about them? What would they say about him? In themselves, these are not diagnostic questions, but they give us clues. They afford us hypotheses.

If he has no love relationship and wants one, has he the power to love, to experience being loved without pulling away? Suppose he has no friend of the opposite sex, except for the one person he loves. Perhaps he likes only those of his own sex, and libidinizes the other. We may wonder whether he truly likes the person he's married to. If his friends are all much younger, then perhaps he hates the notion of getting older, and despises himself as an older person. He is fleeing into youth. Let us say it turns out further that he lies about his age, pretends to be ten years younger. We are on the trail of something big. "Whoever will not be his age / Knows nothing of his age but pain," wrote Richard Wilbur in translating a passage of Voltaire's.

In asking the patient about how he has arranged his life, we are gathering cues about his inner life. The content of his answers does not in itself comprise the diagnosis; from the fact that the person is twice divorced or loses one job after the other, we can't be sure about him. Our real diagnosis must come from the study of the patient himself. We owe him no less. But our scrutiny of his outside life helps alert us about what to look for.

And there are questions we can ask ourselves about the patient that heighten our appreciation of his style. Suppose he seems like a decent-enough person, reasonably attractive, hard-working. We wonder why he's never been able to establish a love relationship. I like to ask myself, "Suppose I had to take a three-day bus ride somewhere with this person. How would I feel?" The answer sometimes heightens my sense of what I would object to in him, or what I would really like more of. Or, "Suppose I were married to this person, what would that be like?" Small failings that I might have overlooked in the hour suddenly jump into prominence. Selfishness I have too easily forgiven would become a problem. Or the person's overconcern with my comfort at his own expense might feel cloying as I indulge in this fantasy. And what could be worse than an all-forgiving nature, with which the patient would be "understanding" even toward a stranger who did me injury! Picturing ourselves as an intimate of a patient can heighten our sense of such tendencies and of how, by their effects on others, they must harm the patient.

It is also helpful to ask ourselves about the patient's emotional range. Do we see in him humor, kindness, rage, love? Does he blame himself sometimes, and is he also able to blame others when they are at fault? Does he agonize over mistakes to such a degree that others feel helpless to reassure him it wasn't so bad? Can he take pleasure? Is he the sort who measures what he gives to others, and who wants quid pro quo? It is never a service to exempt the patient for a personality flaw, since in real life he will pay for deficiencies. A stern list of what we want for him is far more optimistic than a lenient one.

Finally, we need to think about our patient's personal gifts and acquired abilities: strengths of character that have served him well, are admirable, and will remain important in his life. It is incumbent upon us to bring these to his attention. Psychotherapy, owing to its origin as a medical specialty, seems to have devoted too much of its attention and vocabulary to what is wrong with people. In actuality, it is our obligation to recognize such things as the patient's heroism in the face of obstacles, his loyalty to those he loves, his ability to put his feelings into words, and his courage to trust people. These traits are as much a part of his life as those he laments and wants to change. We must not take them for granted, but instead should help the patient become aware of these virtues and accept that he possesses them —and if possible, enjoy that he does. They are integrally related to the rest of his personality.

Many of our patients have the problem that when they were young, no one appreciated what was good about them. They failed to develop an inner voice complimenting them for a job well done. This is partly why their life may seem hopeless: they feel condemned to climb eternally without ever being able to savor their accomplishments. No hand will tousle their hair affectionately, and no voice will say, "Well done." They deny themselves this experience, and find it hard to take love from others.

Such patients are likely to have a problem staying in therapy; they don't see themselves as worth the time or effort. When we pause to admire their excellence, they brush us off. They may even consider us insincere; they hurry off to another topic. We may sometimes wish that they had a little of the narcissist's willingness to vaunt himself, and that the narcissist had a hint of their willingness to dwell on others. Edna St. Vincent Millay once wrote that everything is "a little undersaid or oversung," and our patients' absorption with themselves seems to fall into one of these extreme categories. Lack of self-love seems to underlie both styles, but our therapeutic approach must be very different with these two extreme types, who in recent years have both been described as "anhedonic."

Our shining the spotlight on our patients' good points may prompt them to step instantly out of the light—as if it were deadly. In watching them do this, we see in action a side of them that would have gone unobserved if we had omitted to mention the virtue. Had we noted only their problems and weaknesses, we would not have seen them shunning the light. They must learn to overcome the fear of acknowledging excellence and of having it enjoyed by others. Otherwise they may remain forever ambivalent about excellence, moving toward it and then away from it—as if condemned to an exquisite frustration in which they could only approach what they wanted most and could never possess it. In developing a sense of their own richness of being, they become motivated to enhance that being.

Still another reason for making people aware of their achievement of character is that their greatest strengths are often integrally tied to their worst failings. The loyal person is likely to credit others with too much loyalty and to stay too long in relationships when he should get out. The generous person is liable to give too much. The decisive person may underestimate others, making too many decisions for them. Indeed, as we look at any personality flaw and ask ourselves where it came from, and how it served the person, we can usually uncover some function that the trait served in his life. By underscoring the patient's strengths, we may be laying the groundwork for seeing where he does himself a disservice.

For instance, a patient showed remarkable tact in a complex business negotiation. We compliment him on this, and he thanks us appreciatively. He is proud of his discreetness in dealing with people. But he later finds out that, in fact, he should have spoken up—he overdid a virtue and made it a fault. He was overnice and lost out, and now is sorry. Although we noted his ability in good faith, and not necessarily to set the stage for his seeing this flaw, we have nonetheless done just that. Being thoroughly aware of his gift of discretion, he is well primed to spot occasions when this virtue can become a vice.

Indeed, often a good way to broach presenting a harmful trait, if the patient is highly sensitive about it, is to begin by pointing out the same trait where it is a virtue. Once the person has become conversant with the trait, it is a relatively small step to see how he is doing himself harm by using it inappropriately.

PART FOUR

Motivation

Whoever strives, him we can save.
— Goethe

17

The Search for Motives

Let's think again about the person who can't bear to be complimented. Different people with the same problem might have
different reasons for it. A man tells us that not long ago he saw
an elderly fellow lying in the street; he rushed to the person's aid,
called a taxi, and delivered him to a hospital. It turned out the
person was a diabetic in a coma. Our patient may well have saved
his life. But when we called this to his attention, he blushes. "I
did only what I had to do."

What is his motive for disclaiming merit? Indeed why did
he rush to the aid of the stranger? Our simplest way of uncovering why people act is to ask them.

"I helped him because I couldn't just watch him lying
there," he tells us. Surely this is true. But why not? Empathy. Is
that a satisfactory answer? There are many schools of thought
concerning such acts. Psychoanalysis, following the tradition of
Schopenhauer and Nietzsche, traditionally disbelieved in generosity, arguing that it always derived from some baser motive.
More recently, sociobiology has argued that altruism is inborn,
that it exists as a survival trait in the animal kingdom—as a form
of self-sacrifice aimed at preserving the species. But many people

passed by the prostrate stranger, and only our patient rushed to his aid. No generic explanation can suffice.

"My father was strict. He taught me that we're all part of a team," he said. "If I don't do it, no one will. I felt sorry for the guy."

Our patients tell us why they acted—or why they think they did. They tell us how they recall feeling just before they acted and when they did. Such reports provide a steady flow of information about their motives—fear, anger, love, or whatever. These reports are mostly valid; people usually can sense how they feel. This man described what we might call the pressure of obligation, together with genuine sympathy. He has also told us that not to act would have been uncomfortable.

Admittedly, people sometimes mistake their motives. It's easy to identify those that are logically obvious. "I cursed him because I was furious at him." But some motives are likely to escape recognition, especially those that do not seem logically related to the act. Suppose the truth for someone were, "I cursed him because I wanted him to love me." Such a motive would be harder to identify.

We might start with our own reactions and inquire if the person felt similarly. Or we might ask him how he felt just before he acted, and how he would have felt if he had made a different choice.

Sometimes, we can help patients by giving them the benefit of our vocabulary, but we must be careful not to put words into their mouths. The most we can do is to offer possibilities. A man tells us his wife is always getting into scrapes and reporting them to him when there is nothing he can do. "I get so furious," he says. And he adds, "I don't mind that, but I feel so helpless." Later he tells us another such story. "Again that impotent rage?" we ask. "That's it. Impotent rage! I can't stand it!" he shouts, "I wish she'd stop putting me in that position." Later he uses the term on his own.

Our own precise use of language can help the patient identify his motives. We use the word "sarcasm" to indicate that the intention of an act was to harm another person, "irony" when it was not. But always the final choice of words to express the patient's feelings must be his.

Our readiness to accept the patient's every feeling and motive without passing judgment frees him to express more as time goes by. If we've seen that he has trouble identifying a particular motive, such as anger, we may ask him about it. Our very willingness to accept the motive as a possibility without condemning him makes it feasible for him to acknowledge having that motive.

But we are discussing relatively straightforward motives—if not conscious, then preconscious (that is, able to be summoned up by an act of will). People often sense these motives, are dimly aware of them, but seldom stop to reflect on them. There also are unconscious motives, far more complex, and we need access to them too, because of their sweeping influence on the patient's life.

For instance, our patient who saved the diabetic has no idea why he averts praise. He never knew he did it until we pointed it out. He was very close to his father and his brothers, and the whole family was sad when the father fell ill of emphysema. He remembers his father in bed coughing. He hated the notion of being stronger than the father, who once said, "I love you but don't get too big for your britches." Soon after that the father died and the boy went to work to help support the family.

Before going further, must we say that he is presently responding to a childhood motive? Or can we say that he's responding to a current one? Psychoanalysis has posited the first idea, that there is a "timeless unconscious" in which we harbor certain expectations and pictures of life, secret fears and wishes imprinted upon us, which are still there. More recent schools of therapy, beginning with the social psychologist Gordon Allport, have argued that this is implausible, and instead hold that we must be responding to present motives, not past ones. These psychologists have logic on their side, for what form of evidence would indicate that a person is still reacting to unconscious motives present when he was a child?

But this man felt irrationally that his achievements should always be accompanied by silence, that he owed them to those in his life—and that to flaunt them would make others, including me, feel weak. He even imagined that I might say, "You're getting too big for your britches." And he expected me to cough!

It is not that his unconscious expectations have concretely hardened within him. However, his whole complex of expectations, his unconscious picture of himself and the world, of me and my reactions, does make more sense in terms of his childhood than it does as a reaction to present people and events. The psychoanalyst might say that "he shuns praise" so as not to displease his father or that "he sees the therapist as his father." More recent theorists, at variance with psychoanalysis, would say he fears displeasing me as he once feared displeasing his father. The language that says he fears displeasing his father is very powerful and persuasive; it has therapeutic value if we stay mindful that we are using it metaphorically. It may help him find other elements of the pattern that still exist.

What counts is treatment. How do we discover such an unconscious fear, and how do we help the person overcome it? Here we are at the exact juncture of diagnosis and treatment itself, and can see the inextricability of the two.

18

Uncovering
Unconscious Motivations

Many methods of gaining glimpses into the patient's unconscious have been suggested by psychoanalysts, who were the first to take the issue seriously. Freud's original thesis that childhood motives continue to dominate us provided the impetus. He conceived of the unconscious as a respository for painful truths put there by repression. Not all his colleagues agreed about the contents of the unconscious (Jung, for instance, conceived of it as comprising feelings not necessarily distasteful, but even exotic and fruitful), but they agreed that important truths lie buried there and that the psychoanalyst must somehow get past the censoring apparatus to discover what they are.

Freud utilized hypnosis for this purpose, and later discarded it in favor of other techniques. He discerned that, in unguarded moments, people allow unconscious truths to surface in bits and pieces—in their dreams, or in slips of the tongue or pen, for instance. He hypothesized that unconscious material—such as impulses, and wishes and fears—has an urge to rise into consciousness. These deeply buried impulses come to us, either in disguise or sometimes quite openly. A man blurts out, "I hope something happens to my wife on her ocean voyage," and then quickly corrects himself. "I mean, of course, I hope nothing happens to her."

Psychoanalysis saw that in such "blunders" the unconscious often delivers itself of its truths. By seeking such revelations and piecing them together, the analyst could see past the part of the person that censors the buried truth, and could even reconstruct facts about forgotten childhood experiences.

It seems indisputable that inferences arrived at this way are instructive. But there's a lot of hit-and-miss. One can wait a long time for a slip of the tongue or for a revelatory dream. True, patients tend to dream more while in therapy, or recall their dreams better, than at other times. But we can hardly demand dreams of our patients, and they may not have any for long stretches of time. Once having appeared, these revelations—like Loch Ness monsters—may submerge again for another stretch of time, until they "decide" to resurface. The therapist finds himself in a passive position, waiting and watching for their recurrence.

Actually, patients have the ability to cause their own unconscious "visions" to come to the surface, including early-formed perceptions of existence that appear to have been lost. They can't merely will this material into their conscious minds; the very definition of unconscious material is that the person hasn't the capacity to summon it up at will. However, there is a very dramatic method of making such ideas available, a method so straightforward that the reader, even if not a therapist, can use it himself, and verify that it works.

Additionally, the method has immediate implications for what the patient can do to revise his outlook. It works because of the special relation between our unconscious and our ongoing behavior.

A man uses graphic arm gestures to make a point. They seem almost comical in his case, because he is very tall. All his life he has been criticized for them. I ask him to keep his hands at his side and to report his feelings and any ideas that come to mind. At first he feels strange. The thought crosses his mind, "You won't listen to me." However, he sees that I am listening intently, and goes on.

During this period of frustration, I ask him, "Why does it seem I won't listen to you?" He smiles. "It sounds crazy," he warns me, but I ask him to tell me whatever comes to his mind, as fast as the thoughts surface there, not to judge them.

"I feel small, as if you won't notice me. If I move my arms, you'll listen to me."

He'd learned to use those gestures when he was a small boy. And they worked. His siblings were older and much bigger. He would get their attention that way. Over the years, he'd never known why he used the gestures. Only when he forced himself to stop them, and allowed himself to say whatever came to his mind, did he get a sense of why he'd been using them all along. A minor example? Admittedly. But it contains a very important truth, which, over the years, I have developed into a method to discover unconscious motives.

The person stopping any habitual behavior becomes subject to an illusion, which becomes pronounced as the impulse mounts to resume the habit. I call it *the hunger illusion*.

From the fragmentary feelings and glimpses of motives that come to mind at such times, nearly anyone can deepen his self-knowledge. The reason I chose this seemingly insignificant example was that, as in hundreds of others I've studied, the feeling aroused was clearly an anachronism. Although the man had grown to be over six feet tall, that sense of being physically small and not worthy of notice remained lodged in the particular gesture—and in certain other activities of his too.

Often the technique of stopping a behavior and studying the reactions puts people in close touch with some impression they had dimly sensed, some perception they had held for a long time without identifying it. We can take any instance of a person's routine behavior, of a habit, and study it the same way.

For instance, a man starts to disagree with me and then takes it back. He sincerely belives I'm wrong. Why is he afraid to tell me off? When for the first time he does give vent to his genuine anger toward me, I listen, not responding. I ask him what thoughts he has. He replies that the thought crossed his mind that I would take revenge on him. He didn't know how. It sounded silly to him as he said it, but he felt I would never forgive him.

Over a lifetime this man had withheld objections, starting with experiences in which his parents taunted him for going against them. "We can't think of anything yet, but we're going to take something precious away from you," his father would say. The boy would never know for sure whether they had done so or not. His style of deference at all costs had been motivated by this fear, by the perception of people as vengeful, like his parents.

When another man with the same habit of withdrawing criticism of me finally went against the grain of it and told me off, he had very different moments of experience. He felt that I would collapse, that I was pretending to look strong but must be dying inside. This too proved very instructive about the way he perceived his parents. He had grown up afraid of anger, as if it would be like loosing a torpedo against a battleship.

We've moved from a simple to a slightly more complex case. They have in common that while the habitual behavior is engaged in, it *silences* the true perception that underlies it. The activity keeps the person unaware of its motive. When the behavior is stopped, even for a short time, the real reasons for it—the perceptions, impulses, and feelings behind it—come to the surface. Many of these feelings are apt to seem so outlandish to the person that he discards them. But the material that comes to us by way of the hunger illusion, if we study it and take the pieces seriously, is the most important glimpse we can get into the patient's true unconscious motivations and perceptions.

Alternatively, the "stopping" can be the breaking of an inhibition and starting new behavior. A twenty-four-year-old woman, sexually repressed, forces herself for the first time to try to enjoy a heavy petting session with a man. Throughout she sees images of her dead mother, pointing a finger at her. She can virtually hear the woman's voice repeating sadly, "I knew it. I knew it." Her not engaging in sex had been a repeated choice, and going against the grain of that impulse evoked the historical images. If you want to confront your true unconscious motivations for an inhibition, force yourself to try the difficult behavior if only once, and study seriously the thoughts that come to mind.

Often the patient's discoveries prove surprising, although usually they are in accord with what we have come to suspect from other sources. An extremely argumentative woman, who forced herself to stop arguing with her fiancé, was stunned at how uncomfortable she felt. Quarreling seemed to have a fundamental place in her life, or at least in intimate relationships. That night, after she had been on her best behavior, she dreamt that she was walking hand in hand with her father along a beautiful seashore. The great ocean lay before them and the sun comforted her. In the dream, her father told her he loved her, and she said, "I know. I love you too, Daddy." She woke up sobbing. Her father was dead, and she had never told him how much she cared. When she was still very young, her mother had fallen out with him, and had taken a lover. Her mother constantly disparaged her father, and this little girl felt forced to hide her joy when he would come home at night—out of loyalty to her mother. It seemed safer to argue with him than not to, and so she had always stifled expressions of love for him, being careful not to reveal affection for him in her facial expression or voice tone.

Over the years she combated any loyalty or fondness that she felt for men. She did this by arguing and not letting them get too close to her. As she forced herself to resist this habit, she felt frightened; she imagined that her mother hated her, and it seemed that certain of her women friends would hate her too. Close study of her reactions when she produced "the hunger illusion" taught us more about her real motivation, and its historical contents, than we had been able to learn in any other way.

By the same technique I was able to appreciate why the man mentioned earlier dreaded a compliment. Whenever his boss praised him, he had the irrational feeling that he was committing mayhem. Had my patient said something self-derogatory while being complimented, he would have suppressed any insight. In restraining himself, he could feel his lifelong impulse to crouch physically. In the hunger illusion are buried glimpses of motives. They become vivid, and the person has a sense of possessing a part of his life that seemed lost. The therapist can use this technique repeatedly, having his patient go against the grain and then studying those fragments of experience that accompany the patient's rising hunger to resume the behavior. Every act that breaks with the past evokes the past.

William James was one of the first to point out that the role of habits is to "smooth out" behavior. While learning any habit, we form an elaborate perception, think about the activity, and then choose it, in preference to one or more alternatives. When it seems to work, we repeat it. With repetition, we are able to execute the act with less thinking and feeling. Mentally and physically, the activity simplifies. We become better at it, quicker to resort to it. After a while, we may lose access to our real reason for it. Does a person stand still during his national anthem because he loves his country and is showing respect for it, or because he would be embarrassed to make himself conspicuous through any other action? For most of us, the answer is "both," but the relative contribution of these two motives differs among people. Regardless of the original reason, once a habit is formed we merely repeat the act. This, James pointed out, is the chief function of habits, that they put us on automatic, and free our consciousness to make decisions in new, uncharted territories.

The child—and often the adult—forms a complex perception, which is loaded with impulses and thoughts of different kinds; behind it lies a world view, a philosophy. Repetition of any activity puts the complex motivational pattern behind the activity to rest. Only when we stop the activity abruptly do we experience its unconscious reasons. For an instant, the patient, stopping a habit in midstream, experiences himself and life as it relates to his choices of the activity.

As the person continues to hold out against the activity, his hunger for it first rises and then diminishes. Metaphorically, it's as if the urge cried out to be heard, did so repeatedly, and then gave up. One can see the survival value of this. Any unusual—or impulsive—act, since it is unconsidered and untested, may be dangerous. The same may be said of giving up a habitual act. However, after constant repetition of the act (or the refusal to act), we see that we are safe, and free to explore.

Along with the initial rise of the hunger comes the person's most vivid experience of the imagery of the past, the unconscious imagery associated with the behavior. The woman having sex for the first time "sees' her mother in the room with her. After a while, her mother becomes only an occasional visitor, gradually withdraws, and then is gone.

Consider these two facts together. An activity renews its motive, the underlying perception that gives rise to it. The second, which we've just seen, is that the same repeated activity silences its motive. When the activity is abruptly stopped, that underlying perceptual drive becomes loudly conscious. The point of view, the underlying perception carried forward by the activity, is the very one soon to weaken once the activity is stopped. What the person experiences at the time of stopping the activity, the way he sees himself and life, is exactly what is going to change over time.

The same perception may receive support from other as yet unidentified behaviors. But we have an exciting truth. The hunger illusion gives us the very picture that will fade with discontinuation of the behavior.

This means the man who shunned praise, in forcing himself to endure it, would be erasing the very image that came to him so vividly at first, that of people—including myself—taking vengeance on him.

I have used this method for uncovering unconscious motives countless times. I call it *the method of magnification.* The hunger illusion is a magnification of what the person feels unconsciously. We magnify this underlying perception so that the patient, if he wishes, can do away with it. Naturally, one activity is never the totality. The woman afraid of intimacy with men did more than argue with them to drown her desires. The man afraid of being praised had a more general aversion to success, and we had to discover the other activities he used, in order to restore his early perceptions. In virtually every case, the therapist can tap the same outlook, the same feelings, emotions, impulses, and memories, by applying the technique to a network of activities that serve a common function.

The psychotherapist should have his patient say anything that comes to mind during the hunger illusion, no matter how silly or useless it sounds. I sometimes ask how the person feels about me, how he pictures himself, and what the present experience reminds him of.

The method of magnification has the advantage that the patient is himself contributing to his own process of discovery—and doing so in a deliberate and knowing way. He can use this technique without us, if he wishes.

And, most excitingly, the technique corroborates that we, ourselves, bring the past into the present. The tracks of continuity from our childhood, where such tracks begin, are our own unconsidered but habitual activities. Of course, we've changed some behaviors, discarded some along the way, enlarged upon others. But so long as we go on uninterrupted, our unconscious slumbers. It wakes up abruptly when we break the continuity of our patterns. Then it pours its truths into our associations and into our dreams.

19

Setting Goals

The motivated patient has a clear sense of how he would like to change. He sees that he has some distance to travel. He knows who he is and who he hopes to be. But few patients come to therapy with a clear sense of purpose. The therapist must not only engender it, but help the patient sustain it.

Thus the therapist faces a problem very much like that of the playwright. "Define the need of your character," wrote Sidney Field in his classic textbook for screenwriters. "What does your character want . . . ? What drives him to the resolution of your story?" Unless this is done, the story collapses. It loses direction. If it is done well, and the character's motivations are clear and strong, then every piece of the play or film advances the action. The story can proceed.

The goals of therapy are the attainment of qualities. Our patients may aspire to cultivate self-esteem, spontaneity, the ability to wait before making decisions, independence, courage, consistency, the ability to romanticize life. These are feasible goals. Often the patient may present another kind of purpose for therapy, one that involves changing the way other people behave. For instance, he wants a particular person to marry him, or he wants to make a lot of money. If we are to help him do that, it must be by indirect means. He may be disqualifying himself as a result of character traits that stand in his way. Possibly we may help him overcome those deficiencies. But we can help him only to change himself. We cannot guarantee how any other individual will react to him.

Often our purpose must be to help patients convert situational goals, which they present to us, into personal ones. Success is not to be equated with material comfort or even celebrity. The patient may pursue whatever worldly advantage pleases him, but what it will ultimately afford him is personal, and we must think in personal terms. A young man, not so bright, says he wants to become a congressman. "What would that give you?" "I'd be rich and famous." "What then?" "I'd change the laws and give minority groups a chance, and they'd love me and appreciate me."

One can see lurking in this answer, in the daydream, the desire to feel potent, to have his kindness appreciated, to be loved, to feel a sense of belonging and worth. Studying the patient's ostensible purposes can teach us his real needs. However, we must think in terms of organic goals, of flesh-and-blood ones. They indicate a shorter and surer route to the person's satisfactions than the one he has in mind. Surely, this young man can get much of what he wants without having to collect a plurality in his state, and we can help him. What people strive for is nearly always within them, or else they can put it there.

We may uncover goals sometimes by separating the patient's stated ambition into its component personal meanings. We do this by asking questions concerning the ambition, but of a personal nature. "I want to be a movie star." "What part would you play? Tell me about it in detail. What would the great scene be?" A writer? What would you write about? Who would read your work? How would they react?"

More often than not, the patient comes to us with at least

some situational goals, those that depend on his getting good reactions from other people. He wants to become the chief executive in his company. Perhaps we can help him develop skills of decisiveness or leadership that will improve his chances. But we can't change the way the world responds to our patient. The most we can do is to help him change himself. This requires translating his exterior goals into personal ones. Our real belief is in the patient himself, and in what he can become. We are saying, "What is available to you is you, yourself."

We are, in effect, telling him that we reject his assumption that his life will be a success only if others make it so. We reject that in favor of our belief that he can give importance to life himself. Doubtless, others will respond to changes in him. But he is bigger, his voyage is more significant than what any other person can offer him. As Simone de Beauvoir said, "It is up to man to make it important to be a man, and he alone can feel his success or failure."

Consider this case in which the therapist made the mistake of accepting a goal that was not really proper. A therapist reported that a woman came bursting into his office in tears. Her boyfriend had walked out after she accused him of infidelity; now she felt remorseful and terribly alone. Actually, she had mixed feelings about every relationship in her life, and after a while she felt stifled.

Not surprisingly, she wanted to talk to the therapist about little besides her relationship. Did he think her lover would return? The therapist got caught up in her obsessional concern, did some guessing along with her, and did not help her appreciate that her difficulties were more deeply personal. Whether or not he returned, she had her own suspicious nature, ambivalence, and impulsiveness as problems to solve.

Eight weeks later, she and her boyfriend had a grand reunion. She quit therapy on the spot. There seemed no need for the therapist, who had been a partial substitute for the boyfriend.

She had no sense that there was an enormous amount of work still to be done. The therapist, by failing to give her a real sense of the problem, had left her believing that it was situational. Had he redirected the focus from her situation to the woman herself, she might well have continued to work on herself and profitably.

As our patients free new talents, and enlarge their ambitions, they strive for more. "Maybe I will go to law school after all," a woman of forty-seven tells me. Her horizon has changed. It's a glorious opportunity for someone who, ten years before, had been sitting in a room despondent, day after day. Her new exterior goal is both a symbol of her past achievement and a source of new motivation. It entices her forward. But it requires additional abilities. She will have to develop self-discipline. Every fresh ambition reveals new obstacles that must be overcome. There is a new and healthy tension, the excitement of more work to be done.

The therapist who stays mindful of his patient's goals and needs, and keeps the patient cognizant of them through the upheavals of everyday life, is sustaining the line of the therapy. This sense of purpose is a pillar of the patient's eagerness to do the work.

Every patient presents seemingly different material from one session to the next. A man is sharing a summer house and discusses relationships. The next session there's no mention of them; he's gone home and interacted with his folks. Then there's trouble at work, and he discusses this. Another time he feels the necessity to expatiate on some theory. He's a history buff, and talks about the problem France has had with neighboring countries.

But in much of what he says, we see the same disability and we keep our larger purpose in mind. For instance, this man feels unsure of himself, and presses people for reassurance. They react by retreating and then he feels catastrophically abandoned. He does not yet see the pattern. Our purpose at this stage is to help him understand what he does, as a prelude to giving him vivid insight into why he does it. But what about France? Is his discussion of it a divagation, and are we accomplices to his wasting time by letting him go on? Perhaps. But even as he talks about France, we keep our purpose before us.

Sure enough, in response to a few innocent questions of ours, he goes on about that nation being surrounded by malevolent neighbors, and as pressing for declarations of peace, which it can never fully believe in. He *is* that nation. In talking about history, he is actually working through his own problems, and we let him go on. When a patient recounts a dream, we accept his subject matter as betraying real strivings, needs, and stresses, which may be unconscious. We must regard in the same way other subject matter the patient presents. The pattern of this man's sensibilities predisposed him to his theory of history. His own tendencies and plight identified him with France. "Man is the measure of all things," the ancients would say. And as we listen, we look for the patient in all things.

We might actually be glad when a patient reports a variety of seemingly different experiences and theories, so that we can see a common thread running through all of them. Although the patient may imagine that his sessions are unrelated, they can never be truly unconnected with one another. Our recognizing what they have in common, even when he does not, is something he comes to feel and appreciate. We are a lighthouse for his purposes in life, and continue to operate even when he feels lost. For the patient to see us this way is to confirm his reason for being in therapy.

20

Revealing the Patient's Own Hand

The person who comes for help appreciates that something is wrong internally. He may have some security in his present position, but want to change the state of things without knowing how. Often there's a feeling of victimization, either by the past or by forces in the present. Consider the protagonist of true tragedy. Oedipus finds that a plague has beset his kingdom but has no idea why. Melancholy overcomes Hamlet; although the kingdom is thriving, "Something is rotten in the state of Denmark." Gradually, the protagonist comes to see that choices of his own in the past and in the present have caused the difficulty. There may be conflict over how to set things right, even over whether to believe what he has found out. But the tragic hero accepts and utilizes the fact that he himself has brought on the trouble—he does something and the situation changes. Oedipus ends the plague. Hamlet stops acquiescing in the new regime. He murders the false king of Denmark.

Henrik Ibsen is, I think, the modern playwright most relentless in maintaining this structure in his plays, and he has added details to it that are extremely relevant for therapists. Ibsen's heroes are not royalty like Shakespeare's, but are established as model citizens as the play starts; however, they all hold some dark secret from their past. They have done something amiss that brought them their present social position. In *Pillars of Society,* the protagonist, now rich and respected, has allowed a brother to take the blame for a sexual offense. Hedda Gabler has married a man she never loved, and the one she did love has gone away. In *The Wild Duck,* the protagonist has disowned his little girl. In *Enemy of the People,* a doctor is well respected but has mistakenly recommended the local health spas, which are polluted. Then in each case, some agent of the truth returns: the brother who took the blame, the one Hedda really loves, a congenital blindness that the little girl inherited from her father. In each of these cases, the protagonist sees his past returning, hopes it will go away, and tries to banish it. But he cannot keep it away. It's as if the truth were always there, even when it seemed buried forever; although there is tragedy, there is real relief when the truth surfaces. The "life-lie" is exposed. The protagonist embraces the truth.

Freud's notion of "the return of the repressed" is enacted on Ibsen's stage. Freud himself once used the image of the "impulse to banish an unwelcome guest," and Ibsen has some of his protagonists attempt to do just that. As in Ibsen's plays, the truth needs to find its way to the surface. When it does, the sense of morbidity goes away. The protagonist realizes that all along he has been arranging his own destiny. In the end, the truth proves worth enduring even great hardship.

Many critics argue that classical tragedy requires that the protagonist be responsible for his destiny. Some theater purists have denied the status of tragedy to Arthur Miller's *Death of a Salesman* on the grounds that the hero, Willy Loman, was utterly a victim of forces. I don't think he was; not every salesman is superannuated as he was, or is driven to suicide.

However, psychotherapy does require that the hero, the patient, convert a sense of helplessness into the recognition that he himself is responsible for his psyche. Therapy always fosters the patient's acceptance of personal responsibility for his life. The acceptance of this is the very essence of being motivated in therapy. Motivating patients means helping them discover their own freedom and, more precisely, the hand that they themselves play in reproducing the very outlook they want to change. The patient starts out feeling helpless; he is likely to feel in the grip of powerful emotions. It seems as if his past is within him and that another kind of life is not possible—for instance, he can no more be assertive or joyous than if he wanted to be a bird and fly; or he is the victim of bursts of anger that seem to come over him and goad him into harming those he cares for most. He feels a sense of inevitability. As a result of our work, the patient becomes aware that he is making choices, that he's not merely doing what he has to do but is exercising real options. He further discovers that, although the past is relevant, a certain network of his own choices is restoring his present outlook and ways of perceiving. The discovery of this provides the ultimate spur to his wanting to change. And change becomes possible as he learns exactly which those choices are.

Take the woman mentioned, who feels that every man requires her servitude. She can't distinguish those who truly want her in that role from those who don't. As soon as she likes a man, she feels a powerful impulse to make herself useful to him—to type his papers, to shop, cook, and so forth. Always she has felt this way, ever since her father demanded docility as a condition for love. So long as this outlook feels a part of her, although she is unhappy, she does not feel strongly motivated to change. She cannot picture what change would be like. But, as she starts to see that another outlook is possible, there is hope. When she realizes that choices of hers have kept her a servant, that hope becomes even greater.

The patient's discovery of his own role in perpetuating his outlook is the greatest conceivable stimulus to motivation. He learns that acts whose importance he never suspected are keeping him as he is. He has the power to change, and what remains is only the discovery of exactly what he must do. As with the theatrical hero, he sees that he can save the kingdom. He can save himself.

Patients, at the start of therapy, differ greatly in their ability to recognize the choices they make—and sometimes in seeing that they are making choices at all. Not that we have an absolute index telling us whether an act is truly chosen. Physiologists talk about "voluntary acts" in contrast to involuntary ones, and I tend to follow roughly their lines. By this distinction, it's a voluntary choice whether we leave a room or not; and we voluntarily choose what we say; likewise, it's a choice if we remain silent. There are borderline cases, however. Was it a deliberate choice to be late if one elected to go shopping before an appointment, with good reason to believe it would take too much time? These cases trouble the philosopher more than the therapist. As our patients improve at recognizing their real options, such decisions come increasingly into the domain of deliberate choices.

In contrast, our feelings and perceptions are involuntary. We don't control them—at least not directly. We can't choose not to feel frightened. And many people have tried in vain not to be in love with someone. Our state of mind and manner of perceiving are themselves involuntary. But they are influenced by choices. Any decision to feel different must be implemented by voluntary acts repeated many times for it to take hold.

Patients who are self-reliant tend to appreciate their choices, or at least to acknowledge that they are making real choices if we point them out. At the other extreme are those patients who can't seem to recognize their options.

"How could I stay quiet! He was disparaging my whole work experience and my background." The man who said this was explaining why he did poorly in a job interview. He spoke as if unaware that he had done anything for which there was a voluntary alternative.

"I understand why you got nasty, you've just explained it. But it was a choice."

"It was no choice."

"If someone offered you eleven million dollars to keep your mouth shut and hear him out, you would have done it."

"Yeah, I guess you're right. But I'm glad no one did. He was a son of a bitch!" The man roared with laughter, and I laughed too. But the point was made. Time and again, I would bring to this man's attention choices he had made, as a prelude to helping him see that those choices were affecting him. Moreover, through the recognition of choices, he would make many discoveries about how he really felt.

People often dull the recognition of their own options, in some cases because they are ashamed of something they've done. A divorced man tells us he can't see his son for a week, and we ask him for his schedule. It turns out that he's going to a party one night and to a ball game with friends another. Clearly he is choosing not to see his son. He detests hearing this, but feels forced to agree with it. And curiously, he's glad. He knows he's been avoiding the boy; he's felt wrong ever since the divorce, and imagines the boy will never forgive him. To experience his every choice is to keep cognizant of his alternative. He returns to his son and tells him how much he loves him, and things are easier after that.

Those who spend too much effort trying to please other people are especially prone to conceal choices designed for their own satisfaction. The woman who gave too much of herself, fearing that if she held back, her lover would leave her, found it hard to see that she'd been choosing to please him at her own expense. On discovering that she was doing this, she resolved to stop. At first, when she refused his requests, she made excuses. She would add, "I *have* to go shopping," "It's *urgent* that I see my parents this weekend." She was, in effect, hiding the fact that there were things she *wanted* to do—as if she had no right to her own life. Her next step was to express her real preferences openly, and not justify them.

In sharpening patients' awareness of their own choices, it helps to point out choices they've made that have worked out well.

"You didn't hesitate to disagree with your partner at that meeting. A few months ago you might not have."

"That's true. Strange. I don't feel so afraid of him. I guess you're helping me.

"It's not just what *I'm* saying. It's what *you've* been doing. You're working harder and you're not playing games."

Seeing even small changes in the very direction that changes are wanted can bring elation, and doubly renew the patient's energies to push onward. We can utilize this in the patient's relationship with us. "You trusted me a little more, and felt a bit less embarrassed about the topic. So you confided in me. And now that you have, you trust me still more." I said this to a patient, after he professed to like me better. He understood. Indeed, his very confiding in me motivated him to come to sessions on time, whereas previously he had been late more often than not.

Sometimes we point out to patients choices they have made that have caused regression.

"I feel old, and desperately jealous, the way I used to," a man told me. "And there's no reason, since my girlfriend wasn't with anyone else this weekend. She was alone, doing her homework!"

"How often did you check up on her?"

He told me he'd called her a few times, then hung up when he heard her voice. He'd also had a friend call her for him. On Saturday evening he'd driven across town to her neighborhood, and listened at her door. It's impossible to put into practice such a complex scheme of surveillance without convincing oneself that the plan has some warrant, that it has necessity and value. This man had regressed to maddening himself with jealousy.

Why had he resumed behavior he knew was harmful to him? He'd lost his job and felt inadequate. But to restore his confidence he'd have to act gracefully even in adversity. To overcome his jealousy, he would have to resume living without his old surveillance practices. It was my task to help him see how harmful they were. Always, where possible, we must try to help the patient see how his turns of mind are consequences of real decisions he has been making—and not merely reactions to other people.

We can even point out how our patients' choices, for better or for worse, influence their picture of their early history. What we do now affects our recollections of the past. A young woman who turned to prostitution told me that she used to think her parents were wonderful. She respected them for their hard work and good morals. "But now I feel sorry for them. I think they were fools," she added.

"I know you do," I told her. "But that's a result largely of your having become a prostitute. You're making money fast but there are costs. Your changed perception of your parents is one of them."

Her own choices had elevated in her consciousness a new view of existence. Not only had it accentuated her view of men as shallow and unreliable, but it also made hard-working people who enjoyed each other's company on a Saturday night seem like country bumpkins. Her own life on a farm seemed far away, not just geographically but emotionally. In the same way, the gambler persuades himself by repetition that life is dull without the big risk. Taking his own children to the circus seems boring, and he wonders how other parents can be bothered. It's a very significant truth that our recent behavior colors our view not just of ourselves and other people, but of our values and even our estimation of our own childhood experiences.

As our patients recognize the control they really have, they are likely to feel a surge of desire to go on.

21

The Journey

My right hand pointing to landscapes of continents and the public road.

Not I, not anyone else can travel that road for you,
You must travel it for yourself.
                    Walt Whitman, "Song of Myself"

Ultimately, there can be no replacement for showing we care. Not just the patient is precious but every human being, every center of human consciousness, is indispensible. There is nothing conditional about our patient's importance. We convey continually, "You are the central figure. Your journey, which began even before you had power to reflect on it, is a magnificent one. It doesn't matter where you came from. In the chaos you made millions of decisions, learning, interpreting life as you saw it, furthering as best you could that single conscious being, which is you. You were perhaps sidetracked and alone, or defeated yourself. Or you labored pointlessly in the wrong relationship, seemed almost buried alive. But your aspirations, like your heart, kept beating, somewhere. Every stage of that journey was precious, and I admire that."

And we also convey that, "This phase of the journey, here in therapy, is to be different. Emerging finally from an indifferent night, you will be seen and heard out. Here the searchlight is on you, every detail counts because you count. No matter that others neglected you. The time of trudging through the darkness is over."

We each, as psychotherapists, convey the degree to which we cherish the human soul. And our patients respond. Perhaps they can't pinpoint in words that the therapist doesn't appreciate them, but they sense when this is so. They've always been treated as just an extra. In therapy, they feel the same way—replaceable, perhaps because the therapist would prefer a more prestigious patient, or one who pays more or can tell better stories. The patient senses it in the therapist's bragging, his name-dropping, his exhilaration when big money or a swank party or an expensive vacation is mentioned. Or more subtly, when the therapist shows interest in the patient's being invited somewhere prestigious and neglects to celebrate the patient's own heroic moments. Such a therapist responds to the patient through the mirror of how others see that patient. The patient is not a true soul to him, but a clothed being whose garments declare his worth.

It is to keep the patient conscious of his sense of journey, and of his own ultimate indispensibility, that I hesitate to charge for hours missed. If the patient is truly indifferent or resistant, he'll feel my appreciation of him more powerfully in my not charging. For him to come for a session as a way of getting his money's worth seems costly, because the real reason is to heighten his sense of self. Similarly, if while he's in my office tormented by a problem, and I talk on the phone elatedly with a long-lost friend, how important can my patient's journey be? A great many decisions we make either heighten the patient's sense of journey or obliterate it.

All of us are in a sense tragic heroes, struggling against odds. The ability to perceive people this way should be a requisite for the psychotherapist. This doesn't stop us from laughing, from enjoying the fruits of the islands we visit. Indeed, it heightens our need to do so. But it keeps our own lives, and our work with patients, in the larger perspective. We must highlight our patients' past heroism, and feel exhilarated at their every step forward. As nearly anyone would celebrate a baby's first few steps across a room, we must see exactly what the patient is struggling to achieve in his horizon and celebrate it when he succeeds. To keep his sense of journey alive in his consciousness, we need an unerring light on the path he has to travel. "You stayed alone last night for four hours? Fantastic! I know how hard it was."

The only way we can highlight the patient's real achievements is to stay cognizant of his purposes. True, we may celebrate our patient's being given a raise or getting a new job. But the real heroism, we know, was in those lonely moments of his effort, in what he did that merited the advance. Sometimes, for emphasis, we may even give vent to our natural depreciation of what other people decide he is worth. "I'm overjoyed, but I'm not surprised that they want you to head the new production department. You're doing a spectacular job, and it's obvious you deserve it."

And when he is in adversity, we can also remind him of his journey: "You've been stymied worse than this, but emerged." And we can remind him of exactly when. As Ibsen once put it, "Many a time has luck seemed drooping, and rose up as high as ever." We can point out that luck is a variable, but courage and directed effort are controllable. Out of the controllables comes the patient's real sense of worth.

Unless we can feel the drama of a patient and his journey, we should not work with him. If we can, he will surely know it. In every session we will enhance his sense of the specialness of his life.

PART FIVE

The Therapist-Patient Relationship

There is no rock we can build on except the
possibility of what we may become.

—Hook

22

The Working Alliance

The therapeutic "working alliance" is exactly what its name implies. The therapist and patient work together in harmony. Their alliance is directed toward helping the patient recognize and feel what is wrong and make the necessary changes. Freud once conceptualized this alliance as between the therapist and the patient's "conscious will," which struggle together to defeat the single force of the patient's unconscious.

Where there is a good therapeutic alliance, treatment proceeds as if the therapist were a consultant hired by the head of a firm to handle a special problem. The consultant identifies the problem and pinpoints what the company is doing wrong. Then those who have hired the consultant go to work on the problem itself. The therapist and patient together clarify what must be done, and the patient makes the necessary changes.

Let's look at an example of an ideal working alliance. A young man comes to therapy with the problem of overdependence on his parents. He wants to be free of them and, in particular, to move away from home. He relates well to the therapist. They have a kind of camaraderie that the young man has never enjoyed before. The therapist can use their alliance to help the young man study his overdependence and low self-esteem. Where do these traits come from, and how is he creating them? The therapist and patient together are able to identify some of the patient's attitudes that might lead him into self-destructive acts. Together, they identify the network of behavior that springs from his lack of confidence and that reinfects the young man with the infantile feelings he has.

They work together harmoniously. Little by little, the young man creates a sturdier sense of himself, and moves away from his parents. He stops blaming them when things go wrong, no longer shows off to them or makes small requests of them. He stops reporting so many details of his day to them. He learns to tolerate frustration better. The therapist is there, discussing the patient's feelings with him, experiencing the world through the patient's eyes, helping him appreciate how he was holding on to his parents. The young man used to berate them vehemently when things went wrong; the therapist helps him see that when you kick a parent, you stick to that parent—like the Tar Baby. For the young man, each small act of withdrawal is followed by anxiety, but he gradually learns to endure the gulf between him and his parents. Therapy pivoted around the working alliance and was successful.

However, the variety of ways in which patients depart from the alliance, and use their own unconscious chicanery with us seems unending. During the course of therapy, all patients manifest their problems in the relationship. They cease being our allies at some time. They ask us to do too much, blame us for what goes wrong, refuse to speak to us. A harmonious alliance is rarely sustained, is honored much more in the breach than in the observance.

In particular, we must watch out for a "false working alliance." The patient tells us frankly, "Why should I be dishonest with you? You're here to help me." He admires our ability to arrive at insights, our worldliness, and much else. He answers us directly, comes to the office on time, and assures us he's getting a great deal out of the sessions. Meanwhile he has fundamental fears that he consciously decides not to tell us about. He deliberately befriends us to keep us from doing our real investigation. His telling us how much progress he's making is a device to stop us from delving into sensitive areas. He'd like to get the whole thing over with without having to experience the pain that accompanies real discovery. Unless the therapist spots this false working alliance and intervenes, the patient may quit abruptly. Only in retrospect does the therapist recognize that he never really got to know the person.

Correspondingly, there are therapists who hide behind the illusion of a good working alliance when they don't have one. The patient may be slipshod in his efforts, or even say something sarcastic to the therapist. But the therapist won't bring it up. Such therapists are overly concerned with having their patients like them. They may dread confrontation, as if the first real rift between them and the other person would mean the relationship were over. Their therapy concentrates on problems the patient encounters with other people, and even in regard to those it is always shallow. When the patient blames other people exclusively for what goes wrong, the therapist acquiesces to the extent of not bringing up the patient's own performance. Especially if the patient becomes easily irritated or angry when the spotlight is directed toward his behavior, these therapists may take their cue and not intervene. The therapist, himself, is resisting the therapy! When such a therapist becomes matched with an avoidant patient, a secret covenant may ensue and therapy goes on forever without getting anywhere.

Therapists who have been extremely supportive to patients in dire need are especially prone to enter a false working alliance with them later on. They have helped the person to his feet and don't want to jeopardize their achievement with the newly strengthened patient. It's hard to change tactics, to realize that the person need no longer be treated with kid gloves. These therapists may feel it would be attacking someone who counted on them, and that their own words mean too much to the patient. For instance, the patient once doubted the therapist's loyalty and the therapist proved himself loving and steady. But now another approach is needed. More robustness is in order. If the therapist can't make the change, it would be advisable for him to send the patient to someone else to finish the work that he so nobly began.

We utilize our working alliance with patients at every stage of therapy. But we recognize that there will be continual departures, and that it is a standard and nothing more. The expectation of such an alliance enables us to recognize even the slightest deviation from it.

23

How Transference Works

Our patient comes to develop a complex view of us as therapy proceeds; it is loaded with feelings and expectations of how we're going to react to him. This impression relates only in part to who we really are. The rest is brought forward from his past and superimposed on us. Every therapist has recognized this kind of superimposition, which Freud first identified and termed "transference."

What makes the transference especially revealing is that this superimposed view of the therapist sheds light on the patient's way of perceiving himself. For instance, he may expect us to come down hard on him for mistakes, the way his father did. Implicit is his sense that he himself is really on the edge of acceptability, and had better not make a mistake. It is valuable to think of transference as not merely a way of looking at the therapist, but also as an expression of the patient's self-appraisal.

Psychoanalysis brought us the notion of transference—it was a coup of Freud's to recognize that the patient's picture of the analyst could be used to understand the patient's character structure. However, psychoanalysis interpreted transference passively. Consistent with its view that the patient's outlook

134

becomes ingrained in childhood, it saw the forces of transference as having hardened within the person and as dominating him over a lifetime. The patient himself responded to those forces but couldn't change them. But over the years we have learned that the patient plays a much more active role. By continuing to perform in the only way that once made sense to him, he repeatedly assigns himself and others the parts that were played out in the home.

Let's examine a case in more detail to see how transference operates. Recall the man who didn't tell his therapist that he was going to appear in his first acting role on television. He assumed that the therapist would not want to watch him. The man was imposing on this male therapist an expectation he had formed about his father. As a child he recognized that his father considered him insignificant—he could hardly get through a description of what he did during the day without his father's interrupting him. Sometimes his father would ask him a question, and then while he was starting to answer it, his father would pick up a phone or even leave the room. All through childhood he sensed the father's resentment of having to spend time with him.

Early in life he began acting in ways consistent with what he saw. He talked much too fast—wanting to get in all he could before his father cut him off. He exaggerated in order to hold his father's attention as long as he could. He talked only about events, and never about his feelings. He never complained. Nearing adolescence, he took to name-dropping, and when saying something important he would sometimes attribute it to a prestigious friend, so that it would be taken more seriously.

He continued doing these things. He entered the therapist's office with an unconscious expectation that the therapist would see him as his father did: as an annoyance and a nonentity. Along with this lightly etched expectation was the readiness to act in ways that were characteristic for him.

In the very first session he talked too quickly. When the

therapist asked him about his personal life, he felt uneasy and said little. He did not speak about his own emotions, and held back information that seemed to him to be trivial. He was acting in ways that had long seemed utterly natural to him. But by such behavior he rapidly transformed his earliest expectation of the therapist into a fully blown transference view of him. The patient had no idea of the role his own behavior was playing. It seemed utterly natural to him not to tell the therapist about his TV appearance—when questioned about it, he was actually astonished that the therapist would have been willing to watch it.

There is nothing inherently unhealthy about the process of transference. A patient may bring forward his expectation of success or of being treated well by others—as readily as an expectation of personal rejection. This young man may well have known adults along the way who genuinely cared about him; the problem was that he could not experience their warmth. Also, he might well have discouraged them. Certainly, he let no one become privy to his emotional life and thus could not have experienced the deep good will of others.

Psychoanalysts themselves observed that transference develops as therapy progresses. We now know why. The patient enters therapy with a sketchy idea of what the therapist will be like, and of what his own role will be in the relationship. By acting in the very ways that seem most natural to him, he makes that picture bolder and bolder. Soon the transference is unmistakable.

Transference may be seen as the patient's putting a green lens on a light and shining it on the therapist. The therapist looks green to him, and that is that. No matter what color clothing the therapist puts on, he will continue to look green to the patient. To resolve a transference, the therapist must, by this analogy, help the patient appreciate that he is using a green lens, and help the patient change that lens.

24

Studying the Transference

Freud believed that the patient's problems inevitably manifested themselves in the therapeutic relationship. Study of the transference was synonymous with treatment, and resolution of the transference became equivalent to cure. It was not merely that problems and all repression originated in childhood. The therapist, even if he didn't represent a parent, would take on some deeply personal meanings to the patient.

For example, the patient's fear of bringing up something shameful becomes associated with the therapist, who is patiently waiting for him to talk. The patient's devices to conceal the truth become manifested as efforts to distract the therapist. He praises the therapist, or even falls in love with him. There develops an "idealized transference," very complimentary to the therapist but really designed to get him to call off his investigation.

Every method of repression, every attempt to juggle inner symbols, to surface them or bury them, has its counterpart in the therapeutic relationship. Thus the interpersonal byplay between therapist and patient is like an external map of what is going on inside the patient. There is an isomorphism between inner forces and their exterior representations, a one-to-one mapping, the

way visual reality is reproduced on the retina. The therapist
cannot possibly know all that he means to the patient, but the
patient's dealings with him all have meaning.

This isomorphism gives the relationship between patient
and therapist enormous significance. It is much easier to observe
the external aspects of the relationship than the corresponding
vectors of the mind, which are miniature and covert—and, alas,
theoretical in essence. Whether or not we agree with Freud that
resolution of the transference equals cure, it seems indisputable
that dealing with the transference is about the most powerful
instrument we have, and is often the only way we can gain real
access to the patient.

The best therapists are dauntless in studying this relationship, through their own observations and feelings, and in utilizing it. To enter the relationship deeply with one patient after
another takes not just confidence but also the willingness to be
caught in error. The therapist with something to hide, who
deeply doubts his own ability and feels ashamed may resist bringing things up that would cause discussion of the relationship to
spill out into the sessions. For instance, an insecure therapist who
is haughty or perfectionist may find it intolerable to be found in
the wrong. Such therapists try to hide behind discussions of
patients' outside problems, and give advice on how to solve them
—coaching sessions.

In one case, a woman therapist coached a female patient on
how to deal with her husband, who was having an affair. She
"overlooked" the fact that her patient treated her with stark
impersonality. The patient had treated both parents this way—
they were constant worriers and extremely annoying. The patient learned to ask them for what she wanted and to dismiss
them as people. The patient had treated other people the same
way—including her husband—and now was transferring this per-
functory style to the therapist.

The therapist felt discouraged at being taken so for granted.

But feeling that perhaps she was not helping and deserved such treatment, she rationalized that her patient had enough trouble already and that the time wasn't right to add to her woes. She overlooked the essence of what was really wrong with the patient, which was manifest in the transference itself. She thus settled for attempting to solve a highly specific problem (which, incidentally, proved impossible). When, in response to a suggestion from me, she confronted the patient, the patient responded curtly by saying, "I thought you were here to help me," as if the therapist weren't a real person. When the therapist pressed forward and asked the patient to explain that comment, out came a deluge of the most disdainful reactions imaginable: "Let's not get sidetracked on you. I have more important things to spend my time on." Suddenly, the therapist got a first-hand impression of how the patient felt and acted, and what her husband was reacting to. That session alone cured the therapist of her tendency to overidentify with the patient.

Doing therapy without utilizing the transference is like trying to lift up a huge blanket by only one corner. That we experience an interaction with the patient enables us to see and feel it —to gather it up in many places. Without seeing the transference and bringing it up, we remain too dependent on the patient's account of experiences, filtered through his vision and biases. What we see and sense in the office is at the heart of the matter. There comes a time in every therapy when we must make the patient aware of these perceptions.

The early psychoanalysts stressed anonymity toward the patient, mainly for the sake of the transference. Both the development of the transference and the therapist's ability to identify it seemed to require this anonymity. It was thought that transference would not grow nearly as vivid if the patient knew too much about the therapist. Moreover, if the analyst appeared in too much detail, then whatever transference there was would remain undetectable. How could the therapist know whether the patient was superimposing a view on him or reacting to him as he really was? The psychoanalyst kept a low profile, both to allow the transference to grow and to be able to detect it when it did.

Today, we have come to believe that transference grows even if the therapist is a real person to the patient. Moreover, we can still detect it. We respect the need for anonymity to the degree of not revealing ourselves gratuitously. But we recognize that absolute anonymity is impossible. The patient forms judgments about us from the many perceptions he does make: he knows our age roughly; he sees how we dress; what our office is like; he responds to the values implicit in what we say and in what we don't say. Indeed, so subtle are our communications that we've all been surprised to have patients say things about us that we hardly knew ourselves. A therapist wonders, "How in the world did that patient know I was thinking of getting married?" Perhaps the patient responded to some slight withdrawal by him in the hour, as if, almost imperceptibly, the therapist were closing ranks and forming his new family. Similarly, during the very week a therapist has been worrying about an illness, lo and behold—the patient dreamt the therapist was dying. The patient told him, "I know it's all in my mind, but I'm worried about you. I guess it just proves how much I care about you." Anyone who has been in practice for a while has been astonished by some of his patients' intuitions about him. Before concluding that a patient's reaction to us is transferential, we must always consider carefully the possibility that it may be a warranted insight, although drawn from no more than a wisp of evidence.

None of this disputes Freud's original observation that transference is easiest to discern if we have offered minimal input. The less we do, the surer we can be that what the patient attributes to us is his own production. But we must always take into account that, as therapists, we are interacting and providing real evidence for the patient to respond to.

On the other hand, it seems doubtful that the contemporary

therapist, by interacting more vigorously with his patients than the early psychoanalysts did, is actually slowing down the transference. What the therapist does may actually *accelerate* it. A chance comment by us, even a mistake we make, can become grist for the mill of the patient's transference.

For instance, a woman therapist called an old friend on the editorial board of a magazine and got a job for a young man who was her patient. No sooner did she do this than the man started treating her exactly as he had his mother. There was hardly a thanks. Instead, he began whining about inconveniences, asking her advice on even small matters, blaming her for nearly anything that went wrong, and demanding her approval. Before long, he seemed to take out nearly every frustration on her. By helping him she had opened the floodgates for all of this. She had stimulated the transference by the act, nor did this prove harmful. An accelerated transference can be good or bad depending upon how it is handled. In this particular case, the therapist made good use of it, pointing out its details and studying them.

But the transference is not always so obvious. For instance, a patient had a mother who was warm and concerned—so was the therapist. A few indicative acts by the therapist prompted the patient to express appreciation and to trust the therapist far more than if a blank slate had been presented. By feeling safe and acting in accordance with this view, the patient imposed on the therapist a whole set of expectations and feelings that happened to be warranted. It was hard to see that they were transferential. A view formed in the past but still applicable in the present may pass as being merely a reaction to present experience.

In this case the patient's adaptation to a benign mother made it easy for him to see that the therapist was truly on his side. However, the same adaptation made it hard for him to recognize people who were, in reality, selfish and indifferent to his welfare. He tended to overcredit people with benignity. The result was that he repeatedly proceeded too far in bad relationships. The transference prepares the patient for experiences similar to those he's had in the past. It's as if the transference heightens his sensitivity to some color, enabling him to recognize that color readily where it exists, but disposing him to imagine that he sees that color in places where it is not. A distrustful transference, for instance, prepares him for a world of thieves but not for love.

Transference colors even a person's most vigorous interactions. We see this in marriage, for instance. Someone who, while growing up, never had reason to doubt his parents' loyalty may never pause to consider whether his prospective mate is loyal. He simply credits the person with that quality. It hardly occurs to him that this is a trait to be looked for. This same patient may seem emotionally stupid in not recognizing disloyalty even when it seems unmistakable. He is like an immigrant utterly unprepared for the language of his new country.

Through the transference we may learn a great deal about a patient's past. He overexplains to us, as if we doubted his integrity—he perhaps did this as a child with a parent. He makes it hard for us to disagree with him, treating us as if we were an underling. We wonder who we represent to him. Then we learn that while growing up, he was the oldest son; he automatically assumed the role of commander-in-chief over his siblings and he still unthinkingly assumes that position now.

Also, as we independently learn about the patient's past, we may uncover information that explains the transference. A woman tells us that as a teenager, when she returned from an evening out, her father would cross-examine her. We've observed that she expects us to do the same. She volunteers lengthy explanations as to why she is ten minutes late, and is overly defensive with us, as if we were waiting for an excuse to condemn her.

Transference is clearly an everyday phenomenon. I used to teach the fourth grade, and when I would walk behind the children while they were copying something from the blackboard, certain of them would hunch over the instant I got close, as if they half expected me to whack them for a mistake. By their reactions to me, I could tell which children were beaten and which were not. Transference appears not just in what our patients tell us but in their every act.

25

Resolving the Transference

After allowing the transference to develop, we take active steps to resolve it. There are at least two distinct conditions under which we do this, and for very different reasons. One occurs when the transference itself threatens to destroy the therapeutic alliance, to vitiate the patient's respect for us, and to make treatment worthless: we intervene to defend our reputation to the patient. In the second and more usual case, we resolve the transference because we believe it is ripe and that the patient is ready to grasp his difficulties and can help himself further by understanding his transference onto the therapist.

Our intervention to preserve our reputation to the patient is not self-serving but for his sake. As he devalues us, we sense we are losing the leverage we will need to help him. For instance, we see the patient building contempt for us, more and more, by acts of disdain toward us. He's sarcastic or tells us repeatedly that we can't help him. He insults us. He misses appointments, comes late. He is rapidly proving to himself that we're incompetent and that the whole process is a waste of time. He is bringing some picture of a past figure into the therapy and imposing it on us. Nothing we display about ourselves can possibly unconvince him; he is strengthening the impression of us in his own mind by his mistreatment of us. As Henry Ford once put it, "A man will never forgive you for the wrongs he has done to you."

We may have to intervene in a hurry, to resolve the "treatment-destructive" aspect of the transference before the patient loses utter regard for whatever we say. Perhaps when we confront him, he'll try to run over us, as if he hadn't heard us; but, even so, our comments may stay with him. More likely, if we make our intervention in good faith, he'll hear us, and may even thank us for making him aware of whatever it was we pointed out. Patients appreciate the strength needed to confront them, and feel secure in the knowledge that we won't let them mutilate the therapy experience. We might even explain that, in mistreating us, the patient is reducing our efficiency, and building a case against us. If he switches the topic to how *we* felt when he said what he did, or if he apologizes profusely, we make clear that this is not the point. We merely want him to appreciate the perception he is forming of us, and to study his feelings toward us.

Even when an intervention is well received, and seems successful, we should keep in mind for a long while afterward that the attitude the patient expressed may still be smouldering. It's not merely a matter of smoothing over a personal difficulty between patient and therapist. The patient has an important tendency, one that may erupt at any time, and possibly ruin relationships that are valuable to him. It may help to continue to ask the person regularly how he feels about us. We aren't looking for compliments. We want him to tell us any thoughts or feelings he's had about us between sessions or during them. And we should be ready to construe dreams as possibly relating to us, even if they're about some obvious person in the patient's life, such as a parent or boss or friend.

The kind of transference that blows up in the therapist's face most often is what psychoanalysts have termed the "idealized transference." The patient sees us as able to do no wrong. He dreams about us, pictures us as with him in his private life. He has fantasies about spending the rest of his days with us. Such people have the motivation to withhold truths about themselves —in particular, what they consider their failings—in order to make the best possible impression. They tell us we are helping them immensely, to please us. But their love for us contains the desire to possess us personally, and anger is likely to build as they find out that this is impossible. The higher the pedestal they put the therapist on, the further he can fall. Again, we must ask the patients regularly for their feelings about us, and be on the watch for anything they may have withheld; their anger or their worship may appear in small comments or in their tone, and we can help them express it openly. We must also be careful to resist any tendency to primp or to do anything designed to justify their lofty vision of us.

By far the more common use of transference is to let it grow while studying it, and then when it is ripe, to bring it to the patient's attention. As mentioned, Freud virtually equated psychoanalysis with the study and resolution of the transference. What the patient brings from the past and imposes on the therapist, he thought, contains the whole essence of the patient's problem. He recommended allowing the transference to develop over a period of years. He made clear that a positive transference knits the relationship with the therapist and provides a stimulus for the patient to work on his problems. It became an adage in early psychoanalysis never to analyze a positive transference. For instance, a patient brings flowers to show his appreciation of the therapist. The therapist might ask the patient how he feels, but the therapist would never volunteer an interpretation of the gift, as this would discourage the flow of positive transference that is crucial to the therapeutic process. I think it remains good practice not to intervene or attempt to resolve a positive transference so long as we need a working alliance.

We bring the transference to the patient's attention only when we are sure there are harmful elements that he can now understand or when the time comes to terminate therapy altogether. We watch the patient make changes, one after the other. Perhaps the harmful element is an excessively strong motivation to please us: he is not doing enough for his own pure, personal advantage. Our questioning reveals that he counts too much on us as his audience. We wonder, for instance, how it would be if we didn't respond joyously to some success he reported, and we decide to remain unenthusiastic next time. When we do this, he goes dead in the session. He doesn't know why, but we do. We ask later what he is feeling, and what thoughts went through his mind. He reports nothing about us, only a vague sense of inadequacy and a feeling that life is pointless. He wasn't even aware of these feelings until we asked him our question. Perhaps we do the same on another day, without even telling him our theory, that he is overly dependent on our response and that when he doesn't get it, he feels lost. After collecting more information all pointing to the same conclusion, we present the idea to him, and hopefully it produces a shock of recognition. Little by little, we bring his overdependency transference to his attention, and in our presence, he works at resolving it.

Freud's recommendation that we let transference ripen slowly, and not intervene in ways that might make the transference hard for the patient to identify, seems more important to follow with certain patients than others. For instance, with an extremely argumentative or paranoid patient, if we took issue with particulars, we would obscure the transference. The patient might merely countercharge us with some offense, or find excuses for his behavior, and perhaps rationalize himself into disliking us. Suppose we want the patient to see that certain of his behavior is transferential, and that he is not dealing with us realistically. A man pounces on us for even the slightest error; his anger flares easily, and he becomes accusatory. Above all, we do nothing that could be even remotely construed as provocative. No matter how merciless he is with us, we keep our low profile, never retaliating, or even commenting on his tone. Nearly everyone else in his life has responded to his diatribes with displays of almost equal and opposite passion. That muddied the waters, and he could not appreciate that he himself was the original provocateur. We restrain ourselves instead. Recall how Jackie Robinson, the first black big-league baseball player, turned professional with the resolve not to express rage or namecalling, no matter how many times others abused him. This held the mirror up to them, and their bigotry was unmistakable. We proceed this way. Against the backdrop of our personal control, the patient can often appreciate his own distortions, even without our saying anything.

Then when we do present our point of view concerning his picture of us, it is without recriminations. I prefer to tell a patient who has been sarcastic with me that I know how much he likes me, if indeed it is plain that he does. I remind him of how often he has complimented me, but that nonetheless, he excoriates me for the slightest error. Rather than rush at him like an injured party, I prefer to make him aware of the entire context and then specify the aspect of it that I want him to consider. I find patients quite ready to study their transference reactions when I approach them this way—not always, but as a rule. They usually recognize that they possess the traits we point to, and appreciate our levelheadedness in talking about those traits.

It may help after a patient recognizes the irrationality in his response to us to ask him about a parent. Did he have those reactions toward the parent, toward whom, perhaps, the reactions were justified?

With some patients, the transference evidently contains the essence of the whole problem. With many paranoid patients, for example, the interaction with us is virtually a fluoroscope of what is going on inside of them. The patient feels unworthy, or guilty about something, and accuses us of not listening, or not liking him, or of thinking about something else.

Because the therapist himself has nowhere to hide when the patient is talking about him, there may be a temptation to avoid discussing the transference. It's easier to listen to an articulate patient tearing down another person than to be the butt of his wrath. The therapist who shies away from this role, who resists entertaining the relationship fully, might actually try to divert the patient. The patient is disparaging him in no uncertain terms. The therapist, feeling acutely uncomfortable, might be tempted to ask, "Who else used to treat you that way?" Or, "What does this remind you of?" His aim is to have the patient move the subject away from him and go on to discuss a parent or some other faraway figure. However, if the therapist even suspects that the patient harbors unexpressed feelings about him he should do just the opposite. He should help the patient talk about him. For instance, the patient is disparaging a run of people who mistreated him. He is berating them, one after the other. The courageous therapist comes in at once. "And how did *I* let you down?" Anatole France once said that the secret of life was in the rule, "When you hear the sound of the cannons, go toward them."

The patient may accuse us of ill will, session after session, wholly without warrant. What he says about us may have applied to others in his life—for instance, a father who mistreated him and never listened to reason. Early in life he stopped appealing to his father. His very choice to appeal to our sense of reason contains the hope that we are really not like his father. Ironically, it's as if he saw us both as miscreant and impartial judge who could give him a fair hearing. He secretly hopes that his appeal to our better nature will prevail and we will condemn our own behavior. It's a much harder problem with the patient who is so sure we are like the abusive parent that he doesn't even accuse us of wrongdoing.

The great value of working with the transference is that it colors a relationship that we can see firsthand. When the patient talks about how his parents treated him a long time ago, or even recently, we are forced to make inferences—about his parents and about his role in the relationship. When he's talking about us, we can see and feel the truth or falseness of what he's saying. There's an immediacy and vitality that no hearsay reports can possibly match. We are the ones accused of letting him down, for instance, and not some figure whom we've never met.

26

Resistances

Every patient has impulses to avoid seeing certain truths. He has repressed particular feelings or ideas, and when therapy comes close to uncovering them, he feels the impulse to bar the therapist access to them. The patient finds it hard to obey the fundamental rule of saying whatever comes to his mind, and instead engages in mechanisms of defense. Such active efforts to thwart the therapist in his investigation were called *resistances* by Freud. Resistances are the interpersonal expression of repressions that go on inside the mind.

For instance, the patient might, when a painful truth is broached, become irrationally angry at the therapist, or talk non-stop, or become obsessive about trivia, or overintellectualize, or forget subject matter, or forget appointments themselves. Resistances thus acquired a pejorative implication among the early psychoanalysts as signs of refusal to cooperate. Freud himself became downright angry at patients who invoked resistances until he realized that they were inevitable, and were part of the very problem the patient presented. He realized the necessity of understanding them and dealing with them.

Beginning with Freud's identification of resistances and

discussions of them, there have been exciting developments in our understanding of what resistances mean. Much of what we learned has immediate implications for treatment. In no aspect of psychoanalysis, or of psychotherapy in general, are theory and practice more integrally related than in the study of resistances. The best way to put the role of resistances in perspective is to review briefly some of the history of what we know about them.

The original aim of psychoanalysis was to probe for deeply hidden material, for repressed truths, which were thought to have a life of their own. The purpose of treatment was to uncover such material and to release it, after which, it was believed, the person's symptoms would disappear. By this thinking, resistances were the patient's attempts to retain the status quo. Like the three-headed dog Cerberus, who guarded the underworld, resistances menaced the effort by any mortal to penetrate. The therapist's aim was to steal past the resistances, to "rescue" the repressed material and bring it to the surface. Devices such as free association and the analysis of dreams were used extensively to see past the resistances, to discover what went on in the patient's unconscious.

But before long, it was recognized that the mere discovery of an underlying conflict doesn't do away with the symptoms. "I'm too tied to my mother, that's why I have problems with women," a patient might tell us glibly. He has come away from his former therapy with this insight, but, alas, without anything basic really changing. Early psychoanalysis, upon seeing such cases, argued that intellectual understanding isn't enough: the patient must *experience* the early conflicts. Furthermore, it was maintained, he must experience those conflicts in the relationship with the therapist over and over again. But such an assertion, like any working hypothesis, can easily degenerate into a circular statement. When the person doesn't change, it is simply maintained that he didn't experience the truth deeply enough or often enough. Perhaps this was so, but how could one be sure?

As time went by, psychoanalysis proved less able to bypass resistances, "to see through the veil of infantile amnesia" than Freud had envisioned. He and his contemporaries began to blame therapeutic failures on the unexpected strength of resistances. Then, in 1924, Wilhelm Reich, a psychoanalyst and disciple of Freud's, brought about a whole new approach to resistances with his now classic work, *Character Analysis.* Reich's star has subsequently come crashing down for a variety of reasons—including his mysticism, his sexual "orgone" theories, and his Communism; but his contribution to the study of resistances was a major advance for psychotherapy.

Reich enlarged greatly on Freud's lexicon of resistances, especially including behavior that masquerades as cooperative but is really resistant. For example, the patient agrees with the therapist as a way of throwing him off the scent, or brings in seemingly important material that really isn't; he is on time, apparently eager, but may be playing the game of leaving his true feelings out. Some patients tell us nearly everything but are what Reich called "affect lame"; they don't let on the real meaning to them of what they are telling us. Since Reich's day, psychotherapists have come to appreciate that virtually any activity may be used as a form of denial or concealment—from the self and from the therapist.

Even more important was Reich's understanding of how to deal with resistances. Reich argued against the effort to bypass resistances to uncover what was being hidden. The original aim of psychoanalysts, to plumb the depths of the unconscious, implied that resistances were merely obstacles. The assumption was that if the therapist could steal past them and bring the unconscious material to light, the patient would drop his resistances. Why would the patient employ a complex method of concealment once the truths he had buried were dug up? But patients did just that. They not only sought to bury the very truths they had already acknowledged, but also used the same resistances to conceal a wide range of other material. Their resistances had a life of their own. Reich shifted the emphasis from finding the buried truths to giving the resistances themselves center stage.

He advocated making the patient's resistances the subject matter of therapy at the very start. His recommended method was to begin treatment by identifying the patient's resistances as they appeared, and then making the patient aware that he defended himself and by what means. Do this repeatedly, he maintained, until the patient is steeped in recognition of his resistances and is ready to disregard them. Do not attempt to steal past resistances in order to uproot truths in the patient's psyche. Once resistances have appeared, devote full attention to eliminating them. Only when this is done can the real work of psychoanalysis begin. "Generally," he wrote, "one cannot act too early in analyzing resistances, and one cannot be too reserved in the interpretation of the unconscious."

For instance, a man uses the resistance of falling apart, saying, "I'm utterly worthless," when the therapist comes close to uncovering the man's deeply competitive anger. As a boy, the patient hated his parents for fighting continually, and often had fantasies of their killing each other. Rather than try to discover the exact nature of the competitive anger, as Freud might have done—by looking for cues in the man's dreams or in free-association material—Reich advocated putting aside this ultimate quest in favor of resistance analysis. He would concentrate on the patient's falling apart, and work with this resistance until the patient recognized and discarded it. And as other resistances appeared, Reich would have the therapist deal with them too.

Reich was essentially a Freudian: his theory of psychic forces, taken from Freud, remained closer to that of the master than were the theories of nearly all of Freud's other major disciples. Reich regarded the analysis of resistances as merely a preliminary phase of therapy, although a necessary one, before a truly Freudian analysis could proceed. Thus, ironically, Reich himself underestimated the significance of resistances, even as he gave them far greater weight than any of his predecessors.

As a Freudian, Reich imagined that the psychic forces that lay buried in the unconscious were intact. They simply existed and governed behavior and conscious experience. Buried ideas and impulses had a "charge"—like an electrical force "bound up" in them. It was with this understanding that Reich advocated giving full attention to resistances. What Reich himself did not realize is that unconscious impulses—such as fear, love, and rage —rely on behavior to preserve their force. In particular, the very use of resistances feeds the person's unconscious sense of shame, or fear, regarding the subject matter he is hiding. Thus as the patient gives up his resistances, he is already revising his unconscious state. The very act of releasing the buried truth reduces the "electrical charge" of shame or guilt attached to what has been hidden. What psychoanalysts imagined would be necessary after the patient dropped his resistances they were partly accomplishing by the patient's very surrendering of his resistances.

It was as if Reich were saying, "Get the person to realize that he is wearing a mask. Then show him how to remove it, so that we can begin depth analysis." In actuality, the patient's very removal of the mask enables him to accept his face. Keeping the mask on had been renewing his sense of utter shame. The resistance to truth, whatever it is, feeds the humiliation, and taking off the mask reduces it.

The patient's choice of resistances is as indicative of him as are the truths he is hiding—indeed, his resistances often tell us more about him. The adage, "You can tell more from a person's mask than from his face," is very apt here. Also, the patient's resistances may influence his life far more than whatever they are designed to conceal. There are people who do themselves a variety of harms by their resistances, for example by antagonizing others or not letting anyone get close to them. Not the thing they are hiding but their manner of hiding it becomes their essential characteristic. Recall the man in Paris who had to hide that he was Jewish: his whole personality congealed around his need for overcontrol. His was not an instance of essential character forming in childhood. Yet the principle is the same. His personality style remained even after the truth was out, in this country, where his being Jewish certainly did not have its earlier implications. And it was that very personality style that created problems for him in his dealing with others.

Resistances themselves, apart from their effects on buried subject matter, become the person's nature and determine his fate. As psychology now enters the phase of its full awareness of the psychic importance of what the patient does, our appreciation of the significance of resistance also reaches its zenith. Thus we have Freud and Reich to thank for launching us toward our present appreciation that resistances, and their analysis, are far more important than either of them realized.

27

The Analysis of Resistances

With virtually every patient, there comes a time when we must pause in our search for "deep" truths. We need to identify the patient's resistances and bring them to his attention. His resistances conceal information, and increase his horror over what he is concealing. Moreover, the behavior that becomes a resistance in therapy may wreak havoc with his relationships. Resistances themselves may be so harmful to the patient that, if we have been effective in confronting them, our discovery of truths that lie buried below may be anticlimactic. Resistance are a fortress that "protect" the patient from life itself.

The therapist needs considerable flexibility of mind to do effective resistance analysis. So trained are we to pursue the patient's buried secrets that it is hard to switch our focus and consider as even more important his method of burying them. Above all, we need a dispassionate ego. The therapist who takes it too personally when an insight of his is denied by the patient may stubbornly offer his insight again, perhaps in new words. We must not succumb to the impulse to prove a point, or to say, "I told you so." The therapist, even if he feels this impulse, should merely listen, and study himself, to see what it means. The patient may be subtly accusing the therapist of not liking him, or of not being worth his trust, as an explanation for his withholding material. The therapist's task is to identify the patient's resistance and to study how it affects him.

Curiously, the therapist needs a ready sense of frustration to identify resistances. He asks a question—say, about the patient's sex life, and the patient starts talking about sexual theories, beginning with that of Havelock Ellis and going right up to one that appeared in a recent issue of *Playboy*. The therapist needs the experience of feeling shunted aside; after all, he wanted to know about the *patient* and instead received a scholarly analysis. The therapist needs enough dismay to suspect a resistance, and enough discipline not to lose his equilibrium. We must start out naively—as if the patient were going to tell us all without hesitation and never sidetrack us, so that we become sensitive to the slightest interference.

Unless the resistance is obvious—the patient yells, insists on changing the subject, closes his eyes—there may be a period of treatment during which the therapist feels thwarted—or even inadequate—and suspects a resistance but cannot identify it as yet. There is a sense of chaos, and it's hard for the therapist to know for sure: "Am I lost, or is this patient deliberately sidetracking my inquiries, trying to lose me? And if so, exactly how is he doing this?" The courage to endure this interval of chaos is a requirement. "What is the patient doing that stymies my exploration? How is he inducing in me this sense of futility that I feel?" It is a characteristic of all creativity that the creator must endure such a period of chaos, in which it is unclear whether he himself is failing or the chaos belongs to the act of creation. The ability to endure that sense of chaos is a requisite for artistic originality, and it is required here.

Perhaps the patient seems compliant, even eager. But he remains blank to whatever the therapist says. He's constantly unimpressed, like the critic who continually implies, "You haven't said anything worthwhile yet."

I recall one patient who left me despondent after each session until I recognized his device of saying, "Yes, but . . ." and then going off on a tangent without acknowledging what I said to him. No offering of mine seemed adequate. When I finally caught on, I observed that he used a disdainful wafture of his hand, when he said "Yes, but . . . ," as if he were dismissing me and my efforts with sovereign finality. He seemed always to be waiting for the valid contribution that I might make some day, but repeatedly asserting that nothing I actually said seemed valid. Increasing the subtlety was that he never interrupted, hearing me out to the last syllable.

Over the years, I've had many patients use almost the identical tactic, the same "Yes, but . . ."—agreeing and disagreeing at the same time—and even the same gesture of dismissal. Now I recognize that resistance at once. Dealing effectively with resistances is enhanced by experience, by the therapist's enlarging his own vocabulary of resistances that patients bring up. Spotting the actual resistance is always relieving.

The next step is cross-validation. I deliberately offered comments exactly consonant with what the man himself had been saying. Sure enough, even when I used his very words, he dismissed me and told me I didn't understand him at all.

When the patient resists some topic loaded with shame or guilt, we bring it up to watch the resistance at work. The patient, predictably, talks faster, changes the subject, tells us it's not important, interrupts us, or becomes devastated and seems utterly broken by our mention of it. Whichever he does, whatever resistance he employs, he tends to do the same thing each time we draw close. With this man, it hardly mattered what I said. His problem was that he found it humiliating to be told anything of value by another man. It was as if I were assuming the role of his superior by any contribution I might make. So he fought any contribution of mine. Being schooled in manners, he would let me finish, but he seemed to have a terror of acknowledging that I had given him anything of value. Think how this resistance to potential contributions harmed him in his advertising job, where it seemed annihilation to him to have to carry out another man's suggestion! Others felt the impact of his conflicts, and although he was a talented art director, people, especially men, found him impossible to work with. Each time he fought me, he was reinfecting himself with the idea that to listen to another man would be to annihilate his own identity.

I decided to begin making the man aware of his resistance. He asked me a question, and when I answered it simply, he dismissed me with his characteristic wafture of the hand, and his time-honored, "Yes, but . . . ," followed by going off on a tangent. I brought to his attention that he was dismissing me, and explained how. He became furious. How dare I talk about his behavior when he was asking me something as important as how to save his job! It crossed my mind that this behavior with me was very likely a replica of the behavior that had cost him several jobs. He simply refused to let people know they said anything worthwhile to him, and they found him impossible to work with. Indeed, he did lose his job the next day. But gradually as I brought the resistance to his attention, he took stock of it, discarded it, and kept his next job.

Frequently, when we make a patient aware of a resistance, he resorts to still another one. Usually but not always, the second is more primitive—that is, the patient learned to use it earlier in life than the resistance we pointed out. Just as we temporarily drop our quest for hidden subject matter in favor of focusing on a resistance, we may find it necessary to postpone our efforts to bring the first resistance to the patient's attention when he presents another. The rule is we always deal with what the patient is offering us at the time, thus peeling away layers of resistances.

When the patient starts to discard his resistance—in this case, when the man forced himself not to dismiss me, and actually responded to my comments—the reasons for the resistance rise toward consciousness. The method of magnification has real value in studying resistances. I asked the man how he felt about me, just after he had given me a real hearing and actually agreed with a criticism I made of him. He replied at once that he felt that I must be secretly laughing at him, that I probably felt triumphant over him. He saw that I had given him no reason for this belief. However, his mother had constantly explained simple things to him and underestimated him. Both parents would remind him over and over again of how much they had done for him. When he excelled in college, they would let him know how hard they had worked to get the money to put him there. He had resolved to become independent as soon as he could, and developed the habit of never letting people know what they had done for him. It seemed that whatever anyone gave him would have strings attached. He had the sudden thought that I was going to raise my fee—a thought that had never crossed his mind until he began acknowledging that I was helping him, and that he was really changing.

Recall that the hunger illusion, evoked by breaking a behavior pattern, is the very picture of life that is soon to fade as the old behavior is discontinued. By acknowledging me, this man taught himself that I (and, by implication, other people) were not waiting to claim things from him the minute he admitted we had given him something. We were not stingy and resentful of his success. After a while, allowing people to feel useful to him became much easier. This was why he improved all his relationships and kept his next job without difficulty. His very discarding of the resistance had a profoundly curative effect on him.

Pointing out resistances must be done simply and dispassionately. The patient may object that we are wrong, but since resistances are inveterate habits, he will surely come to see instances of the behavior that we have mentioned to him. The key is to watch the resistance for a while, perhaps acting in ways that incite the patient to invoke the resistance, before we bring it up. While stung by an insult or any form of rejection, we have little power to make our presentation equably. As we develop a thorough appreciation of the resistance, we can view it more dispassionately. It ceases to feel like our problem.

It helps for patients to appreciate the impact that their resistances have on their own lives. For instance, the patient can see that his hiding something deepens his shame and distrust of other people. In allowing people to discover him as he really is, the patient is learning to accept himself, as he has perhaps never done before.

28

Countertransference

How we respond to a patient is always, to some degree, the result of what we bring to the experience. We are never purely objective instruments, but being human we have a history and a disposition that affect our response. The part of our reaction to a patient that is our own particular import, our bias, is called *countertransference.* Often we need to decide to what degree our experience of a patient is countertransferential and to what degree it is real.

Every countertransference, like every transference, tends to heighten certain perceptions and has its own particular blind spots. Recall the analogy of the colored light. Perceiving through his colored lens, the therapist sees certain colors readily, even if they are only lightly present, and sometimes when they don't exist at all. And he is oblivious to certain other colors, because his own projected color blocks them out.

Certain forms of countertransference are extremely common. Perhaps the most usual is the tendency to see people as needy, accompanied by a desire to do things for them. Such love of the underdog seems quite natural for one in the helping profession. Some bias toward seeing patients as helpless and toward offering them too much is likely to go unnoticed. But when the tendency is pronounced, the therapist can see the patient only as a victim of mistreatment. He may offer too much advice or even concrete aid, and is likely to be overcredulous when the patient blames other people for his problems. In this state, the therapist may overlook even an extremely grudging and thankless nature in his patients, and does not appreciate their failure to act in their own behalf.

Also common is the countertransference stemming from unresolved rivalry with the patient or jealousy of the patient. The therapist may be marvelous with those less educated or poorer than he is, but is unable to root for the patient who seems to have more already. It's easy to see how we might fall prey to this kind of countertransference bias. For instance, we have a childhood history of rivalry for a parent's affection. In other instances, our present lives cause the problem. We've worked hard, grown up poor, and we still have to get up early in the morning to make enough for our mortgages. And here comes this smug, narcissistic little rich man's son, seducing women at will, breaking promises, taking no one seriously and buying our time so that he can discuss the merits of summer resorts we'll never be able to afford. Or even more germane to us, he's built a business or written a successful book that gives the lie to our best efforts. We're like Salieri with Mozart, or like would-be painters being employed by a young and more successful artist to supply the right frame for his masterpiece. We've got to look out for envy and anger.

There is also the countertransference fear of intimacy. The patient loves us, and for good reason: we've opened up the doors of happiness for him, and we have been devoted. He talks intimately, expresses warmth toward us easily. For the therapist who grew up in a cold climate, where affection was scarce (and many of us went into the field for this very reason), such intimacy is disquieting. We should be able to talk to our patients about their love or sexual feelings for us without freezing up. But in this case, although we may refer to intimacy, perhaps espousing its value intellectually, our patient is the one who expresses it easily and we have trouble with it. His problems are elsewhere, and when he tells us he loves us, we shy away. When he buys a present for us, as a token of affection or appreciation, we refuse it, or accept it ungraciously, not because it is uncalled for therapeutically, which we might say, but because we simply aren't comfortable in the climate we advocate.

Every conceivable human bias may appear as a form of countertransference, threatening to distort the therapist's perception of his patient. The therapist feels certain impulses more than he ought to, and finds particular modes of treatment especially difficult. We each have certain patients whom we find it especially hard to confront, to say something that would make us unpopular. Our hesitancy might be induced—for instance, the patient has been hinting that if we disagree with him, he will consider us incompetent and will quit. But even so, we should recognize the threat and not feel stymied by it. Where there is a countertransference obstacle, we find it hard to meet this patient head-on and say what needs to be said.

How can we decide whether we are under the influence of countertransference? Some forms become quite evident to us but others are difficult to identify.

Sometimes we can see easily that we're in the grip of a countertransference reaction. For instance, we feel desperately in love with a patient. We are obsessed by concerns over what he'll think of us, and we feel possessive. Surely nothing the patient did accounts for such detail and intensity of response on our part. Every therapist has had the experience of thinking about some patient too much, on holidays and weekends, not productively but obsessively. When he does things out of character for a therapist—for instance, walks in the park in his old clothes or starts to go out on the dance floor—he pictures the patient observing him. Or when he imagines some royal success, he imagines impressing that patient. The patient has assumed a role in the therapist's life that other people once possessed.

Aside from the intensity and detail of our reaction, we may suspect a countertransference problem if we recognize that we have had much the same feeling toward many patients. A therapist finds himself resenting a number of his patients or feeling sorry for one person after the other, and being afraid to confront them. In the first case, he's afraid of revealing his resentment, of saying something bitingly angry; in the second, he's afraid of crushing the patient, whom he regards as fragile. Every countertransference inhibits the therapist somewhere. It always interferes with the ability to confront the patient squarely. Also, every countertransference has its blind spots: there are things about the patient that we can't see. I once told the psychoanalyst Theodor Reik that a therapist we both knew "loved his patients." "That's too bad," Reik replied. "Love is blind, you know."

Just as we expect a range of perceptions and reactions from our patients, we must expect them of ourselves. Has there never been a patient whom we recognized as a scoundrel, an exploiter of other people? If not, and we've been in practice for a long time, we're probably subduing our capacity for seeing people in that light. Or, for example, it may be that we hold a countertransferential bias toward some set of people—such as minority group members, or women, or children. We superimpose on them a consistent bias, and don't see who they really are. Can we recall instances in which the woman in a relationship has been unfair to the man, or seemed to us to be the one who cut off the communication unfairly? Or has it always seemed that the man was at fault?

We also learn about our biases from the accusations our patients make of us. They might tell us we're naive, or too polite, or unfair to a certain group. They may not be accurate, but if we hear the same charge repeatedly, they're alluding to something real. A patient once told me that I had a prejudice against the children of rich families. I seemed less sympathetic with their victimization than I should be. I studied the reaction, and came to the conclusion that I did indeed hold a prejudice, but it only indirectly concerned those children. It seemed to me that I too quickly assumed that their parents gave these children too much, and that the parents expected too little of those children. I was primarily annoyed with the parents. Not that I always made that mistake, but I tended in that direction.

There's also a lot to be learned about ourselves from what our patients don't tell us, and from what doesn't happen in our sessions. For instance, a therapist reports that all his patients are polite toward him. He never has crackling sessions, in which his patients criticize him harshly—the kind his colleagues describe. His countertransferential bias leads him to befriend patients and to become overly polite toward them. He praises them too much and solicits their favorable opinion. Not surprisingly, they respond by withholding information from him so as to protect their reputation with him. As a result, his sessions are insipid, and a number of his patients become bored and quit. Some tell him that they can't afford his fees, but he later discovers that they've gone to someone else and haven't wanted to hurt his feelings. When a patient has gone for good, this therapist becomes able to recognize that he never liked the patient as much as he pretended to. He becomes aware of issues that he failed to deal with while the patient was there.

A good antidote for this kind of distortion is for the therapist to ask himself, while the patient is still going to him: "How would I feel if this patient suddenly quit?" "Why might this patient suddenly quit?" "What would I then wish I had brought up with him?" Therapists with an acute dose of this pseudokindness countertransference may find the very questions painful. They are tempted to reply that they can't even imagine the patient quitting, things seem to be going so well. But then the patient does quit! Being taken utterly by surprise is nearly always evidence of countertransference distortion, especially if it happens repeatedly.

Along with biases in perception, there are overintensified impulses in countertransference. For example, the excessively sympathetic therapist finds it hard not to offer his patients advice and solace, and perhaps finds it difficult not to help the patient when the patient is struggling for words. Similarly, the therapist with a rivalry countertransference may find it hard not to defend himself when the patient accuses him of a blunder. Instead of asking the patient what such a blunder might imply to him, the therapist gets caught up defending himself and his behavior. There is always compulsive behavior involved.

The therapist must study his own behavior both to diagnose his countertransference and to begin curing it. For instance, he decides that he's giving too much advice to his patients. He would do well to pass the resolution: None of that behavior for the next session, or the next week. It may be excruciating to stick to his resolution—and without his realizing it, he may lapse into giving advice, and talk far too much. Far from inducing that urge in him, the patient may be annoyed at his giving the advice. The diagnosis is made. He is caught up in a countertransference reaction inducing him to behave that way.

To learn more about himself, the therapist should, while restricting himself, study his reactions. The thoughts that come to his mind may be familiar to him—or utterly unexpected; but they will surely be informative. "If I don't jump in with advice now, he will think I'm stupid." Such a reaction is especially telling if the therapist also knows that the patient is annoyed at him for giving the advice. The therapist's fear of appearing stupid is an import from the past. In another case, the therapist might feel, "If I don't help him now, he'll feel lost and be utterly crushed." And in still another, it might cross the therapist's mind, "He'll think I don't love him." From such fragments of thoughts, the therapist can get a sense of what his true motivations are.

Similarly, the therapist may discover in himself the impulse *not* to do something. For instance, not to confront the patient who hasn't paid him in months. The same method of disobeying the impulse means, in this case, to do the thing—as to bring up the matter of money.

Patients who induce certain feelings routinely are most likely to impart those feelings to the therapist who is, for reasons of his own, ready prey for them. In some cases, the patient can all but immobilize such a therapist. For instance, the patient is still playing the child disappointed by a parent; the therapist has a countertransference dread of disappointing those who count on him. It takes systematic efforts for the therapist to see what is going wrong.

The therapist's very discovery of a countertransference relieves some of the pressure. As we come to appreciate our own bias, we free ourselves from victimization by our patients. We can study explicitly what is missing in their private lives, and set to work at trying to satisfy our needs. Ultimately, as we give up the countertransferential behavior—not just with patients but with people in our own lives, we gradually free ourselves of the bias. We become more effective as therapists and have a distinct sense that we are traveling lighter than before.

PART SIX

The Tools of Treatment

By request and such fair question
As soul to soul affordeth.
                                    —Shakespeare

29

Listening

Nearly everyone underestimates how rare the good listener is. What seems easy to do, and what we expect of others, namely to pay full attention to what we say, to hear us out, is a surprisingly unusual talent. Like many animals, we come on this earth with what seems an instinct to communicate. But try to think of an animal—dolphin or chimp or bird or man—who instinctively pays full attention to another of its kind when it communicates. Teaching a child to pay undivided attention to what we say for more than a few seconds takes time, and many adults have never learned it. Add to the art of listening the ability to communicate, "I hear what you are saying and it matters," and the number of true listeners is further reduced.

There are patients who find it almost impossible to hear us out without bursting in and trying to finish our sentences for us. Even after we've pointed this out, they find it stunningly hard to let us finish; some may automatically put a hand over their mouths, as if to help them stop from breaking in. Other people appear to be listening but are really responding to associations of their own while we talk. We no sooner finish than they go right to their own topic, as if we weren't there. Chekhov was the first writer to understand this truth about human nature—often his characters did not respond to what the previous speaker had said. At first, audiences thought he was mad, and then realized that he was merely capturing the pattern of everyday conversation.

Hardly better are those "listeners" who use what we say as a springboard for talking about themselves. Our auto accident reminds them of a near miss that they suffered years ago. They go from what we say to something vaguely like it in their own life: "Parallel communication" is reminiscent of parallel play when little tots are first put in the same playpen and do their own thing, barely looking over at one another. Among adults, in what seems like a group discussion, the spotlight is really going back and forth as contestants grab for it, prefacing their interruptions by some statement that pays minimal homage to what the other person has said. When the party is over and the various couples drive home in their cars, they perhaps remember moments of pleasure, but feel unfulfilled. They feel inexplicably lonely, not realizing that they have been cut off repeatedly, unacknowledged, and not knowing that they did the same to others.

To the extent that we can't listen, we fail to make a real connection with other people, even loved ones. How many of us, after people we loved are gone, feel that somehow we never got the chance to be as close to them as we wanted to! Not only this. We lose out on the chance to see life honestly through the perspectives of the many people we know who have different vantage points. The real wisdom that they might have brought us, a deepening of our own values, we do not accept. It is all too true that, as one of Shakespeare's characters put it, "Wisdom cries out in the streets and no man will listen."

As psychotherapists, we will see a great many patients who have never been listened to. Their parents paid attention only when they liked what was being said, if at all. Even if their parents were skilled at listening, they considered the child's concerns to be trivial, and exercised their option of not listening without loss of status. One thing that power quite often corrupts is the readiness to listen. Whether one is boss, or an acknowledged expert at something or the head of a household or a parent, it becomes too easy to decide whether and when to listen, and to whom. Many of our patients would be quite different today if only someone, some adult, had taken the time to hear them out, to listen to their thoughts and feelings, and to communicate that they mattered, whether the listener felt the same way or not.

By expert listening alone, we can help our patients arrive at new insights and actually improve. For ages they wandered without anyone knowing who they were, perhaps longing for love as much to satisfy their need to be seen realistically as for its other benefits. Now a light is shining on them in the darkness, the therapist's light, and under it they flourish.

Carl Rogers, the nondirective therapist, has been the main champion of listening as being in and of itself therapeutic. The patient, he feels, has a "self-actualizing potential," which flourishes when another human being gives him the opportunity. Rogers emphasized the importance of communicating that one has heard, of "reflecting" back to the patient the deep, underlying feelings in what he has said. Therapists of virtually all schools are Rogerian to some extent, and certainly in the early sessions they make contact with the patient mainly by listening. Interestingly, the behavioral therapists have, in the last decade, reinterpreted Rogers' method of reflection by saying that choices the therapist makes actually reinforce particular ideas the patient has voiced. Even to say "uh huh" at a particular time is not merely a neutral act, one encouraging the patient to keep talking; it is, they argue, a reinforcement of what the patient has just been saying. Perhaps there is no such thing as pure reflection, which would express simply, "I am with you," without conveying any attitude toward the subject matter.

Granting that our very listening has an effect on the patient, we can use the process of listening to tell the person, in effect, "I am not shocked." Kinsey had a rule for his sex researchers, which was, "Never lean forward, never lean back." The experts on his staff, especially Wardell Pomeroy, were masters at communicating a nonjudgmental acceptance of whatever practices the person reported. Others who instinctively violated that rule had to be dropped from the interview staff. We can use listening in a very deliberate way to color certain subject matter with our own equanimity, and this can help the patient a great deal. It should be remembered that in some cases the patient has harbored some deep secret for ages. Although a fact, such as that he masturbates or is homosexual or is having an extramarital affair, may seem commonplace to us, to him it is earth shattering, in part because he has kept it a sectet for so long. We are releasing the person to reconsider it in a whole new light by countenancing his presentation of it, by merely listening. Whatever our impact, we encourage the patient to explore new territory. And he comes to think of us as a comrade on his journey to places he has never visited before.

We show that we are listening in various ways. In the questions we pose, in the interpretations we make, and in our very recollection of details, we communicate that we have heard and heeded what the patient said. Remembering some name the patient brought up in a session a long time ago can do a great deal to let him know that we are there when he speaks. If we slip, it may communicate that we don't really care about him the way we should. Often, as therapists, we realize that our mind has wandered and our memory with a patient is poor. It may be right not to communicate this to the patient, but we ought to know it ourselves. As we take pains to find out certain facts that we are sure the patient already told us once, we ought to ask ourselves why we don't remember them. Is there something about this person himself or what he is saying that makes it hard to remember the material? If we constantly forget what the patient tells us, the reason almost surely lies in either his presentation or in some countertransference problem of ours.

The solution is not simply to write down details. Instead, it is to study why we block out what he says, and to tackle the problem in ourselves. Nothing is more discouraging than some blatant piece of ignorance on our part. I heard of a case in which a man spent his first session talking about his father's death, and three sessions later, while he was talking about his mother, the analyst broke in and said, "You've talked a lot about your mother. What about your father? How come you don't talk about him?"

On the other hand, it's important not to be bullied by a patient because we've forgotten some detail that he expected us to remember. Usually, we'll recall the things that matter to us because they're germane to our purposes. An Adlerian, who emphasizes the birth order of children in the family and its relation to the subsequent personalities of those children, will almost surely remember that order. An existentialist therapist might not, and moreover would be more likely by far than the Adlerian to forget the names of the patient's siblings, and so forth. We all make mistakes, and forget some of the things we've been told. This doesn't mean we're not doing the job. We may be doing it far better than the person who writes down all the inert facts of a case and is oblivious to the patient's style in the sessions and to what is really going on.

The good listener should concentrate on the emotions of the person talking. We listen for words and tones suggestive of emotions and we watch for facial expressions. For instance, a woman talks grimly about life but when she mentions her brother, her face lights up. She herself isn't aware that this happens. Our sensitivity to this unconsidered facial expression cues us in and we ask how she feels about her brother. She replies that she's proud of him, and loves him. He has always been a source of great joy to her, but she let him recede from her life. She vows to see him more often, and thanks us. We may return to what the patient has offered us nonverbally as a conception that he can use, as a piece of the puzzle of his psyche that seemed missing.

Sometimes we can feel a tone quite different from what the patient's words imply. For instance, a man tells us that without him his wife would be penniless. He sacrifices for her continually, but she is unappreciative, sarcastic, and will not lift a finger to make his life easier. He has no intention of leaving her, although he offers not a single reason why he should stay. Their children are grown up and married. After every story of a heroic sacrifice by him and of how thankless she was, a smile comes to his lips. Why the smile? It seems to say, "See how victimized I am!" He takes pleasure in the fact that any listener in his right mind can see that he is trod upon and deserves better treatment. Yet he isn't pleasant to be with. He is getting real relief out of loathing her and even out of sacrificing for her. She affords him the chance to be an heroic underdog, and the excuse to wallow in. With another woman, he might be obliged to muster good cheer, to become a more positive person, and he fears having to do this. Perhaps he would fail.

Close listening has revealed the secret benefits of his staying with her and being exploited by her, and also the long-run penalty for both of them. The choice is up to him. Will he go on plucking these rather shallow benefits from the relationship or give them up, as a prelude either to improving his marriage or getting out of it? There is a history to his neurotic system of dealing with his wife. His mother was deeply respected in their hometown, considered an excellent wife and hostess, but the patient and his siblings knew she was a serious alcoholic and an irresponsible person much of the time. He grew up with the fantasy that the neighbors would learn the truth, but felt too much loyalty to give it out. Early in life he had learned to bear suffering, to see himself as downtrodden, and to feel misunderstood. He still pursued pleasure in this form, and was afraid to seek it more directly.

Listening attentively, we can often hear emotional tones quite different from those in the patient's ostensible message. The patient is telling us how happy he is, and yet we feel a flatness in his voice, or anger. He says he's looking forward to some event, but we don't feel it. Not that we should interpret at once, or tell the patient what we think he is "really feeling," but what we hear can prompt us to ask questions and choose directions that otherwise might never have occurred to us.

As careful listeners, we should go slowly and dwell on critical moments even if the patient implies that they are unimportant. A man is talking glibly: "Oh, that was the summer my mother died, but the real thing I wanted to tell you was . . ." The therapist may let it pass for a moment, rather than sidetrack the patient, but we must go back to the topic of his mother's death and what it meant to him. We have many questions to ask, and he will surely appreciate us in the long run for not being party to his downgrading of such an important event in his psychic life.

As listeners, we must never be accomplices to the patient's downgrading of his own importance. For us to allow that the death of his mother is unimportant would be to condemn our patient himself as a nonentity.

We do the same if he glosses over some honor received as if it were unimportant. Perhaps he doesn't expect other people to care that he won a scholarship to finish college. He mentions it in passing. But we break in at some stage and ask him about it, perhaps commenting to the effect that he must have been good and worked hard to achieve it. We must not join his dismissal of his own accomplishments, but rather counter the tendency and point out that he does dismiss his achievements.

Some patients downgrade themselves by switching the subject away from themselves—for instance, by praising other people. When the patient moves from something of importance to him to a lengthy discussion of other people, even his own children, the time may come to break in. "I am glad about John but you had started to tell me about your project, and I want to go back to it." Or we may simply ask about the details of that project.

As Carl Rogers taught us, listening is far more than a passive method. By reflection and by occasional questions designed to focus the patient on himself, we are imparting a quiet emphasis, letting him know that his psychological life is what we care about most. We are there to learn about *him*. He is worth it, whether he thinks so or not.

Reporting back to the patient what he has said is our way of indicating that we have been listening. The use of reflection is one of those nearly invisible techniques, and it is extremely powerful partly for this reason. The whole technique of reflection can be misused easily, and it needs to be looked at a little more closely.

To reflect is to hold a mirror in front of the person, enabling him to see himself. Often we merely rephrase what he has said —but more tersely, almost by way of summary. This helps the patient get a grip on what he has been saying and see its importance in his own life. Sometimes patients who have been free-associating literally ask us to tell them what they've been saying, not necessarily the detail but the gist of it.

By reflecting, we can keep the flow of feelings and ideas alive, without introducing our own input. For instance, a patient who has been talking productively is suddenly silent. He seems to be thinking over what he just said. We judge that his silence is itself productive and let it go. But then we get the sense that he is stymied, feeling increasingly uncomfortable, even confused. We want to show we're there, and to focus on his feelings but not interfere with his flow. As the silence continues, we decide it would help to join him in what now seems like a painful void. We highlight the feeling that has dominated in what he's been saying. "So you're angry at your wife, and you've been angry at your boss for days, and you say it's been miserable." "Yes," he goes on to amplify. We have helped the flow.

Usually we reflect a mood or feeling. "You're really stymied right now, on all fronts." He replies, "I sure am. And I have every reason to be, wouldn't you say?" And he goes on to explain.

But a word of caution. Sometimes what seems like reflection can become a dangerous weapon if used by a therapist who holds a bias, and, consciously or not, wants to manipulate his patient.

A therapist treating a woman thinks that her marriage is destructive and that she should divorce her husband. He believes that the only thing standing in her way is that she doesn't appreciate how much her husband is harming her. Using, or rather misusing the technique of reflection, he chips away at the marriage. When his patient complains to him about her husband, he highlights the complaint by "merely reflecting it." Actually, she loves her husband and senses that all along she has been contributing to their troubles by being infantile and provocative. For instance, she spends their money in sprees, provoking him into the exaggerated position of denying her the right to have money in her possession. He demands that she report to him every dollar she spends. Their relationship is extremely complicated and needs painstaking analysis before any decision should be made about whether to continue it. However, the therapist, responding to his own bias, reflects back to the woman only her dissatisfaction with her husband: "He sounds infantile." "I wonder why you stay with him." Soon it seems to her that the only sensible thing to do is to leave the marriage.

In cases like this one, the patient usually develops an unarticulated sense about what the therapist wants to hear. After a while, this woman withheld from the therapist reports of glorious weekends with her husband and good sex. As often occurs, the distortion was fed by both parties. The therapist, under the influence of his bias, was not substantially different from a parent to whom a young married son might complain about his wife, but who doesn't get to hear the wife's side because the son doesn't do it justice.

In such cases, the distance between therapist and patient changes at time goes by. They either become closer, and gradually the patient responds to the therapist's influence and makes the decision the therapist wanted. Or the patient comes to feel increasingly uncomfortable and dishonest with the therapist, hiding more and more of the truth; he might turn on the therapist in rage or quit suddenly.

Reflection can, as Rogers made clear, serve as a powerful tool to show that we are listening to the patient's every word and understand him. But for the very reason that it is an almost invisible tool, it can be harmfully misused. Whereas a patient can reconsider a therapist's interpretation or opinion, or discuss it with friends, it is hard to controvert what seems like mere reflection of what one has just said. It is hard for the patient to identify that part of his message that the therapist failed to reflect. Therefore we must be careful, as we listen and reflect, to see and highlight the real essence of what the patient is telling us. We are only as good as our genuine involvement with the patient's welfare and our freedom from bias.

30

Asking Questions

Along with listening, the very essence of treatment is to ask questions. A good question gets the patient to do the work, which is always preferable to our doing it. By what we ask, we not only orient ourselves but also convey what we consider important. Our patient will come to ask himself at least some of the questions we put to him. Therefore, we may think of our every question as a model in detail and emphasis.

By our questions, we are letting our patients know that we are in touch with them, that we see where they are. A timely question makes an excellent bridge. There are patients who, especially in the early sessions, depend upon our questions for the confidence to keep going. Some who would otherwise feel lost thrive on a steady supply of questions from us, and may, when a thing is hard to talk about, actually request that we ask them about it. Beyond showing interest and conversance, our questions can provide reassurance to patients and allay suspicions that may lurk in too long silences.

The therapist who can't think of anything to ask the patient may seem indifferent or out of it. Important topics are gone as fast as they appear, and seem to have disappeared forever, when a quiet question would have sustained them. As we go along in our profession, we learn to ask more and interpret less. We've all had the experience of posing a question that we thought we could answer, only to be astonished that the real answer hadn't occurred to us. And even if we knew the gist of the answer, having the patient tell it to us in his own words has value. His words have connotations to him, and import extra meanings that we might not have suspected.

On the other hand, an inappropriate question may betray some bias or preoccupation of ours, or indifference or stupidity. Such a question can sidetrack the patient. Every question we ask should have a purpose, if not several, and should be defensible in terms of what we want to accomplish. Also, just as we need the ability to ask timely questions, so do we need a sense of when the patient is reaching for thoughts or feelings of his own, at which time we should be quiet and let him do his productive work.

What gives our questions their central importance is the basic understanding behind the therapeutic relationship. Our patient has agreed to tell us whatever comes to his mind. He may hedge, or repress something or tell an untruth, but his part of the contract is that he say what comes to his mind when we ask him a question, and at other times too. We have the right to ask him whatever we want to. Granted, he may not answer us directly or logically. What comes to his mind may be a free association to our question, or to us. But this association may itself be worth much more than the answer we sought, and we need the flexibility to pay full attention to it, whatever we imagined we were looking for. If we're not satisfied, we can always ask the same question again, as often as we want, so long as we don't drum it at the patient or make a personal cause out of getting our answer. Like good lawyers, we ought to rephrase questions that don't get through.

Most of our questions will tend to be "open-ended"—that

is, to admit of a variety of answers. Usually, we avoid "yes–no" questions, although there are patients frugal with answers, who do their best to respond with only one or a few words. Some of our questions amount to requests of the patient to amplify: "Would you please tell me more about it?" We are asking the patient, in effect, to keep talking and to put in details. The experienced therapist, who is unafraid to appear ignorant, is ready to ask very simple questions designed to get the patient to break down his thoughts into morsels, so that the patient himself can better digest what he is saying.

There are instances in which therapy goes nowhere because the patient has the habit of passing over his really crucial ideas by containing them in pat phrases. The whole therapy is humdrum, and both patient and therapist feel bored. However, some pointed questions might get the patient to take apart those phrases, and the result would be a release of energy, like that from smashing an atom. For instance, a man keeps saying flatly that he is "confused"; a therapist too easily satisfied with imperfect understanding of the patient would let him go on, hoping to arrive at some discovery. A better therapist would insist on knowing more. For instance, when the patient says he's confused, the therapist asks, "Between what and what?" Whenever a patient describes an ambivalence or uncertainty, or any condition in which he feels himself in two places at once, the therapist should be sure that it is made clear what the two separate positions are.

Often it turns out that there is no conflict at all. For instance, a man told of his sadness in sending his son off to college. He loved the boy, and an era of life was ending. He experienced more emotion than he had for a long time. On the other side of his conflict were his doubts about whether his son could live successfully away from home. Patients often bury strong feelings by finding spurious counterbalances, as this one was, and then merely reporting themselves as "confused," or "uncertain."

Having broken down the communication into its raw elements, the therapist can then go on to draw the patient out on either of the positions taken, or on both in turn. In this case, the therapist had the man go on to talk about his sadness, and what the loss of his son would mean to him.

Two questions that we are likely to ask early in treatment are, "What brought you into therapy?" and "How would you like to change?" Therapists find their own words for these questions, but most ask them in one form or another. They are open-ended. The patient can talk about a friend who recommended that he go for help, or about a symptom, or about his belief, or disbelief in therapy. We can then get him to amplify or be more specific. The patient may talk about changing in ways that only indirectly concern our purposes. He wants to get a good job, become rich, or make a wonderful marriage. Little by little, questions can help us focus on the task at hand. Why is it that he doesn't have those things now? How can therapy help? Is there anything about him which, if it were different, would make him more likely to achieve the ambition he mentioned? He must suspect so, or else he would not have chosen to come to us. By questions we convey what we can do, and what the focus of our efforts will be. We can't produce a satisfactory mate, but insofar as the patient is stopping himself psychologically from finding one, or disqualifying himself when he does, we can help him see how and then he can do something about it.

A form of questioning developed in psychiatric hospitals and used extensively with projective tests is called "testing the limits." The method entails asking a sequence of questions, each more direct and leading than the one that went before. We go from very open-ended questions to increasingly specific ones. The method becomes especially useful with a patient who doesn't appear to see or feel something—or at least doesn't report it. We want to elicit the knowledge if he possesses it, without suggesting that knowledge to the patient.

For instance, a woman reports a series of incidents in which people took advantage of her. We suspect that she felt angry, but she has never acknowledged that she felt this way in any context. When we ask how she felt, she answers, "Fine. I understand why he did that to me." "Any other reaction you can recall?" "No." "Were you upset in any way?" "Not at all."

We let the matter drop, but plan a return. Why has she selected these anecdotes to tell? She must have some underlying feeling about them for her to have saved them over the week and then presented them to us. Besides, her phrasing, "He did that to me," implies at least the possibility of a reaction that she hasn't yet put into words. Before long, out comes another story of her being victimized. We ask similar questions, but this time go one further. "Were you upset or angry?" She thinks carefully. "Yes, I was." "At what?" She goes on to tell us, but hesitantly. We have found the emotion, but it took a lot of work because she was covering it over.

Testing the limits has the value of eliciting information while imposing a minimum of our own point of view. We might use the method to study the patient's unexpressed attitudes toward us, first asking about them generally, and later going on to ask more pointed questions.

For instance, we suspect the patient is angry with us, although he has never told us as much. We've got to get this attitude out in the open. If the patient has a history of burying his misgivings and simply fading out of relationships, we can ill afford to fall silent when there are signs he is doing the same with us. It is never right for us to join his refusal to discuss something unpleasant in our relationship in the hope that it will "blow over." The experienced therapist knows that nothing ever blows over in relationships. "You've been late several times in the last two weeks. Any reason?" "No, I just couldn't get here." We go on talking and the patient, usually voluble, gives us one-word answers to whatever we ask. "Why so brief? Is there some feeling you have about me?" "Not really." If we think the word "really" hints at something more, we might go on. "Tell me. Did I do something wrong? You don't sound like yourself." "Well, you always take the other person's side when I tell you what happened. Like the other day, when my cousin made that terrible criticism of me, you said . . ."

Now that the patient is criticizing us openly, we listen. We have, by escalating our questions in this way, brought out a noxious attitude, one that was poisoning him and the relationship. Nothing is cured. He is still prone to bury misgivings, and to let them fester inside of him. But at least this one is out in the open and now we have a chance to help him. To some extent at least, he has learned that it is possible to express his complaints to us, and therapy is less likely to come to an abrupt end.

We might approach some challenge in the patient's life by much the same method. He's going for the big interview and solicits our advice. "What do you expect at the interview?" If he has not formed a detailed picture of what it will be like, and he may not if the whole episode looms as very unpleasant, we might ask, "What could go wrong?" "What are you afraid you might do that you might be sorry about afterward?" To this, let us say, he answers, "I'd lose my temper and tell the interviewer off." "What would prompt you to do that?" "I don't know." "Well, what might he say that would touch you that way?" "He might refer to my not being a college graduate, which doesn't really make a damn bit of difference, and he knows it." Our questions can help the patient prepare himself for contingencies, and more important, learn about himself and his vulnerabilities—important learning even if those contingencies never arise.

We each tend to ask questions in our own special provinces of interest. Being familiar with a certain pastime or activity, we're likely to form judgments from how the patient carries it out. A psychologist fond of cooking found it significant that a patient, also a diligent cook, used a prepackaged soup for his in-laws after an argument. Indeed, the patient admitted, he had not fully forgiven them. Another therapist might not have asked for details of the dinner, but perhaps would have responded to other hints of this type.

I'm always curious about whether the patient has heroes, and if so, who they are and why. We each contain within us at least some stirrings of hope to be like our heroes, to embody their values and virtues. They are organizing forces within us. A particular personification of courage gives us courage. The person without heroes is forlorn, wandering, empty—incapable of heroic transference or of bringing forward the image of himself as a hero. Our patients bring forward not just images of significant adults they knew, but of movie figures and heroic characters they read about, and impose those images on their present lives. I often question them about these figures, and what they have meant to the person.

I think it is significant when a patient asserts—as it is fashionable to do—that there are no heroes, that all people have clay feet, that everyone has his price. Their error is in concluding that clay feet—fear, uncertainty, even folly—disqualify heroes. In their minds, realism and romanticism stand as opposites, when indeed our very frailty is a requirement for us to be truly heroic. Only mortals can be heroes; the gods are eternal with nothing to lose. I try to help every patient who needs such help to accomplish the fusion between realism and romanticism.

It's valuable to make our questions concise and respectful. We can ask the same thing looking conspicuously like a psychologist or in a more conversational way. For instance, a professional interviewer might ask, "What did you think of the movie?" But we might better ask, "Was it a good movie?" Either way, we will find out how the person reacted to it, but in the former, the focus of the question is on the patient, and in the latter it is on the movie. The latter form is less self-conscious, and much more effective, especially since we ask many questions of the person. If we are clear about our own purposes, we need not fear that the sessions will sound like ordinary conversation; indeed, it will be easier for the patient if they do. Our expertise need not be expressed in the form of our interrogation but in the aptness of the questions we ask.

There's a paradox attached to questioning. Although a good question creates a bridge to the patient, and brings out precious information, it is also true that every question "creates a gap," to use the words of the therapist Jean Balderston. No matter how accurately the person answers, there is much unsaid. A simple question requiring a "yes" or "no" might seem answerable, but even with these, one often feels that qualifications are needed. And with an open-ended question, it is hard to imagine how any answer can avoid "leaving a gap." The question itself creates the gap, and only part of it is filled by the answer, no matter how comprehensive it seems at the time. When patients go home, our questions are apt to resonate in their minds; they think of more they might have said. Questions create what seems like a vacuum, and the mind rushes to fill it in, but never does completely. This is what makes apt questions so serviceable in keeping therapy moving forward. They stimulate thought.

It is largely for this reason that, in many fields, among the greatest contributors are those who posed critical questions. The philosopher Kierkegaard once announced that living in an age of discovery, his contribution would be to pose problems to which others could find answers. The mathematician Karl Gauss, considered in the very first rank, used to comment, jokingly but accurately, that he left behind more unsolved problems than the number of those he solved. Freud too left behind a great many questions to be answered, some semantic, others imaginary, but many of them very real. The result in each case was a flood of interest in the kind of thinking contained in the questions.

We do the same with our patients. Our questions, which are never completely answered, are like therapy itself, which never gives our patients everything. But as with those questions raised by life itself, they inject value into the experience and intensify the surge toward fuller understanding.

31

Describing the Patient

While the patient is talking, we observe various tendencies. We offer brief descriptions, sometimes tentatively. "You mean you went from home to marriage, and then lived with a lover, and have never in your life lived alone for more than two months. That's interesting."

"That's right. I never have. I guess I'm afraid to be alone. Even now, I seem always to be with people, at work and in the evenings. Do you think it's a problem?"

"It's a fact. If you're afraid to be alone, you're certainly losing a kind of freedom. Let's keep looking at it."

The description opened up a subject.

Description, which goes one step beyond merely reflecting to a patient what he has told us, is a technique the therapist ought to rely on. We offer brief descriptions, sometimes tentatively, not just to check our own understanding, but also to help the patient organize his material and to let him know we are there. With reflection, we are reliant on what the patient has reported—a fact or a feeling. In our descriptions, we can collect information from various sources, which the patient himself may not have thought to organize. We heighten particular elements of his life, calling them to his attention. We impart focus, but quietly. In every description, I think, are the rudiments of an interpretation. But description is a far more conservative act than interpreting. With a description, we may be wrong, far from the mark, in which case the patient will tell us, and the result is that we learn some new fact. The person might have said, for instance, "No. I lived alone for three years, which I didn't tell you about." Whatever interpretation we were formulating in our own minds may still be apt, but the facts are not what we thought they were.

If we make good descriptions, the patient will utilize them for self-understanding and will go on to make his own interpretations, which may be more accurate than ours. We have not forfeited the right to interpret later on. And, as mentioned, it is always better when the patient does the work.

By description, we can call attention to whatever we want. For instance, we describe some way of thinking that the patient may not be aware of: "Whenever the topic of your children comes up, you immediately start talking about money difficulties." The patient might reply, "Yes, I know I do," or "Do I?" From there, the patient might go on to tell us, "I'm worried that I won't have enough money to send John to college." After that, we might help the patient discover that money isn't the real issue, that a sense of not giving her son enough is more general. A simple observation by us helped the patient start to unblock deep concerns.

Nearly always, the best approach to a resistance is to bring it to the patient's attention by describing it. A patient acts flippant and changes the subject whenever we talk about some particular topic. Rather than push it uphill, we reintroduce the subject to evoke this very behavior, and then point out precisely what he is doing. "I've gotten to know that when you joke about a thing and say it isn't important, it may be very important." Before long, his very use of the resistance becomes a cue to the patient that he is uncomfortable about some topic and wants to bury it.

The very camouflage becomes a signal that the thing must be important and worth looking at.

Bringing a resistance to the patient's attention, by describing it on the spot, gives him possession of the resistance. For the first time since childhood, he can decide consciously whether he wants to go on employing that resistance. In the end, he is almost sure to decide against it, if we repeatedly help him see it and are fair with him. Thus, describing resistances is the ultimate key to helping patients unblock and talk about what is really important to them.

We describe the glorious as well as the self-destructive. We bring to the patient's attention admirable qualities that he may not have recognized in himself. "I admire your loyalty. How you cared for your father while he was dying, though he was never that good to you!" And this sets the stage for us to describe difficulties attached to that admirable trait. "You really stuck with people who took advantage of you. 'Once a friend, always a friend'—that seems to be your motto." As mentioned, we will observe that some people may show virtually the same discomfort, and try to change the subject when we describe their greatness, as others show when we describe an undesirable trait. And we may go on to describe their reaction to our descriptions of them.

Descriptions, ideally, like any intervention, should be brief and to the point. They can be quite powerful. For instance, I might point out, "Though you say you like me, Arthur, you've said four very sarcastic things to me this session." If the patient asks what they were, before we tell him, it would be ideal if he could tell us. "What do you think they were?"

Several warnings are in order about describing people. One is that we should not readily describe the patient's loved ones or friends, or people in his outside life—unless we are doing it essentially through the patient's eyes, using substantially the point of view that he has presented. For instance, we may perceive a patient's mother as a tyrant. It is one thing if he sees her that way, and reaches that conclusion. Even as he disparages her, he may love her, and we help him house the two reactions to her. But if he doesn't or hasn't yet accepted his holding that view of her, then our calling her a tyrant can be injurious to the patient. In some cases, we may mobilize defense of her and delay his arriving at our "discovery." He may wonder if he hasn't misled us. Our characterizations sink deep. We have branded his mother, and even if he agrees with us, he himself feels branded, and may become afraid of us.

If our patient is telling us emotionally about how his mother has been mistreating him, we can certainly reflect what he is saying. We can even ask, "Has she been tyrannical?" in context. But we're talking about her *behavior*, and not summing her up with a single, glib description.

The second warning is that, in describing people, we should never imitate them. It is tremendously insulting to a patient, I think, for a therapist to copy a whining voice tone or a slumping posture. The ingredient of mockery makes such a description a bitter experience. What we gain in vividness, we lose in trust. The patient may laugh with us, but after leaving the office he remembers having been imitated and feels humiliated. Imitating people is a nonverbal insult to them, even if we use their actual words.

Consider how thin the boundary is between description and interpretation. We say to a patient, "You have a way of lowering your voice when telling me something really good that happened." Pure description? In a sense. The patient sees this and can hardly avoid wondering why he does it and what it means. We are inviting him to interpret this piece of behavior, the implications of which are almost surely more important than the behavior itself. But suppose we had said, "You have a way of lowering your voice when telling me something good, as if you're afraid someone will overhear us and take it away from you." This time we see description combined with interpretation, presented in the form of a simile. One step further would be for us to say, "Take it away from you as your mother did when you were a child."

We may think of three techniques—reflection, description, and interpretation—as on a continuum with regard to how much of himself the therapist injects into his comment. When reflecting, the therapist introduces himself the least. The choice of what to show the patient is based on what the patient has presented in the session. The therapist comes closest with this technique to "holding the mirror up to nature." Naturally, the therapist's own point of view influences what he chooses to reflect. But he injects himself less than with other interventions.

Our descriptions, even those that sound like quiet articulations of what the patient has presented to us, entail a greater contribution from us. We decide what to highlight; our presence is implicit in the particular data we consider important and in how we pull it together. A brilliant description has the ring of being a mere comment on nature, the way a brilliant line of poetry seems like a mere statement of something that was always obvious to us. But the description is really a creation that bespeaks the therapist as much as the patient.

Think about Hume's assertion that all we really know are the sensory images impinging on us, and Kant's inference that the very translation of such blind events into meaningful wholes bespeaks our existence. In the same way, our very ordering of the patient's behavior and free associations bespeaks our existence and shows our hand as much as his.

In interpreting, which we shall come to soon, we do more than reflect and describe. We consciously impose our own view on what the patient has presented. Interestingly, the art of reflecting accurately and of describing is likely to require more wit and soul in a therapist than that of interpreting. I have seen practitioners in the field, of inadequate intelligence, and dedicated followers of some party-line theory—Freudian or Adlerian or Gestalt, for instance—who make the same interpretations, year after year, to all their patients, and need hardly listen to what the patient has told them in order to do this. A machine could, in theory, crank out such hackneyed interpretations and many patients would accept them. But accurate reflection and description —which pave the way toward major discoveries—both require real sensitivity and judgment. Truly accurate interpretation is, of course, an important tool and requires adeptness, too. But accurate description, done by an expert, can achieve much that interpretation is intended to do, and more effectively. Not only does description invite the patient to participate more than interpretation does; the method of ongoing description is less flashy and subdues the contrast in status between patient and therapist rather than highlighting it.

32

Interpretation

Interpretation may be likened to a valuable
drug which has to be used sparingly if it is
not to lose its efficacy.

Wilhelm Reich

Interpretation was the earliest hope of psychoanalysis. Deep in
the unconscious regions of the mind lay buried truths that influenced the patient; the purpose of Freud's therapy was to uncover them, reveal them to the patient, and thus free him of
profound irrationalities and misconceptions. Once the right interpretation was made, it was hoped, the woman's frigidity
would melt away, the person suffering from psychological lame-
ness could discard his crutches, the writer would find himself
unblocked. Some lurking memory was the missing link, and the
aim was to discover and present it to the patient in the form of
an interpretation. Virtually every book on Freud's life recounts
how he came to lose faith in the curative power of interpretations
alone. His patients would find the truth unacceptable emotionally, or else their problems would persist regardless of their
reactions.

There remains a real place for interpretations in treatment, but, as the preceding quote from Reich makes clear, they should be offered sparingly. A timely and well-phrased interpretation can help a patient to insights that will change his life. Good interpretation can help a patient discover his motives, separate the past from the present, and ideally help him see how he himself reproduces the past and creates his psychic destiny. The ideal interpretations are those the patient can immediately use to understand and improve his life.

Reich's analogy between interpretations and potent drugs was as prophetic of the drug culture as it was accurate about interpretation. In his day as now, many practitioners used interpretations as a way of strutting their stuff to impress the patient. What they said often sounded magical. It attributed something the patient could see and feel, the problem he had long recognized, to supposed unconscious dynamics; or to events whose existence might have been real but whose significance had to be taken on faith: "Your impotence stems from unresolved conflicts formed in childhood, when you wanted to seduce your mother and were afraid your father would find out and kill you."

Professionals sometimes dispensed such interpretations before they had really gotten to know the patient as an individual, and commonly made the same interpretation to one patient after another. Such seeming profundities made them look good, in suggesting a depth of perception and knowledge that the layman could hardly hope to equal or even evaluate. Unfortunately, this mistake is still made sometimes, and these formulations impress a great many people who, in our age of miracles, are ready to accept one more, especially when it is backed up by an authoritative tone and diplomas on the wall. The patient, although not undergoing real personality change, contents himself with the notion that at least the therapist understands his problem in its depths. Indeed, his very failure to change seems to testify to the deep-rootedness of his problem and the likelihood that the therapist is right. How can he be expected to realize that if he brought the same problem, or dream, to another professional across the street, he would receive a substantially different explanation of it?

Often such interpretations actually lead the patient to feel more hopeless, and to perceive the cure as further from his reach than he had thought. The standard psychoanalytic interpretation, in ascribing the problem to buried sources, in effect tells the patient, "You are a victim of forces within you. The problem will remain until something is done to explore those depths. Meanwhile, all you can do is to keep coming for therapy and to cooperate until those depths are plumbed and the mechanism is repaired." The psychoanalytic notion that the adult is formed, and that a psychic determinism renders the patient helpless, is implicit in every such formulation.

An example shows how such interpretations give the patient the sense of being more removed from cure. A woman has fought with her husband and driven him away. She has done the same with a lover afterward. It is discovered that as a small child she had a desperate rivalry with her brother, a year older. Their father made a contest out of everything, and withheld affection if the girl misbehaved. The therapist tells her that unresolved competitive feelings toward her brother still haunt her. No wonder she can't form a loving relationship with a man: not until something is done about the cause will she be able to do so. With this new understanding, she should hardly expect anything to improve fundamentally until the real, underlying problem has been resurrected and resolved. She develops the impression that, at long last, she is making progress. At least now she knows why she has the trouble! The interpretation seems validated by her very inability to have overcome the problem on her own. Its roots were too deep. Mere behavior on her part, no matter how new or carefully chosen, could not possibly alter the underlying mechanism. While announcing the cause, the interpretation also persuades her that it is a cause she cannot remove. Ironically, what she has learned from the interpretation is that the only hope is for her to put faith in the therapist, to keep coming back, and to cooperate. The very essence of psychic determinism, for which psychoanalysis is famous, is lodged in every such interpretation.

Over the past half century, psychotherapy has slowly been moving away from psychic determinism. Cut and dried interpretations, which ascribe a problem to underlying forces, or to childhood, are remnants of the earliest form of psychoanalysis, which preached the patient's essential helplessness.

Certainly, many personality problems, if not most, owe to unidentified impulses and feelings, to unconscious forces in the person's character structure. However, a person's behavior affects that unconscious "field of forces." New behavior by the woman *can* enable her to overcome the unconscious rivalry she still feels toward her brother. Similarly, new patterns of choices can help every patient. The mere ascription of an apparent problem to unconscious forces, even where accurate, fails to make this clear. It misrepresents by neglecting to add that new behavior can alter the underlying outlook.

The purpose of interpretation should be to increase the patient's recognition of his own power over his psychic destiny —to reveal to him levers that are within his reach. Ideally, once we as therapists arrive at an interpretation and decide it would be good for the patient to see it, we should help the patient reach it on his own.

Many of us entered this field to make interpretations. We were impressed by their magic—they seem to produce light where there was darkness, and we may pride ourselves on being able to see subtle connections and to reveal them. We'd like to use this ability, not just to impress the patient, but also because it may be a talent of ours that is a pleasure to exercise. Our art is not merely that of making discoveries; it is that of helping the patient lift his awareness so that he can make the same discoveries.

As when building a bridge, we work on both sides of the broad river that rushes in between. For instance, our interpretation relates a past experience to a present one, to some neurotic tendency of the patient's that started long ago and is still in evidence. Understanding the roots of his tendency will help the patient conceptualize it in the present and deal with it. Back and forth we go, between the past and the present, heightening the patient's appreciation of his experience and behavior at both times. When the two sides of the bridge become solidly constructed, it becomes easier for the patient to make the connection.

The woman has talked at length about her competitive feelings toward her brother. She has recalled thinking many times that the home wasn't big enough for both of them. She described similar rivalry toward her former husband; the two of them fought over trivia. She remembers feeling terribly angry when he would pride himself on his good looks, and primp in front of the mirror, and when he would exaggerate his expertise in a story to the children. It is still hard for her to let a man have his day. We want her to appreciate that as soon as a man seems to be faring well, she feels in trouble, and that this reaction of hers is irrational and has a long history. It began in childhood, where there was real warrant for it.

She came to us confused about why her relationships with men would collapse before long. She recognized her tendency to get furious at them, but it seemed to her that they misbehaved and deserved her fury. She was in that state common to patients who, while blaming their troubles on others, secretly suspect themselves of having the problem. We certainly resisted making any interpretation at the start. How could we relate her competitive feelings toward men to those experienced in childhood, when she did not yet appreciate that she was competitive? So we did what had to be done. We helped her study her own reactions to men in her present life, especially toward her present lover. The other day they visited a friend of his, and she felt burned by his getting so much attention.

Our helping this patient build the bridge entailed heightening her emotional awareness of her tendencies in the present, while enlarging her appreciation of her childhood context— what the conditions were, how she felt, and how she reacted to them. She has been unconsciously reproducing those childhood associations over a lifetime. For her to understand the nature of the past will be to help her conceptualize what she is doing in the present. The only way she can sever those past associations is to single out all such behavior and stop reproducing the past. She will have to teach herself, by new behavior following insight, that a man's being in the limelight does not mean there will be less light for her.

We ask quiet questions bearing on her competitive urges and distortions in the present. Was she neglected the other day? Why does she think so? And if she was neglected by her lover's friend, why did she direct her fury at him in the car going home? What had she wanted him to do? She tells us she wanted him to defend her, to be aware that she was neglected, and to say something. Perhaps. We are not going to argue the matter. We show caring for her by empathizing with her experience of neglect. It's not easy to be among strangers and to feel utterly out of place and hopeless. And yet, why the hopelessness? She didn't even venture subject matter of her own when she saw they were talking about him. This very failure to assert herself suggests to us, although we don't say anything at the time, that there are historical roots. In the home, any attempt to rescue herself from oblivion was met harshly. "I told you to keep your mouth shut," her father would shout at her, when he decided she was talking too much. In addition to her rage, she brought forward that early sense of hopelessness that discouraged her from trying to overcome her exclusion. No wonder the rage! All other avenues seemed barred.

As we contemplate the bridge we want the patient to build, we go on clarifying our interpretation to ourselves. We see new details that make it seem more accurate. With some other patient, we might see contradictions and scuttle it entirely. But with this young woman we feel almost certain. We encourage her to keep talking about the interaction with her boyfriend in the car. As she does, she gets the sense that perhaps her reaction was not wholly warranted, that her accusations of him were excessive.

Concentrating on the present, we ask her what comes to mind when a lover is being given what seems more than his due. In telling us about her feelings of rejection and her anger, she may herself come to see the similarities between the present and the past. If we have enabled her to discuss at length her feelings back then, she is most likely to make this connection. We may not even have to make the interpretation. Even without us, our patients very often feel something familiar about the kind of trouble they encounter. They dimly sense that the past is recurring. We capitalize on this vague sense of continuity. "Yes, it was like that," we agree. "There's a long history of your feeling that there isn't enough room for you and the man in your life, if he excels."

Nearly always, it is valuable to say something at once, reminding the patient that he is bringing the past with him, and need not do so. Since our whole therapy is geared to helping the patient see how he sustains and produces his own outlook, there is little risk that the patient will feel more helpless as a result of seeing this relationship. In any event, we will go on to help this woman see that she is reproducing the past, by acting in much the same ways she did as a little girl. True, she can't help the feelings of rejection and resentment, which seem almost overwhelming when she does so. But to know that they are anachronistic and to resist acting on them are major steps. Having arrived at the insight, she will slowly teach herself by new behavior that she need lose nothing when the man in her life gains status or respect. By acting in accordance with the interpretation she has reached, she will terminate those terrible expectations from the past. After a while, she will be able to endure her lover's being praised, even overpraised, by people who care about him. And some time after that, she may even come to enjoy his pleasure in the experience.

A very powerful method for helping the patient see the roots of a present tendency is to evoke the hunger illusion. First we spot crucial behavior by which the patient is reproducing past expectations—for instance, here it was the woman's assaulting her boyfriend when he got the limelight. Such behavior, which springs from deep associations, simultaneously keeps those associations unconscious. So long as she indulged her wrath at such times, she was masking its true motivations and its associations to her past. An activity itself keeps the motivating reason for it unconscious. Therefore, having spotted the behavior, we ask the person to restrain it and to make note of the feelings and reactions that come to mind. This woman reports vivid feelings of rejection and resentment, perhaps dotted with very particular details, which made more sense about herself when she was a child than now. The rush of reactions that comes to mind is very informative, about the past as well as the present. "And what would have happened if you had begun to talk about your job?" we might ask her. "They would have said 'shut up.'" Our patient's very words, which would be more appropriate in the mouth of some past figure than a present one, will help the patient appreciate that a past association is operating. Use of this method, already described, is invaluable in building a bridge.

Just as metaphors are usually more effective than similes, or long-winded locutions, the briefer we can make our interpretation, the more effective it is likely to be. Recall the patient who lowered his voice when telling us something good that was in store for him. Suppose that, instead of merely describing this, we chose to interpret it. We might say, for instance, after he did this, "Shhh, let's not let your father hear." This technique has been called interpretation by "joining" the patient. If we're on target, the patient might laugh with us, and we have given him an important insight. Ideally, we can make nearly all our interpretations metaphoric and quick, bringing images from the past right into the present, on the spot where they are relevant and when the patient can accept them.

Once an interpretation has been made, it is much easier to make it a second time. A quick reference suffices to underscore it, and show its relevance. In this last example, we weren't reading the patient's mind or telling him how to feel. Our interpretation of the man's lowering his voice was made after many long discussions of his relationship with his father, who, the man now realized, threatened to take away from him what was precious. The ghost of his father still haunted him, and the interpretation called attention to that ghost, and to behavior by which the man, unknowingly, was resurrecting that ghost.

On occasion, we may even use interpretation as a form of reflection. A man who had long been a top executive in his company was feeling angry and disheartened at the placement of an incompetent above him. One session he began by telling me about the father of a secretary in his office who apparently, after being fired, had taken a hatchet and destroyed most of his own home furniture. "Imagine that!" my patient said. I responded as if he had been talking about himself. "It really sounds miserable to be trapped in that job of yours." "It sure is," he replied, as if he'd been talking about himself all along. "I'd like to throw every typewriter out of the window." He went on to talk about his despondency, and not long afterward, did quit his job and took another. In retrospect, I feel my interpretation actually kept me more on his track than if I had responded literally to what he'd been talking about.

Logically, there are two forms of interpretative statement that therapists can make. The classical form attributes a choice to something not immediately controllable: "You are late to your teaching job because the principal reminds you of your father, whom you fear." Conceivably, this may be true, but it runs the risk of being invasive and humiliating to the patient. Its main danger is that unless much more is also said, it adds to the patient's feeling of helplessness. His being late may seem less under his control than before he discovered the reason. Any interpretation that attributes an act to its unconscious roots may leave the patient at a dead end and feeling more helpless than before. The classical interpretation is useful only if the patient also sees that he has the power to change the unconscious patterns.

The second kind of interpretation, *the action insight,* goes in the opposite direction. It attributes an inner state—for instance, a feeling or way of perceiving—to the person's behavior: "No wonder that principal seems more like your father than when you started the job. You hide from him in the lunchroom, or else curry favor artificially with him, and now you're arriving late." The action insight here shows the patient how he himself is assigning to the school principal a part like that his father played; moreover, it shows the young teacher, who uses guile to survive, how he is making himself feel inadequate and a delinquent, just as he did in the home.

On the other hand, we may be dealing with someone who denies the validity of anything we say. Are there other ways to work with him—for instance, to ask him a sequence of questions that may lead him to his own discoveries? Or, we may decide to bring to his attention that he is resisting; we point out to him that each time we've suggested a possibility, he has dismissed us at once. Until we do this, he may deny the validity of anything we say, or if his is a compliant resistance, he will accept what we say but won't utilize the insight. It doesn't matter how ample our evidence is for the interpretation; if the patient isn't ready to hear it and take it seriously, then we have more groundwork to lay before we make the interpretation again.

With still other patients, interpretations are counterproductive. Among these are patients prone to intellectualize, whose resolution and spirit seem utterly buried under words and ideas. These patients would love any kind of formulation from us, the more elaborate the better. They would enjoy debating psychological theory with us as a substitute for examining themselves. We should be especially wary of interpreting anything to these patients, lest the whole therapy become buried under the pale cast of thought. Like a surgical operation, every interpretation requires timing as well as touch, and the measure of its success is not how well it's done, but whether it helps the patient.

33

Giving Advice

Giving advice is, nine times out of ten, a substitution for psychotherapy, and one that turns out to be extremely destructive. It does considerable harm, and very seldom any good. It's like going into the water and pulling a swimmer out because we don't like his form. If he were really drowning, that would be one thing. But to treat him as if he were going to drown is to undermine him, and to reveal a panic in us much less justified than whatever anxiety he might feel. Seldom is a wrong decision irremediable, and in making the decision for the person, we are depriving him of the chance to develop.

We're also declaring our own bankruptcy. We're admitting that we really don't know how to help him arrive at his own best decisions, and that we have to take the controls. Among the other outcomes of giving advice is that we foster dependence. Not surprisingly, patients ask us for more advice, and may soon start telephoning us at odd hours when they are unsure of themselves. They get angry when we stop. Often, for the therapist who acts as advisor, the first half-dozen sessions are full of interesting subject matter. But then, when the patient runs out of questions about what to do, therapy comes to an abrupt halt. The patient quits, truly believing that there is nothing more to do, when in actuality, therapy has never really started. When we hear a therapist complain that his patients quit after a few months or so, a leading contender as explanation is that he has been giving them advice, and the subject matter ran out.

Of course, we may think that some patient is mired in a rotten marriage, or that he ought to choose a particular career in preference to another. We root for him as we would for any friend, or for the protagonist of a movie or play. But we are not puppeteers. Our focus should always be on the inner life of the person, on how and why he makes decisions, and on helping him to run his life better. The beginning therapist will, almost surely, have to remind himself that his real focus must be on the patient's development, and that every time he substitutes himself for the patient, he impairs this development. If the patient needs us to tell him to leave a marriage, then he doesn't want to leave it enough himself. Perhaps he will never leave it, and our advice may even be wrong because he has deleted facts, and doesn't want to leave it. If we think that his leaving will be a real solution, to that degree we imagine that people's problems are circumstantial. Whatever brought the person into that marriage may bring him into a similar one next time, or he may choose an alternative just as damning. In telling him to leave, we are implicitly accusing him of the inability to know what he wants. It's too bad that so many of our patients think their problems owe to circumstance, and beseech us for advice, as if their very next decision will make or break them. Their very sense of emergency, and their readiness to ask others to take over, is a basic part of what is wrong with them. By giving them advice, we abet them in their worst misconceptions, and foster this misemphasis.

Recall, once again, the principle that the motivating feeling, attitude, or belief that prompts an act is strengthened, reinforced, by the act itself. In turning to us for advice, the patient is, even before we reply, telling himself that he is inadequate and needs us. He is sending that message to his mind. He is weakening himself and giving us undue importance. A right decision accrues to our credit; a wrong one becomes our fault. Once he identifies us with a decision, and makes it on our recommendation, the decision can no longer afford him the satisfaction or sense of independence that a successful venture of his own would have.

Why do therapists err far too often in the direction of giving advice? In some cases, they're unclear about their purpose. But more often their giving advice is as much for themselves as it is for their patients. The therapist is compensating for a sense that he's not giving the patient enough. He feels at a loss when it seems that the patient isn't making progress on his own. The therapist starts to worry that the patient is feeling disappointed with therapy and might consider quitting, and so he gives his advice out of a desire to have the patient come away with something. It consoles such a therapist to think that at least, owing to his advice, the patient has improved his life. He now knows which summer resorts to go to, and may be living in an apartment that he would not have found but for the therapist's counsel on how to look for one. The therapist imagines the patient asking himself whether, as a result of going into therapy, his life isn't truly better, and now it seems that the answer will be yes.

Another motive is to prove that he's really the patient's friend, that in his time of adversity the patient can count on him. The patient is in pain, feels lost. The therapist, taking on too much sense of responsibility, wants to offer relief: he starts to resemble the parent who is unable to allow his children to make mistakes and suffer the consequences. Therapeutic love becomes overprotectiveness. The therapist with this difficulty becomes easily manipulated by any patient who feigns helplessness. Many of our patients will test us by saying or implying that we let them down. Even when we were careful not to favor one choice over its alternative, they may rebuke us later, and swear that we did.

It's as if they were saying, "You got me into this mess. Now get me out of it."

Surely, some patients will beseech us for our opinions about what they should do, and will act hurt when we don't give them a substantial reply. But our task is not to fill voids in the patient's life. That is their challenge. Ours is precisely the opposite. It is to evoke reactions from them and reveal voids where they exist.

We may feel a strong impulse to give advice to certain patients. They beseech us for ideas about what we should do. But as with any induced feeling, when we have the urge to act, we should restrain ourselves and study the impulse. Rather than satisfy it, we should go precisely in the direction that intensifies the urge—in this case by adhering to the rigorous rule that we won't give advice. We will soon become acutely aware of what the patient is doing that evokes our urge to advise him.

Close scrutiny reveals his technique. For instance, he exaggerates the stresses he is under, and conceals resources available to him other than depending on us. His tone and posture convey a false innocence. He adopts the part of ingenue, and assigns us that of the experienced master. No wonder we felt like rushing in! The more clearly we see what he is doing, the easier it becomes for us to restrain ourselves. We must turn our attention from the "calamity" he is describing, which seemed to crave our intervention, to the attitude he is assuming with us.

If we've given advice, the patient may become angry with us when we stop. We'll get him to talk about that anger if he has it. This will help surface his true expectation of us and his disbelief in his own ability to make decisions. He may become very demanding for a while, regressing to a performance that he used as a child. The clearer we see this process, the more insulated we are against the urge to run his life. We bring his demanding style to his attention. Gradually, the whole therapeutic balance will recover, with the patient assuming responsibility for his decisions and reaping their rewards.

Therapists who make the mistake of giving advice to one patient tend to make it with many, if not all. In rectifying it, they teach themselves, as well as their patients, that they really have something to give worth a lot more than the kind of counsel the patient could get from a newspaper article or a call-in show.

Closely related to the actual giving of advice are various ways that therapists, knowingly or not, endorse particular choices their patients have made—as if by reinforcement to steer them toward what's best for them. For instance, a woman is in love with a man who lies to her and exploits her. She's a nervous wreck, and her own career suffers greatly while she holds onto him. The therapist doesn't tell her to leave, but gradually she comes to see that it's hopeless. Still, she hangs on, trying to picture that someday he will change. Her own self-esteem is at rock bottom. Finally, the man gets tired of her, and makes things so bad, she decides to end the relationship. There's no contact between them for a month, after which he sends her flowers and a note, in which he says ambiguously that he still thinks about her all the time. It arrives when she has just started showing signs of regaining her confidence.

The therapist is careful not to advise her, but cannot resist asking, "Are you going to call him?" "No," she replies at once. "Hooray!" says the therapist. His position on the matter is clear. Doing this is less dangerous than offering direct advice, but runs a little of the same risk. She may rely on the therapist's judgment to save herself, when it would have been better to rely on her own. Another therapist, feeling the same way, might not have commented, but from his bright smile, she could have made the same inference. And even if he said nothing and kept a poker face, the patient in such a case would almost surely have been able to infer his preference. Some degree of endorsement would be evident. It is false to imagine that the therapist can ever fully delete his preferences on all matters in the patient's life. Reinforcing what the patient has decided to do interferes far less with the benefits of those decisions than giving direct advice leading to those decisions.

All we can do is to try to avoid giving endorsements as much as possible. And where our preferences are evident, we should make clear the grounds for them so that the patient can make an independent evaluation. For instance, the therapist may have helped the woman see how anxious she was while in the relationship, how much her other friendships suffered, how inadequate she felt. By contrast, the therapist can help her see that in the man's absence she has resurrected her friendships, sleeps better, looks prettier, feels whole again, and is more confident and effective. While with him, she loved him but hated herself. Without him, although she still longs for him, she likes herself much better. Now, when the therapist communicates, perhaps involuntarily, that he is happy she has renounced the relationship, at least she knows what he is reacting to. It isn't merely prejudice against the man, but the desire as well to see her using her full faculties and getting the most out of life. More than this single relationship is at stake. What she is learning is to evaluate decisions by their impact on her feelings and the ability to do the things that matter to her.

The therapist with a strong bias ought to recognize it, and tell the patient about it rather than influence him unwittingly. A man describes his new office in glowing terms, and observes that the therapist looks unhappy. "I guess you think I shouldn't have gone off on my own. I wasn't really ready to leave the firm." "No, that's not it," the therapist confesses. "I just hate modern furniture. I can't help it. That's my prejudice. So please don't judge by my reactions."

Our first obligation with patients who press us for advice is to study them. Why are they asking for it, and what do they expect of us? Have they a pervasive distrust of their own judgment, or do they ask only in a certain context? Theoretically, it might be that the person simply doesn't know how psychotherapy works. He pictures us as experts in daily affairs and imagines that he is there to get our opinions. But there is always something wrong when an adult stands ready to make major decisions simply because another person recommends them. The kind of person who would quit a job or reject a lover or berate a parent merely because a stranger, no matter how well informed, tells him to is abdicating responsibility for his life.

Often the desire for advice was learned with a parent who was extremely anxious, and who became panic-stricken when things went wrong. The parent displaced his anxiety from himself onto the child, and stood in judgment over the child's every decision. The child found it easier to ask, "What shall I do?" than to act and then hope his choice was satisfactory. The parent may have been punitive, but the fact that the parent himself suffered ostentatiously over the child's mistakes was enough to drive the child into asking for guidance. As an adult, our patient lacks confidence and fears making mistakes. He hopes we'll steer him on course, and if not at least his mistakes will be ours, not his.

Sometimes, the patient who asks us hasn't the slightest impulse to take our advice. He is merely paying homage to what he thinks is our desire for importance in his life. The child of the overanxious parent sometimes learns to do this. Growing up, he found it best to ask his parents' opinions, even if he'd made his decision, or actually done the thing already. Such patients are calculating, reminiscent of those theater producers who ask their backers for delicate opinions about staging and casting, with no intention whatsoever of even considering what they say. They're asking us for advice to keep us happy. With them, as much as with the anxious seeker of our advice, we lose a great deal if we rush in and fill the void.

Once we have good comprehension of what the patient does with us, we bring it to his attention. Why is he asking us? He has much better access to the answers than we do. Sometimes this is all the person needs. He virtually wanted to have us throw the ball back to him. I'll never forget a telephone call I got while on a radio show in Chicago. It came from a woman over a thousand miles away. She spoke briefly about her sex life and then asked me if she was a lesbian. "Do I prefer women, doctor?" Realizing that I was addressing a multitude, and not just her, I took the approach of scolding her for asking a distant stranger a question that she was in a much better position to answer. What she could decide, neither I nor any other expert could ascertain nearly as well. Psychologists have often been lampooned for answering a question with a question, but in effect, the strongest vote of confidence we can render may be to tell the person to decide for himself.

Instead of giving advice, we sometimes ask the patient what his options are. "Are there other possibilities?" "You mean, not go to the party." Perhaps the therapist had something else in mind. "That one hadn't occurred to me, but what about it?" "Well, I never thought of that," the patient might say, overlooking that he just did think of it. We can then go on to explore that and other options that come to his mind. Less often, and when this method fails, we might bring an alternative to the person's attention, not recommending it, but asking him to think about it and decide for himself.

"Suppose you didn't go to the party, how would you feel?"

"Are you suggesting that I stay home?"

"I'm not suggesting it. It depends on why you don't want to see those people. Why is it such torture?"

The danger here is that since the suggestion comes from us, it smacks of our endorsement to the patient, even if we merely asked it to have him consider the possibility. Outright suggestions from us are loaded with danger, and should nearly always be avoided, if there is even a slight chance that the patient will discover those alternatives on his own. And if we make them, they should be very lightly hinted, and the patient allowed to run right past them, as his way of voting them down. The argument for them is that all people have occasional blind spots regarding available alternatives, and our identifying a few possibilities may help the patient appreciate them in other contexts. We should always remember, however, that the failure to think of an alternative that might seem obvious to someone else is likely to be indicative. The person may well have an emotional stake in not seeing that alternative, and we may go on to investigate why he has that block.

When asked for direct advice, it can be shallow and insulting for us merely to return the question, as if we were sending back a letter unopened. "Should I look for another job?" "What do you think? Should you?" The patient is asking us for more than mere advice; he wants our involvement in the matter. Our tossing back the question, without putting our own mark on it, is as if to say, "Not only won't I answer you; I won't even consider the question." We can help the person study aspects of it that might help him reach a decision: Why would he look for another job? What are the arguments against his looking? How will he feel in retrospect if he does? If he doesn't?

Perhaps he's unclear about events bearing on the decision. He has summarized them to us, and not thought about them enough himself. We ask for more details. "The boss said you were going to be fired? What were his exact words?" Filling us in helps him consider more precisely what he ought to do. For instance, it turns out that the boss merely threatened to fire him if his work didn't improve. There will be time to consider whether to look for a job. Meanwhile, the very question has sidetracked him from the real issue, which is how to save his present job.

As we investigate the advisability of his making some decision, we should take into account that patient's particular tendencies. How has he gotten himself in trouble in the past? For instance, he tends to act impulsively, picking up the phone and telling someone off before he has considered the full implications of venting his spleen. He has made rash decisions in the stock market or in relationships. Almost surely, he underweighs the benefits of conservatism, of doing nothing. Another person who tends to postpone too much should be suspicious of that impulse next time. There are people who overstay in relationships, wishing later that they had paid more attention to the handwriting on the wall. When they catch themselves saying they really aren't bothered by something done to them, they should be suspicious, knowing that this tendency to minimize has gotten them into trouble in the past. We can help people appreciate the patterns of their lives, and take them into account when making new decisions. To recognize their most common ways of erring is for them to be on guard against repeating them. This helps restore perspective when new and confusing decisions loom. There are some patients who would do well to follow the rule, "When in doubt, keep quiet," and others who follow that rule too much already and should err on the side of more radical action. Patients, indeed everyone, should learn their own tendencies and take them into account when decisions appear hard to make.

It's always valuable to ask whether a decision needs to be made at once. Often the patient has put himself under unnecessary pressure, or is being unfairly pressured by someone, and is afraid to demand the time required. "You mean if you don't agree to marry him this month, he'll walk out of your life!" That in itself is a danger sign. We wonder about the advisability of marrying such a person, or of marrying anyone under duress. There's an adage in the marketing field, "If you need to know right away, the answer is no." Often we can help our patients see that they have more time to reach a decision than they realized. The achievement is in making sure they give themselves the time. And, the need to choose isn't always real. The person can do both things, perhaps not at the same time, but sequentially. Always, as we help patients by asking questions, we are teaching them what to ask of themselves and to make better decisions.

There would seem to be two major exceptions to the rule about not recommending behavior. One is that we may do so, but only temporarily, for the purpose of having the patient make crucial discoveries about himself. We may ask a patient not to do something, and less often to do something, in order to produce these associations. We might ask a patient, for instance, not to talk about himself on a date, in order to study the thoughts that come to mind. He reports fantasies of being terribly neglected, or considered stupid, and along with them details that are very reminiscent of a childhood in which anyone silent was bypassed. Now he knows far better why he engages in compulsive self-reference. It is best, as a rule, to study these associations when the person has himself decided on a strategy of behavior unusual for him. But there are times when actually asking the person to go against the grain leads to valuable insights. Where the person seems absolutely rooted in certain behavior—for instance, a man refuses to go out into the street alone and doesn't know why he's afraid—we might ask him to take a step, even a small one, toward the dreaded stimulus, just for the sake of self-study.

In the following instance, I recommended a single act in order possibly to learn something, and I learned much more than I expected to. A woman, whose father died when she was very young, recognized that she became highly critical of any man she began to fall in love with. She put forth different theories, and reported that her parents' marriage was idyllic. One day, when she was about to leave, we noticed a red scarf on a chair, which a previous patient had left behind. I noticed that the woman pulled back as if it had been a cobra. Seeing her reaction possessed me to suggest, "Try it on, just for fun." She protested that the owner would object, which I knew to be false. and then, as fear entered her countenance, she said flatly, "I hate scarves."

THE HEART OF PSYCHOTHERAPY

"You don't have to, of course," I replied, "but I would like to see you do it." At that, she took a deep breath and put the scarf on her head. As she did so, she went into shock, and suddenly recalled an episode in which her father, coming home drunk, accused her mother of infidelity and tried to strangle her with her scarf. But for the interference of an older brother, who knows what would have happened? My patient told me she had always avoided scarves, but considered it an innocent taste preference and nothing more. She took it off slowly, realizing that at least some of her fear of intimacy must have derived from seeing her parents' relationship, which she had misremembered as idyllic after her father's early death.

How complex is the human mechanism, and the plexus of associations we have, for it to be valuable to this particular woman to wear scarves after that! Doing so was a symbolic statement to herself that not all men are violent, the way her father was. Wrapping a scarf around her neck signified taking a chance on a man. She noted that it was harder to wear a scarf in men's company than in women's, and that observation made perfect sense to her. Perhaps not one other woman in a million who disliked scarves had the same reason for the aversion. Here it was clear that my advice was not to improve her life, nor was it intended as permanent, but only to help us learn about her. When asking a patient to do something for this reason—for instance, to spend a few minutes among people who are frightening or to forgo a practice like being critical, we should make clear that this is our purpose. Our patient may return to his prior pattern whenever he wants to. Sometimes when a patient is in a rut, getting him to act in another way, even briefly, can produce a flood of feelings and ideas that break the ice. Although the person returns to his former pattern, he now has a sense of why he is this way, and other possibilities continue to beckon.

The second exception to the rule about not recommending behavior occurs when we truly believe that the patient is in a crisis that is more than he can handle. We might send a patient to a drug-addiction center, or tell him to discuss what is wrong with his next of kin. If we're up against someone contemplating murder or suicide, we may have to intervene, informing others —perhaps even the police. With a child or a psychotic or brain-damaged adult or a drug addict or drunkard, we may elect to make a unilateral decision. It may console us that other people, and very likely the patient himself were he to have his full faculties, would want us to do so. But here we are exchanging our role as therapist for that of responsible human being given special knowledge and ethically bound to make use of it. Although the patient may resent us and distrust us afterward, we impose our will.

When we do decide that a patient is really dangerous to himself or others, and is no longer bluffing? No simple formula is possible. We take into account the patient's prior history and what we consider his rationality and seriousness in the particular case. But once we do intervene, we must realize that we have very possibly lost his trust, and perhaps even undermined his trust of the next therapist he may have to work with. Perhaps no more sensitive decisions will ever confront us in this profession.

34

Recommendations and Favors

We've probably all departed at times from the mainstream of our work, whatever our guiding theory, and done extratherapeutic things for our patients. These have ranged from being generally encouraging, or teaching them something they needed to know, to doing them an outright favor. Ideally, when we offered such benefits, it wasn't because we were at our wit's end or felt forced to act. We chose the occasion, recognizing that what we did wasn't at the core of our work but something extra, offered with possible dangers in mind as well as benefits. Above all, we've acted for the patient and not for ourselves.

When it is absolutely clear what a patient wants—for instance, to go among people instead of staying in bed for days at a time under the covers, or quitting a drug and trying life on one's own—usually there is little harm in the therapist's rejoicing with his patient at success. In lining up with the patient's best interest, for the therapist to say, "That's great," when the patient reports a period of high achievement won't blur the focus of therapy. The patient is acting for himself, but his success is also a gift to the therapist. The therapist isn't getting anything out of it apart from joy at seeing the patient succeed. Perhaps the patient has had few if any allies. In mustering the heroism to give the therapist something, namely some accomplishment, he is succeeding for himself. This is quite different from the therapist's applauding a choice in any way questionable as to whether it's what the patient truly needs and wants.

The same holds for a deliberate favor. Suppose a person, friendless and in the throes of depression, sees little reason to try to improve himself. Over the months, we exhort him to lift himself. A better life is just ahead, if only he will put forth more effort. For a time we see over the mountain, and he doesn't. But with us as guides, he tries to climb that mountain. He endures confusion and pain, motivated mainly by our descriptions of a citadel of people who will accept him.

An opportunity comes along. We hear of a job in the very field he is preparing for. A wonderful chance to learn carpentry, to make some money and work alongside people who can teach him a great deal. Do we tell him about it? Do we recommend him for the job, knowing that in the past he broke promises, quit in the middle of things, let people down?

Therapists would differ here. Purists would say, "Telling him about the job is not our role. He may grow dependent, and if he fails at it, he may resent us. We would go down together. He has come this far on his own. Surely there will be other chances."

Others would advocate telling him. They would regard this as giving him a noble reward for his blind toiling when there were few prospects ahead. They would argue that if the reward seems too far off, he may not be able to last long enough, and quit on himself before he reaches it. They maintain that telling him is providing evidence that the therapist really believes in him. With such a chance, the patient will trust the therapist more and try harder. He will properly appreciate such assistance as a sign that the therapist believes in him. He cannot truly fail, even if he proves unready for the particular opportunity.

The therapist must make his own decision, of course. But there can be real value in lending a hand. The patient knows that our offer is off the beaten track, that we have transcended our role for his sake. He is likely to "work" harder in therapy, and if in the past he sometimes doubted our sincerity, he becomes less prone to do so. If he misinterpreted our comments as hypercritical when we touched a sensitive area, he may trust us more now, knowing that we want the best for him. Our relationship may deepen, whether he takes advantage of the opportunity or not.

Above all, if we do transcend our role this way, it must be only after the patient himself has put in real effort. We aren't giving him something merely because he demands it. Our helping him is a continuation and reward for what he has done. It's as if to say, "There are people who will join you when you do your best, who might not otherwise be there." If he is the kind of person who blames others when things go wrong, or who takes the attitude that the world owes him a living, we surely should not come to his aid in this way. To make this judgment, we watch closely how he reacts to us. Is he appreciative? Does he blame us when things go wrong? Does he mistake our motivation and accuse us of manipulating him? We have unquestionably altered our relationship, at least for a time, by entering his life this way, and we must be prepared to inquire into his reactions to us.

Concerning nearly any favor we might wish to do, we should ask ourselves why we feel the impulse. If it comes from a sense that we aren't doing enough for the person, then we should absolutely not do the favor. Only if we feel that we could easily not do it, and that our relationship would remain the same, should we consider it. There should be no hint of the motive of buying the patient's esteem when we do the thing.

Also we should be careful that the motive for our act isn't self-serving. If it is, we certainly shouldn't give in to the impulse.

This is true whether it's merely praising the patient or impressing him with anecdotes. Many who do these things rationalize that they're doing them for the patient. To a bystander it would be quite clear that the therapist is doing them purely for his own self-aggrandizement.

If there's an iota of doubt as to why we want to do the "favor," we should not do it. Our not doing it can hardly interfere with our work, but our doing the thing may be extremely destructive. A woman therapist felt deep sympathy for a young man, an electrician who had been very troubled. She found it hard to see why her patient was fired from one assignment after another. It turned out that her own home needed electrical wiring, and she decided to give him a chance. Rather than start him off on a small job, she gave him the task of rewiring her whole basement. He began eagerly, but after buying the wrong equipment, he failed to appear. She telephoned him with concern over her basement and with worry about him. However, he never did come back—to finish either the assignment or his therapy.

I think it would always be ill-advised for a therapist to introduce a patient to a prospective lover or mate. Perhaps the patient has complained that the right romantic partner is hard to find, and this may be true. But the therapist's aura will hover over the relationship. The reverberations are incalculable and should be prohibitive. Our task should be to help our patients utilize available opportunities, and when it comes to romance, we should never play matchmaker.

What we do can sometimes backfire, and afterward we kick ourselves for going beyond the boundary of psychotherapy. Usually, the reason for our misjudgment was that we underestimated the transference. A male therapist, for instance, calls a female patient in the hospital, or visits her after an operation. She construes this as romantic desire toward her. He had reason to know she might. An error? Admittedly. But that same therapist, more than the stickler for rules, is likely to have given marvelous hope to a dozen other patients by his transcending the requirements. The very fact that our kindness is gratuitous and risky is what makes it special and memorable to the patient.

35

Utilizing the Patient's Past

Psychotherapists have in the last half-century gradually reduced their emphasis on studying the patient's childhood and on the utility of dream analysis. For a number of reasons, theoretical and practical, the past as a domain and dreams as a way of descending to that domain have come to occupy a smaller place. There is still a coterie of therapists who dwell on the past. And Jungian analysts still center their treatment in the interpretation of dreams. But an increasing number of therapists deny the patient much time to go over his past; many consider preoccupation with it as irrelevant or as a downright avoidance of the present.

Patients themselves talk less about their childhoods than they used to, and bring in fewer dreams. It was always recognized that they tended to produce recollections and to dream more for the therapist who rewarded them by his involvement with such subject matter. Besides, they come to sessions less often—in the beginning of psychoanalysis it was five times a week; now it's often once or twice, or even once every two weeks. There are proportionately more daily events and more ongoing decisions for the patient to talk about.

Perhaps no one would deny the relevance of at least some

childhood experience to adult personality. But this doesn't automatically tell us how to utilize those experiences in our treatment, even if we knew which they were. Of interest to us is what we can do with such knowledge when we have it. How do we employ the patient's past to help him overcome a problem?

For instance, we have good insight into how our patient, a man of thirty-five, came to distrust women. His mother had many clandestine love affairs, which his older sisters knew about but which no one ever mentioned to him. Women dominated in the home. His three sisters chatted together continually, but addressed their younger brother and their father only when necessary. Our patient grew up appalled at the women in his household. He seemed unable to take things lightly, the way they did. To them the truth seemed a pawn, to be pushed onto any square that offered advantage. Later he watched his mother coach her daughters into marriages with wealthy men, whom they led around—at least this was how he saw it.

No wonder our patient has a morbid fear of falling in love! As soon as he feels tenderness, he feels endangered. He soon finds fault with the woman and rages at her. Often his diatribes send the woman he is with into shock. If she becomes compliant or goes dead on him, waiting for his thunder to abate, his whole sense of being a bull in a china shop makes him feel miserable. Yet he professes a deep desire for a wife and children, and feels that something is wrong with him. To this day, he unconsciously renews the sense of himself as unworldly, and not worth listening to. He sees all women as holding men in contempt. He expects betrayal, and would virtually never ask a woman for anything.

We learn this history from many sources. For one thing, his parents are still alive, the mother still harrassing her husband, telling him what to do and where to go. On holidays he visits them and watches them together. Moreover, his memories of the past are very clear, and he is able to document them richly with examples. That he brings past expectations with him is also clear.

He is presently engaged to a woman and yet he feels almost sure that she would let him down in an emergency. He still overstates and repeats himself; he's accusatory without knowing it, as he was in childhood. Many of the feelings that come to him when he cherishes this woman are reminiscent of those he recalls having had while growing up.

As is common when a patient forces himself to break with the past, the flood of associations that came to this man's mind provided a rich source of information. For instance, he forced himself, while in bed with a fever, to ask his fiancée to bring him things. Each time, he would feel sure that she was going to forget what he wanted. Lying there, he recalled that his mother had forgotten more than once, and had even failed to take him to the doctor when he had an appointment. Recalling this, he had flashes of anger toward his fiancée, and then was stunned when she came back with the medicine. He vowed that no matter how hard it would be, he would do his best not to bully her.

The case for the relevance of this man's childhood is incontrovertible. But how may we use our knowledge to help him?

Merely recognizing what his childhood was like is a starting place. Back then, he had no basis of comparison. The women he knew represented "all women." His identity-in-the-home he took to be his universal identity. In therapy, his recognizing what was unusual about his mother and sisters was in itself freeing. Merely to appreciate what they were like, something he could not do as a little child when there was no basis of comparison, was to lay the basis for picturing another kind of woman, one who might be worthy of better treatment.

In realizing the nonuniversality of his history, he could consider that he might not be the ignorant child he had always pictured himself to be. Perhaps his fiancée was not like those first women he knew in his childhood. The very recognition of what life was like in the home starts the patient considering that he himself may not be the person he thought he was.

As we study the past, and especially how the patient perceived it, we should ask in particular, "What did he expect of others? And how did he himself act?" For instance, this man expected aloofness, and used big guns in an attempt to arouse a response. He shouted, exaggerated, accused, repeated himself—especially when addressing women, but to some extent with men. We help the patient try to appreciate his reasons for such behavior. He can then see that those reasons need not apply in his current life, even though he still feels that they do.

Such understanding helps a patient identify the anachronistic behavior in his present life—and his anachronistic expectations of himself and other people. Next he must undertake to change that behavior, since only in this way can he truly break with the past. The critical questions are: How did the patient see himself and others back then? What did he actually do? What method of survival did he choose as his way of coping with the challenges he saw? Although he almost surely has refined his techniques, he is persisting in at least some of that behavior. Such behavior provides the tracks of his perpetuation of himself from then until now. As he stops pieces of this behavior, past images will come back to him. Fragments of his early history will return in the form of irrational thoughts. Not only do such fragments teach us about the patient's past, but also as we piece together the patient's past conditions, we can make sense out of those fragments. The patient feels less daunted by them.

For our young man to recall that his mother might well "forget" a medicine he needed was a big help when he felt suspicious of his fiancée. Such knowledge strengthened his resolve not to telephone his fiancée to remind her. Had he done so, he would have renewed his suspicion that she was like his mother. Thus, the knowledge of his past helped him see the difference; it helped him endure his own irrationality; it guided him toward the very behavior needed to break with the past.

Although not absolutely essential for his therapy, knowledge of the past was useful at every phase.

The patient's past can affect him in a variety of ways, some of which, upon discovery, prove quite surprising to him. In many cases, the adult's personality evolves partly out of a deliberate effort on the child's part to make himself as *unlike* one or both parents as possible.

For instance, a parent brags, and is ridiculed behind his back. The child wants to avoid a similar fate, and so learns to understate his plans and not to mention his accomplishments. Or the parent is chaotic, an alcoholic who has terrible outbursts. One such father kicked a dog who strayed across the yard, and his tiny son never forgot the incident, and backed into an exactly contrary identity. In his desire never to be like his father, he became overly modulated and never touched a drink. He never told others what to do. By adulthood, he was much too passive for his own happiness. His boss underpaid him, and at home his own children ran roughshod over him. His first efforts to discipline them brought terrible feelings of identification with his father, and the picture of himself as hideous. It was then that he recalled the incident in which his father had kicked the dog, and his own resolution never to do anything even vaguely like it. I would say to him, when he put forth even the slightest hint of authority where it was needed, "Did you kick the dog today?" That was exactly how he felt. My reference to his past heightened his recognition that his reactions were not necessarily appropriate to his own present behavior. Realizing the story of his childhood helped free him to act differently.

And sometimes, even the worst of childhoods becomes a fertile soil for the growth of very important skills. The early demise of a parent may draft a child into the role of adult long before others his age take on responsibilities. The child develops a precocious independence, which serves him all his life. And though an utterly unresponsive parent is dismaying, the parent who pays attention only when the child is reporting big moments may unwittingly nurse in the child a faculty for vivid speech. The child feels forced to use metaphors and irony and exaggeration as a flare in the darkness. He becomes a master at rubbing two words together and creating fire. When working with patients, especially those whose childhoods were full of privations, I always try to help them see the special skills they develop and not merely the losses they incurred.

Finally, an understanding of the patient's early relationships, especially with the important adults in his life, can help us appreciate his inner voices. The child hearing a parent's voice may honor it, and go on hearing it—in Freud's language, he "introjects" it. (We now know that the child's own behavior keeps that voice alive.) Growing up, the child tells himself, for instance, "You're clumsy," or "You're beautiful," or, "You are chosen to educate mankind." The child whose mother was stern may become unduly stern toward himself. The child who grew up feeling that nothing he did was ever sufficient may hear a voice that asks mockingly, "Is that all?" The child who experienced profound mother-love may offer that love to himself. He hears a forgiving voice when he blunders and a consoling one when things go wrong. A woman physician told me that after performing a long surgery, she could virtually hear her mother's voice saying, "It's all right. You did what you could for that patient. You can rest now." This woman's mother had been unmarried and brought her up alone, and was very devoted. The mother died long before her daughter ever got her medical degree. The fusion of past and present was in the voice.

To more than one person unloved by his parents, I've said, "You'll have to learn to become a good mother to yourself, to be the parent you never had." Knowing exactly what they missed out on in childhood can help many patients recognize what is still missing in their lives, and enable them to put it there.

36

Dreams

The earth, and every common sight,
To me did seem
Apparelled in celestial light,
The glory and the freshness of a dream.

Wordsworth, "Intimations of Immortality"

While in graduate school, I had an unforgettable nightmare. There was rich land, full of vegetation, and running through it were creatures of all shapes and sizes. I loved their vitality and variety. As I kept looking, I could see that all this was contained in a huge glass bowl. Then there was water, miniature oceans, and in them too were creatures eagerly swimming everywhere. But as I kept looking, the proportion of water increased, the creatures became fewer. And then, to my unspeakable horror, the creatures were gone. Not a single hint of life in that vast ocean. I woke up trembling and sweating. Being a psychology student, I got myself to free-associate to the dream. The rich soil and animal life, it seemed to me, were my talents. "My God!" I thought. "I'm afraid of death." I was going to a rather traditional analyst, who added that I was afraid of not being productive. That made some sense. But it was nothing radically new.

The interpretation, that the dream represented a fear of mine, bore no implications for what I could do.

A year later, I made friends with the psychotherapist Louis Ormont, who has since become a group psychoanalyst of wide repute. When I told him the dream, he gasped. "You're afraid you're in danger of throwing it all away." What he said came down like a lightning bolt from the sky. I had great desire for accomplishment, but I also did too much socializing, with the result that I was perpetually preoccupied or exhausted and had to drag through the days. I could easily throw it all away, whatever talent I had, for something less valuable. It wasn't death, or even the erosion of time, that I feared, although I despised them both. It was myself. I feared *my own impulses*, which had so often been centrifugal to my purposes. I could feel the risk of my turning rich life into sterility.

It wasn't an utterly new idea. I had gone through childhood hearing about my father, whom I didn't know. He had converted an excellent opportunity, intelligence, good looks, and education into fifty years of afternoons in bridge clubs. But although the idea wasn't new, the interpretation seemed thunderous to me. I could feel its rightness, or at least its value. The terror I felt about what I might do with my life seemed perfectly expressed in the dream. I have since recalled it over and over again, and used it to help stay on course, or at least near course.

My own therapist had used the dream merely to describe a fear. The interpretation was inert. My friend had related it to my own impulse—to an unrecognized impulse of mine to act in a way that would do me great harm. Whether I secretly wanted to harm myself, or would do so as a byproduct of giving in to the impulses of Dorian Gray, was not the point. The dream pinpointed an impulse at the threshold of my own recognition, and the interpretation brought it out. The vividness of the dream became the vividness of my own insight. I am convinced that it has helped me gain mastery over my own life.

The earliest uses of dreams were for discovery of deep truths, not ascertainable in any other way. Included were insights into the patient's latent fears, impulses, childhood wishes, and memories of childhood experiences. Dreams were also used to understand transference fears and desires. The early psychoanalysts might devote many sessions to a dream, and one analyst, Stekel, is said to have sent patients home when they came to his office without a dream to discuss. The interpretation of dreams by using standardized symbols—a waterfall is a memory of the father urinating, a turret is a woman's breast, and so forth—has fallen into disrepute. Today, a great many psychotherapists avoid dreams entirely, and even among psychoanalysts there's a tendency to play them down, to deal with them if a patient brings one in, but not to solicit them. Whereas dreams were once used to prove theories about infantile etiology, this is done much less today. One can "prove" nearly anything by making the fitting interpretation, and few experts accept such proofs as they once did.

Not surprisingly, because dreams were so heavily relied on, and often so illogically, dream analysis fell into disrepute. But there can be real value in the use of dreams. We can use them for hypotheses, and also as sources of information on the threshold of the patient's awareness. Jung long ago warned against interpreting dreams far in advance of the patient's ability to perceive the truth or falsity of what we discover. He maintained that where the mind knows something, or almost knows it, we can use dreams to help the person learn it with his heart. We can help the patient face up to the truth of what he already senses. However, we never bank on dreams entirely, and because interpretation is so subjective, it would be folly to base a theory wholly on what they "tell" us.

Ideally, an interpretation should reveal not merely a feeling but something the dreamer is actually doing in his life—or is afraid he will do. So what if I was afraid of my talents being wasted! I knew this. But that I myself had impulses to waste my life, that was another story! The terror of the dream became my terror over what I myself could do, and might be doing already. How was I sabotaging myself and my ambitions? Why was I?

Certain principles, well known in psychoanalysis, are that the dreamer creates all the events, all the characters. *He* is all the people, and determines the outcome, much as a novelist or playwright is all his characters and determines their outcome, although he may have the illusion while creating his piece that they are determining that outcome.

Many analysts who work with dreams feel that therapists should definitely not interpret every dream presented to them, lest the patient present nothing else in his sessions. Upon sensing that the therapist gives extensive attention to dreams, some patients will start bringing them in as gifts, making them increasingly complex, as if the therapist were a puzzle enthusiast. Also, one should never simply construe elements in a dream as symbols, but should ask extensively about the patient's associations to the dream. There are *day residues* in every dream, elements that the patient recalls from recent events.

The therapist who interprets a dream should do so first for himself. He may wish to keep the interpretation to himself, perhaps never making it to the patient. He should construe his conclusions merely as a premise—for instance, that the patient is grappling with a particular impulse or feeling—and cross-check this premise during the weeks or months to come.

Besides, he may not wish to dwell on the dream and thus reward the patient for this "gift." If the patient is someone who lives too much in fantasy, he may wish to discourage that approach to life. Or the patient may be telling him something: "I dreamt that I punched you in the mouth and your whole face was bleeding." "I dreamt that we had sex and you were impotent, a terrible disappointment." The therapist might wish to ask the patient openly whether he has such a feeling toward him. If so, why the indirect communication, when the ground rules specify that the patient say whatever comes to mind?

If we do wish to interpret dreams, it should ideally be in order to bring out impulses or wishes of the patient's—like my impulse to act in ways that might dry up my life. Merely to tell the patient something about his early life, or present situation, offers little.

Consider the following dream, as illustrating this all-important aspect of dream interpretation.

A woman dreamt, "My lover and I were in a newly decorated apartment, on banquéttes of tufty leather. Suddenly a stranger entered and held up a mirror shaped like a lollipop. I didn't want to look into it, but he insisted. As I did, I felt weaker and weaker. My mind was intact, but I collapsed to the floor, and my lover had to pick me up."

Most vivid in this dream was the terrible sense of helplessness, of weakness, this woman felt. One could easily say, "You are afraid of becoming weak, of collapsing and having to depend on a man to pick you up." This was true, and she knew it. All her life, she had been independent. She had supported her husband economically, by working long hours in a job, and she had almost single-handedly raised the children. But, we must remember, she created the event in the dream, brought in the stranger with the mirror. Whatever looks like fear in a dream we should consider as possibly a wish. She was stunned when I asked her whether she might have an impulse to collapse, to depend on a man, to be weak for a change, instead of always forcing herself onward independently. "Absolutely! That's it!" she assured me. She went on to tell me of fantasies that this lover would take care of her, and a growing sense that her independence shouldn't require as much as she gave. She felt embarrassed to admit wanting this, and yet recognized it as a real wish of hers.

This interpretation was made about an impulse whose existence was on the threshold of her own awareness. How can we be sure that this dream, and my dream too, didn't refer to early infantile events? Perhaps she wanted her father to take care of her. Perhaps, for that matter, I was dreaming about my father and not myself. The answer, it would seem, is that truth manifests itself in many places, and thus we have our choice as to where we point it out. The woman doubtless wanted me, her male analyst, to take over, to relieve her at least in part of her burden. She had moments of wanting to collapse in my office, with its soft couch, which might have been the prototype for the "banquettes of tufty leather." And the lollipop shape of the mirror suggests childhood, although she'd seen a mirror somewhat like it not long before. In support of the transference interpretation would be the notion that I was holding up a mirror in front of her, in which she could see herself. Again, it is not a matter of one interpretation being right and the others wrong. Her unacknowledged impulse to rely on a man, to disburden herself and have a new kind of relationship, might be manifesting itself in many places, and if so, it would almost surely appear with me.

Perhaps, as traditional analysts maintain, every dream contains information about the earliest years of life; in every dream there is a wish and a defense against that wish. But this is not tantamount to saying that a therapist can always read those elements, no matter how profoundly he understands his patient. Sometimes we can, but more often we cannot, even after we've questioned the patient at length for his every association to elements in the dream. One thing is sure, however. Dreams, many though not all of them, are full of dramatic exaggeration and powerful emotion for the dreamer. We see citadels and beautiful vistas and we fly or fall from great heights, and the experience is often ecstasy or terror. We may have in our audience parents long-ago deceased, or kings and princes, and when we forget our lines, or do beautifully, whole multitudes may tremble. In fact, even when the events don't seem to warrant much feeling, the dreamer may experience unspeakable emotion: tearful joy or overwhelming sorrow. For the patient who is emotionally dead, or who is numb in some particular region of his life, the discovery of any parallel between real life and a dream can be invaluable. Dreams hold the key to dramatizing what is really important in the patient's life, to helping him experience the significance of what is going on inside of him. I have sometimes retained a metaphor from a dream, and used it over and over again.

A woman, unhappy in her marriage, was toying with the idea of beginning an affair. She seemed blithely indifferent to the risks of getting caught, almost without conscience or fear, as she met the other man for increasingly flirtatious lunches. She recognized that if she went ahead and her husband found out, he would never take her back. She would be alone with the two children. The other man was married and would not join her. Still she went ahead. She dreamt that she was walking along the edge of a cliff. To the left was a terrible fire, on the other side was an abyss. A wrong step and she would be burned alive or dashed to pieces. She tiptoed along, with great trepidation, and reached the other side. Her first association was that her marriage was fire and brimstone, full of angry arguments and burning accusations. Looking at the dream herself, she volunteered that she was walking an incredibly narrow path. She had better watch where she was going. There was no need for me to say anything. The dream itself, her own view of it, released profound emotion, which she had been repressing, and I considered that enough for the time being. Dreams often have the value of allowing the dreamer to feel and experience something he had recognized only intellectually, if at all. They enable the heart to grasp what the mind already knows.

We've all had dreams that reminded us that we felt much more deeply about someone than we'd recognized. We understand the German poet Heine's verse from "Lyrical Intermezzo":

My old love comes in creeping
From death's immense domain.

She sits by my side, and, weeping,
She melts my heart again.

In the same way, we may get a sense of how much we fear someone. And yet, we must be careful in interpreting the mood of a dream. A patient dreams that his mother died. It was tragic, and he wept. He feels sad all day. Is the mood a decoy, as Freud would have suggested? As arranger of the dream, did he want his mother to die? He killed her in the dream. But even here, all the therapist can do is to ask the person for his associations. Just as the mood may be displaced, so may the object of the impulse, if there was one.

This brings us to what many modern psychoanalysts consider the most important use of dreams: understanding the transference. What does the patient think of the therapy and of the therapist? More precisely, what are his impulses as pertaining to his treatment?

The woman treading a narrow path between the abyss and the fire was also tiptoeing with me. She was extremely careful not to say many things that came to her mind. For instance, she would never admit that she hated someone, or even disliked a person she knew. She might hint such a feeling, but would take it back in a hurry, even deny the very words she had used. I used her dream to help myself see how careful she was. My work with her centered mostly around her various resistances to experiencing the depth of her own emotions and concerns. Her arguments with her husband seemed always concerning trivia, and left them both unsatisfied. She had lost a lot in life by default. When she began to see how much she hedged even with me, I used the word tiptoeing, and she accepted it easily, using it herself. Later, I reminded her of the dream in which she had tiptoed and made it to the other side. That couldn't happen in real life, where the essence of fulfillment was the bringing into reality of her whole emotional being. A hesitant passage is itself a failure. There is nothing that makes people feel more hopeless and alone than their own facade.

Many dreams lend themselves to transference interpretations. A man dreams he's on stilts, looking down at me. If he stops to talk to me, he'll fall over, so he keeps walking. Does this patient see me as dangerous to his balance? That was his association. We went on to talk about how I might endanger him. He was a sculptor, who feared that he might listen to me, make himself subject to my overpowering will and lose his creativity. Behind that fear lay an impulse to please me, and the notion that unless he did exactly what I wanted him to, I would withdraw from him. Coming in touch with that impulse—to stop and fall off his stilts—helped him see that if I made such a demand, he had no need to pay attention to it. His work was more important than any directive about his work that I might give him.

Another man dreamt that he was in a traffic jam. Everything was at a standstill. I wondered whether he felt his work with me was at a standstill, and if so, why he was causing such a standstill. It turned out that this man was afraid that I would despise him for his homosexuality and had avoided telling me that he was having sex with another man. He had sensed that he was sabotaging his own therapy by this concealment, but the dream made it seem mandatory that he tell me. His refusal to accept his own sexuality was the standstill. He felt great elation in seeing that it was he, not I, who had been causing the traffic jam.

Always, whether we actually interpret the dream for the patient or not, we think in terms of impulse. The dream may describe an inner reality—that is well and good. But mere description of a reality never attaches so keenly to the person's ongoing life as insight into an impulse the patient can recognize. Jung and others have talked about the prognostic power of dreams. A man dreams that he has a terrible skiing accident. The therapist advises him to be careful, not to go out on the slopes alone. But he does, and after one near mishap, plunges to his death. This is not astrology; insofar as the therapist could see ahead enough to warn the patient, he was predicting an outcome from knowing something about the patient's impulses. The ancient Greek adage, "A man's character is his fate," was what allowed the prediction to be made.

A patient of mine felt cheated by a business partner, but while giving the evidence to me and others, kept denying that this was really happening. He then dreamt he was in a bathtub and his head was being pushed under water by his partner. Purely descriptively, one might say that he saw the malevolence of the other man in the dream. But, again looking for an impulse, I considered the possibility that he *wanted* the other man to cheat him. Not that he wanted to drown; what he wanted was some outright event that would allow him to draw his conclusion about the man without any possibility of its being wrong. He was inviting the man to prove himself unworthy and giving him too many chances for dishonesty. Actually, the evidence against the partner was already overwhelming; there was no need to sacrifice any more money for further proof.

I mentioned earlier that a major mistake of reasoning has been to conclude that simply because a person *caused* an outcome, he secretly *wanted* that outcome—as if people had perfect control over their actions and the effects of those actions. A man may be in a traffic accident or lose all his money gambling without having secretly longed for that result. If it befalls the gambler that his father dies of a heart attack over his losing so much money, it need not follow that the gambler wanted that either. However, the dreamer really does have control over the outcome of his dream. A patient reporting the dream that he lost all his money and caused his father to die may be reporting a real impulse. It may either be an impulse for the outcome he created, or the impulse for an activity that he fears might produce that result. That is, he may want his father to die, and thus dream of having killed him this way. Or he may want to take a gamble, which activity he associates with killing his father, who is against gambling.

Finally, the hunger illusion may stage a vivid appearance in dreams. The person who breaks an accustomed pattern of behavior, or who pushes himself to try something new, may become flooded with unexpected feelings and thoughts. His reason for beginning the activity and his present motives for it both make themselves conscious as the impulse heightens. Very common is the pouring into a dream of an ocean of these renounced thoughts and ideas. The person may dream about why he began the behavior and what it means.

For instance, a man has played life extremely close to the vest, never taking chances. He doesn't know why he is this way, but it has cost him a great deal. He starts doing things differently, taking gambles. He is frightened at first, feels the impulse to retreat, to play it safe. He decides to take his family on a summer vacation, which he will have to pay for in the fall, never having done anything on credit before. It is relatively safe, and called for. He has money surely coming in after the summer. But doing this is very hard for him. That night he dreams that he has played for high stakes at cards, lost, and killed his father. The dream highlights his motive for having played it safe in the beginning and over the years. In a sense, he has all along been honoring his father by his conservatism. In actuality, his father, somewhat senile, doesn't know what he has done and doesn't care. But by the new behavior, he has activated his father of years gone by. His father appears as he did when the boy was young.

Time and again when patients report their dreams, I ask myself what they are doing differently. From the dream I can sometimes see which patterns they have begun to break. I consider whether the dream may hold clues as to what that behavior means to the person. It's as if the old behavior were pleading in the dream, as in waking life, for the person to resume it.

Often we face an inconsistency between the outcome of a

dream and the mood of the dream. The dreamer sobs over an experience which, because it is his dream, he himself brought to pass. A young man dreams that he has left home. His father, searching the streets for him, is struck by a car and seriously injured. The problem arises whether to regard the dreamer as wanting the outcome in real life (his father's injury) or simply wanting the behavior associated with that outcome (to "leave home"). As always with dreams, we ask the patient for his associations and reactions rather than tell him anything. And we select the interpretation, if we make one, that dovetails with everything else we know about the person.

The study of dreams, like that of the patient's early childhood, was surely overdone in the early days of psychoanalysis. Even today, there are therapists who interpret every dream brought to them, who capitalize on the fact that no one can disprove a dream interpretation. Many seem more determined to impress the patient with their expertise than to cure him. The very far-fetched nature of what they tell the person gives it a kind of credibility to certain patients. Such therapists appeal to narcissistic patients, who love the fact that the ramblings of their unconscious mind even while it is sleeping are taken so seriously. Many patients enjoy passivity and want others to do the work for them—even to predict their future. Those who purvey the far-fetched will always find ready prey among the illogical, and among those so distressed, and so desperate, that they will turn even to magic as an answer. Still, dreams, which are repositories of deep feelings, if used as hypotheses, can have real therapeutic utility.

37

The Therapist as Model

Whatever our underlying theory, in helping the patient we use ourselves as a model. From simply observing us, the patient forms conceptions of how to live and act; and may unconsciously go on copying our example for a lifetime.

Every patient makes judgments about his therapist, and although we may sometimes call them his projections, the fact is that we do declare ourselves in a variety of ways. Even if we don't talk about our personal lives, or interact with the patient outside the office, we present a very consistent picture after a while. Our patients sense the degree of genuineness of our ethics, and get a strong impression of what we emphasize in life. They watch how we handle our own blunders and cope with their attacks on us, and how we field questions. They know when they're putting us on the spot. It could be by anger or by an open sexual overture. Although we may never touch our patients, they get to know if we're the sort who touch other people easily, what our attitude toward sex is, and whether we're afraid of sickness or death. While the patient is telling the story of his life, we are revealing not necessarily the dates and places important to us, but the spiritual nature of our own journey.

Once we start talking about ourselves—for instance, tell the patient that we're divorced, or married, or have children, or vacationed in a particular spot—we must expect the person to mull over what we've said and to interpret it. He may feel competitive toward the people close to us. If we've done well materially, he may envy us or our mates. If what we mention seems like a weakness, he may feel sorry for us, or become condescending. We've taken up his time in the hour and burdened him. We can't control the person's associations afterward, and he may attribute nearly anything we say to what he's learned about us. "Well, no wonder you say that. Your own marriage apparently wasn't so happy." It would be folly to start defending ourselves at this stage.

A good principle is that it's never wrong not to talk about ourselves, and it is often wrong to do so. No matter how innocent our comments may seem to us, they may find fertile soil in the patient's neurosis. Once we've said something, we can't take it back. Every therapist ought to have the experience of not talking about himself throughout the course of at least one whole therapy.

Why do therapists so often discuss their own lives? One reason is that they want to look good. They brag indirectly, hinting at how well they've done, so that the patient, who may have doubts about what he's getting from therapy, will persevere. The therapist knows that the patient would rather go to a winner than a loser, and the therapist communicates—sometimes not so subtly—that he's a winner. Talking about oneself for this reason is never acceptable. It often makes the patient feel worse about himself. "Your children go to fine private schools, and mine are off to a much poorer start in life."

Sometimes the therapist, being from a poorer social class than his patient, wants to impress that patient that he's an equal. He talks about his recent life, as if to say, "I, like you, am from a wealthy family." So the therapist pretends he's unimpressed by the patient's lavish indulgences. But this way of justifying his right to work with the patient is unnecessary. Even if the patient doesn't see through the pretense, it achieves nothing. The therapist whose patients engage in ostentatious displays of wealth should bring those displays to the patient's attention and study their meaning, and ideally will never compete with them himself. The real issue for the patient is whether he is being helped, and we must stay true to this purpose, no matter how envious or dazzled we become.

The third major reason that therapists discuss themselves is to offer support to the patient. "I myself was poor." I myself am homosexual, and was in the gay march." "I had your problem of doing poorly in school, and in the end I straightened myself out." This seems to me a noble motive, and yet self-revelation for this purpose too may backfire. "So you don't know either what it's like to be heterosexual," the patient might retort—or think. If we need examples of heroic accomplishment, we are better off using people other than ourselves. Moreover, to whatever extent that patient dislikes himself for some trait, he will dislike us for that trait too.

However, if there is any reason for us to talk about ourselves, I think revealing a weakness is the best one. Often we can gain a person's confidence this way, and can help him see that, even if he doesn't share our failing, he can do well in spite of some other failing of his. If he tends to idealize us, sometimes we can help him by showing a weakness. But even here, self-revelation is second best. Preferable would be to help him arrive at confidence, and stop idealizing people *generally.* We can use the relationship to help him see what he does and why. But it's best to help him resolve the problem without our having to reveal the actual facts about ourselves. We should do so only after considered judgment.

Ideally, a crucial revelation about ourselves may be highly therapeutic in spite of the risks. Years ago, I showed a patient, doing poorly in school, my own college transcript, which shows that I did badly. It inspired him that I could have overcome that start, and he went on to get his doctorate. Later I tried similar demonstrations when working at a drug addiction center, and there too had good results. But sometimes I've said too much, and now am always mindful that once a thing has been said, it can't be erased. To refrain from saying something is to leave oneself time to reconsider it and the option of saying it later if we wish.

A fundamental rule is this: Don't talk about yourself if you feel any pressure from the patient to find out about you. "Are you married? I must know." "How would it help you to find out?" "I'd know you had my experiences." The patient is mistaken who thinks that the whole process of therapy would go more smoothly if only he knew some fact about your life. Whatever his problem, it would remain, and almost surely he would before long feel the need to know some further fact. Such a patient is nearly always the kind of person who deals with what goes on inside him by trying to learn about the outside, or by controlling other people. That very approach is one reason why his problems persist.

Before talking about his own life, the therapist should make sure that he can refrain from doing so. The only way he can be sure is by resisting his impulse for at least some sessions. He should also consider whether there is any impulse on his part to show off, to improve his status with the patient. If so, he should investigate that impulse. Is the patient making him feel unworthy? Is the therapy unproductive? Or does he have the problem generally? Little can be more embarrassing than having a patient properly detect the therapist as showing off. Denying it won't help, when the patient and therapist both know it's true.

When a patient pressures us for personal facts, it's best to explain that we don't talk about ourselves. I usually explain that it interferes with the process. Although the patient may think he would be better off in possession of some fact about me, he is mistaken. Nearly always, when I explore why it feels vital for the person to learn some particular fact of my life, we uncover a need of his that becomes much more important to look at, in his view as well as mine.

In general, if we are to discuss an incident in our lives—for instance, to let the patient know that we too were rejected and know what it feels like—it is best to take the incident from out of the past, not from yesterday. This way, we're not still smarting from the rejection, or flushed with the triumph. Then, clearly, we selected it to talk about only because we think it's relevant to the patient's immediate experience.

Some patients dislike the imbalance in the relationship, the one-way flow of information. They're supposed to tell us everything while we sit back and tell them nothing. But this argument, though understandable, should not be compelling. Their purpose is different from ours. And often, I've observed, the charge is made against therapists who seem emotionally detached. If we're evidently engaged with them in the sessions, emotionally involved, we are giving enough; and they're less likely to feel this misgiving.

I think there are some things that therapists can, and sometimes ought to, reveal. I might answer a patient's question about whether I saw a movie or a television show. It saves time when the patient talks about it. Our patients know we have daily wants and satisfactions. They get a sense after a while of whether we cook or go to the opera or know anything about ballet. But we must be ready to draw the line.

And what if we've slipped, said too much? We told a parent that we too went through a divorce and had to worry about our child, but things came out well. At the time, the patient was contemplating divorce from a loathsome mate, and feared being out in the wide world alone with a child. But now the person has gone back, tells us he's deeply in love, and feels sorry for us, and for anyone who is in our spot. Even worse, he tells people about our divorce, and asks their opinion about whether he should go on working with us. We're left to wonder whether we spoke out of some desire to encourage the patient to leave his mate, which he surmised unconsciously, and for which he is now punishing us.

Nearly always, however, if the relationship is good, we can ask the person what our "blemish" means to him; and by discussing it, we can go beyond it. Certainly, once a patient has abused even the smallest confidence, we ought to put him in the category of those with whom we don't talk about our lives, at least not for a long time.

It's a very different story when the patient finds out about us in some other way. He investigates, or even follows us, or simply happens to see us in daily life. Some lonely person, who wants us to help him break out of isolation, sees us joyously walking down the street with loved ones. It's painful to the patient, and perhaps to us. Who wants to be an agent of contrast, making the person feel worse by comparison? Still, we can't help this. We can't shield the person from the facts of life. And if our patient feels crushed, it is merely because a truth has become inescapable. Most important, when we do meet a patient anywhere outside the office, we should be polite and friendly, though brief. Then, in the very next session we should refer to the meeting, and ask the patient to tell us any feelings he had at the time or afterward. If we met the patient unexpectedly, perhaps we were less than composed. Rather than guess how the patient felt about seeing us, we should ask. Above all, it would be wrong to defend ourselves against any inference he might draw. A male therapist was seen escorting an unattractive woman to the theatre, and assures the patient, "She was just a colleague," as if to say, "Don't evaluate me by that woman. For romance I have someone far better looking."

There is one time when it seems positively indicated for us

to talk about ourselves, and that is when we may behave unusually during a session. "Sorry. I have a terrible toothache—just developed. If I wince, it isn't because of what you're saying." Here the aim is to avoid burdening the patient.

Nearly all therapists talk about themselves from time to time, and not necessarily for the good of the therapy. Although we in private practice spend time with people all day, we are remarkably isolated by the necessity to dwell on those who come to us. It's as if our every feeling is primarily an instrument to understand the other person. Ideally, when we do talk about ourselves, and it's not for a therapeutic purpose, we choose neutral subject matter, and don't run on too long.

We reveal ourselves not just by our reactions, but by our very failure to react—for instance, if we are not appalled when the patient talks about a sexual perversion or something unethical, this tells him about us. We are to some extent a model for him. How we respond to death or illness when he reports it, how we deal with emergencies, what we laugh at, even the way we sit and gesture, may have meaning to him. Patients are likely to copy us in unexpected places. Probably all human beings should live as if they were going to be a model for others, anyhow. For the therapist, as for the parent, this would seem especially important.

As illustrations of this, let's look at three particular forms of behavior that we engage in, which are likely to have special meaning to the patient: how we handle our own mistakes, how we respond to attacks on us, and how we reply to questions from the patient. With all three, the patient very likely expects us to act as his parents did—more particularly, the parent of the same sex as we are. His approach has been fashioned largely out of that expectation.

We all make mistakes. Chief among the therapist's are being late, forgetting an appointment, scheduling two people at once;

then there are mistakes that can occur within the therapeutic hour, such as getting a name wrong, forgetting that the patient told us something, or insulting the patient by obvious inattention.

Much more damaging is the crime of falling asleep in a session. To fall asleep seems to require a combination of inattention and disdain. The therapist who does this should apologize, not charge for the hour, and consider seriously whether to continue working with that person. He has profoundly insulted a human being coming to him for recognition, and the effect may be ineradicable.

Perhaps even worse is betraying the patient's confidentiality, already mentioned; this can undermine the whole therapeutic relationship.

When we make a mistake, our only course is to apologize. "Sorry I was late." This is called for even if we're only three minutes late. It asserts that the patient's time is important to us, and that we are mindful that we had an appointment. A few times over the years I have forgotten an appointment entirely—usually when it was not at the person's regular hour. There's nothing left to do except ask for the patient's mercy, and if the person has a lot to say on the subject, to hear him out. We may have touched some terrible chord of memory, reminded him of past neglect that he always felt was deserved. The same with scheduling two patients at once. Someone has to go home, and it's usually the person who scheduled the appointment last, although I've sometimes made it the person whom I knew would be least affected.

After a blunder, the most serious crime we can commit is to make excuses or to blame our mistake in any way on the patient. No other human being puts us to sleep or causes us to be late or to forget a name. To blame the other person, even by innuendo, is to say that we're not responsible for our actions. By implication, he's not responsible for his. The excuse is likely to do more long-run harm than the blunder. Recall Othello, after

committing murder, imploring his jury to "Nothing extenuate."
It meant more to him to preserve the dignity of being held
responsible for his actions than to slink away as less than a man.
That must be our position too. By providing a heroic model, we
may actually do the patient some good. We help him see how to
handle mistakes, and to recognize that they aren't calamitous. At
best, our response to our own mistakes, if we admit them freely,
can be liberating to the patient.

We are again a model when the patient attacks us. Perhaps
we have done something wrong, although most vehement attacks on therapists are disproportionate to the therapist's actual
blunders. We've said something to a woman that, we now realize, was somewhat sexist. We hadn't thought about its full implication. Apparently, she has. Now she harangues us, telling us we
shouldn't be in the field, accusing us of every conceivable form
of contempt and incompetence. Our impulse rises to defend
ourselves. For instance, we want to make a depth interpretation
to the effect that the woman is displacing her anger onto us: "I'm
sorry your brother got all the advantages, Mary, but don't take
it out on me. I'm on your side."

To do this would be a misuse of our role. If we're wrong,
it befits us to admit the error. "Yes, now that you point it out,
that statement of mine was sexist." Or, "I'm sorry my mind
wandered." "Oh, you say I stopped abruptly last session. I'm
sorry." Even if we aren't sure, it's best to admit that the error
might be ours. This is most apt to happen on a schedule mixup,
in which case neither we nor the patient may ever be absolutely
sure whose fault it was.

But our admitting an error doesn't warrant the patient's
attributing malevolence or incompetence to us. He ought not
ascribe any motive to us, any more than we should to him. When
he does, he is merely acting upon his license, in fact his agree-
ment, to say what comes to his mind. "You really don't like
women, do you?" a female patient may charge. We may ask her

why she thinks that was our reason. Perhaps she can cite five other reasons for believing it, in which case we may promise her we'll think about it. More likely, if the person doesn't forgive us, his attack is more than a reaction to our mistake. Especially if we've admitted the mistake and not defended it, have given ground, his refusal to forgive us indicates something about him. After hearing him out, it may be helpful to distill our error from his torrent of interpretation and abuse: "Yes, I was late. I repeat that I'm sorry, but you're not warranted in what you're accusing me of. I'm not trying to avoid you. You're bringing that into the picture, and it just doesn't belong here."

It's seldom a good idea to analyze the patient's overreaction just after we've done something amiss. Too often our going into his reaction becomes a form of escape for us. It defuses his upset, and sets a poor example. The most we can do is to identify the limits of our culpability. If he keeps making reference to our error, we may bring this to his attention in the future, and point out that he's holding on to his grievance. We may ask if there's any way we can make a comeback. In the most extreme case, we may have to tell the person that he can quit if he really wants to, but if he stays with us he ought to consider why he wants to punish us.

Every accusation by the patient gives us the chance to demonstrate how to take criticism. We should encourage the person to say what's on his mind without defending ourselves. We can't know whether he's right or wrong until we hear him out. If what he says is vague—for instance, he tells us only that he has an "impression" about us—we should ask him what gives him that idea. What did we actually do that makes him feel we're bored by him, or being seductive, or angry with him, or that we prefer another patient? Whether we agree or not, we should assure him that it's good he told us his reaction. We're glad he brought it up, and we want him to continue doing so. We hold as significant any feeling about us that crosses his mind.

This applies to any general characterizations of us, no matter how uncomplimentary. If he even hints at dissatisfaction with us, or with the therapy, we should try to bring out what's on his mind. A patient says to us in passing, "You're a very lonely person." "Why do you say that?" When we understand why, we should ask him how he feels about it. Not until we've heard him out in detail, and thought to ourselves about his reaction, should we look for his motives. For instance, he thinks us lonely because he wants a place in our lives, wants us to need him. Rather than parry with this interpretation, we can make use of the insight at another time. It's vital that we never explain away any impression of his until he fully expresses it. We can elicit that same impression about us, the need to be useful to us, from future comments of his.

Meanwhile, we learn a great deal about his style of speaking to people from the way he criticizes us. For instance, we see that he's overinterpretive, punitive, sarcastic. All of this can be used later on.

Especially if the patient has always been hesitant to criticize authority, we do wonders for him by encouraging him to say all. He may speak tentatively, then withdraw what he started to say. "Don't take it back. Maybe you're right. Maybe you're wrong. Please finish." Such a patient, if he's right, may feel guilty, expect us to topple over or to get furious. After encouraging him to tell us what he thinks about us, we may do well to ask him how he feels. And also, "What do you think I feel?" "You hate me." "Why do you think so?" When he tells us, we may ask what he thinks our reason is for the reaction. It's our job to liberate tentative people. His freedom to speak openly to us becomes his freedom to think critically about other people. Many patients without this freedom had parents who would emotionally disown them for such thoughts. Such patients have gone a lifetime cleansing their perceptions, and blaming themselves when faults lay elsewhere.

With people who overreact continually, we can do our best work when we have been absolutely innocent of any wrongdoing. We don't argue our case, but get them to deliver theirs. Like a wave, it may collapse on itself. Even with paranoid patients, unless they're psychotic, the freedom to tell us their misgivings is a valuable start, although we can't expect their paranoia to go away so easily. Every act of trust liberates them a little, and their delivering their worst is, paradoxically, an act of trusting us. Even paranoid patients know when they've given us an excessively rough time.

Our handling of attacks by patients, and by people generally, is fundamental both for our sense of self and for the image we project in the world. There's almost no better circumstance in human existence for creating personal dignity, and demonstrating it, than being falsely accused. Whenever a patient attacks us, he recognizes, whether he says so or not, that we had getaways. We could have used the sovereignty of our position as therapist and we disdained this avenue. Because we came forward unafraid, he is much more likely to do the same.

Questions too pose their challenge, often a subtle one. Our position allows us the easy option of not answering any question on the grounds that it won't help the person to know. However, certain questions merit an answer, whether or not answering makes us uncomfortable: "What are your credentials?" "How long have you been in this field?" A great many questions are reasonable, but we just can't answer them—at least not as definitively as the patient would like: "Can you help me?" "How long will it take?" "How did I get this way?" "Have you seen people with my problem before?" We may need a lot more information than we have before we can tell the patient what he'd like to hear.

Our first rule, I think, is never to discourage questions—and certainly not by implying that they're stupid. Perhaps the person has asked us before, and the repetition is annoying. That gives us no right to act disdainfully. Always, I think, we should either answer the question or explain why we can't. Whether we can help the person remains to be seen, and will depend upon how hard he works at defining the problem. In the end, it will be up to him, and his efforts also determine how long it will take. That we can't answer the person doesn't imply that his question is in any way amiss. Often we've got to get the person to be more specific. "What do you mean by 'your problem?' " "Alcoholism." "Yes. I have been able to help people with drinking problems. But every problem is different; it will depend on whether you are willing to make the necessary sacrifices."

We may need to ask the person questions of our own to clarify his question; however, it is nearly always wrong to simply throw back the person's question to him. "How long do you think therapy will take?" "What do *you* think?" Merely tossing back a question to the patient, for which psychologists have sometimes been lampooned, runs the risk of making us look overly detached, or even disdainful. On the other hand, we might want to emphasize that the patient himself has the final say about his feelings and motivations, and often, over the answer to the question he asks us.

Sometimes the patient, afraid to possess some reaction of his own, asks us, as if for permission to have that reaction. "Don't you agree that my wife is terrible?" It would be a pitfall for us to answer this kind of question. We might help the patient see what he is asking us to do. He surely shouldn't need expert testimony about the merits of someone he loved enough to marry. He has some feeling, and shouldn't need us or anyone else to validate it.

It is always our right to ask the patient what he's thinking, or why he asked a question. After months of therapy, for instance, the patient suddenly questions our credentials. We answer him squarely, never substituting a study of him for the kind of response he deserves. But we wonder if he hasn't developed some recent feeling about us, perhaps doubt of our abilities, that is implicit in his question. After answering him, we might ask why the question. Or we might ask what feelings he has toward us.

The patient's questions are often a resistance. Rather than talk about something sensitive, he becomes unslakably curious about us. Still, that doesn't give us the right to downgrade what he asks. We answer him with dignity, and then go on to study the resistance, as we might study any other. In answering him, we are serving as a model. We would like him to take all people seriously, and critical moments for doing this are when people turn to him with questions.

As therapists, we exemplify our view of mental health and of personal dignity. Our honesty and respect for people are manifest everywhere and not only in the contexts I've mentioned. The cynical patient may disdain us for what he takes to be pointless honesty or optimism. Still, we must hold fast, for our own sakes as well as his. We offer even the cynical patient some vision of a citadel of people who care and who welcome others who do. His striving would not be in vain. If we succeed, he comes away with even more than he dared hope for out of treatment.

PART SEVEN

Beginnings and Ends

Why do we have to accomplish our human lot?
Because it is much to be here . . .
And because they apparently need us,
Those things of the earth,
Whose transience strangely concerns us.
                                        —*Rilke*

38

Crisis—The Limits of Therapy

Psychotherapists nearly all face an occasional crisis. Some patients threaten suicide, and a few may talk about murder. Will the person really do it, or is he just using a figure of speech, saying, "I'd like to end it all"?

A crisis is any situation threatening grave danger—usually so serious that if it occurs it will be impossible to remedy. Our problem is whether or not to go on in our role as psychotherapists, disdaining to interfere and allowing the person to keep talking, as if it were mere thinking. The alternative, if we think there's a serious chance of the danger occurring, is to violate our role as psychotherapists, and to "betray" the patient by interfering actively in his life. We might call a loved one of his, or even the police. Were we sure either way, we would know what to do.

The problem is we never can be sure. To simply wait and see may be to allow a tragedy. To intervene may be to undermine the person's trust in us. On finding himself on a hospital ward, locked away and under observation, our patient may regret that he ever went into therapy. The instant we enter his life actively, we have risked his trust for the greater good—or for what we consider the greater good.

Complicating the situation is that there is no ultimate preventive. If the person really wants to kill himself, or anyone else, he can do it. He can't be contained or monitored forever, and if he trusts us and likes us, he may be worse off having lost that trust. On the other hand, he may be thankful for our interference. Many patients who tell us these things do so in order to have us protect them, either by analyzing those impulses away or by literally stopping them. The patient may have told us so that we would call a loved one, who would protect him.

There are centers devoted to handling crises. People on the brink of suicide, and many who just want attention, call a hot-line. Experts who answer may talk them out of it, or keep them on the phone long enough to summon help. But those experts have less to lose than we do. The patient hasn't formed any relationship with them, at least not one comparable to that with us. He is unlikely to feel the same sense of being betrayed.

Crises arise in many forms. A few years after getting my doctorate, I had occasion to work with a woman in her early twenties. She was attractive, pleasant, extremely promiscuous, and ready to try almost anything so long as it didn't demand much postponement of gratification. It was during that period when few people, indeed few judges in magistrates court, knew the difference between marijuana and hard drugs. Possession of even a few reefers often brought long imprisonment. My patient smoked pot regularly, and used people's ignorance about it as an excuse to discount everything else that society stood for. Our work was slow, but it did result in her enrolling for a course leading to a hairdresser's license.

At that time, this woman began living with a man who was a heroin addict. For a while she resisted putting the needle in her arm, but apparently he wanted company and would rhapsodize about the experience. She knew his life was an utter waste, characterized by misery between moments of pointless elation.

Then she told me she had tried it, and I could see the handwriting on the wall. Although I argued against it, and got her to promise not to do it again, she continued. However, she wasn't happy with this lover, or with their life together, and had mixed feelings about staying with him and continuing what she called her experiments with the drug.

Her father was paying for treatment. She was close to him, and gave him permission to talk to me. I told him that I couldn't reveal confidences. He was understanding. He informed me that he had just sold his business, and was going to live in Florida, faraway.

In retrospect, I should have told this man it was urgent that he request his daughter to go with him. I realize now that she would very likely have welcomed this opportunity. Even without giving him details, I might have conveyed that it was urgent that he do this. She would have escaped the relationship and would have been in a place where she didn't know where to buy the drug. The break might have made all the difference. Unhappily, the real story was that I did nothing. She went deeper into the habit, stopped therapy. I met her a year later. She had left the man, and become a prostitute to pay for her habit, which was ravaging her. I never saw her after that. Conceivably, she rallied. Others have. But if she did, it would be no thanks to me.

Why was I so remiss? Looking back, I blame my incompetence on my own dogmatic belief in classical therapy. Sometimes, we've got to acknowledge that we can't handle a challenge all alone, or by the traditional means. To intervene seemed to me an admission of failure. Not that I considered that possibility consciously. But I was motivated by wanting not to fail. I had visions of my patient becoming successful as a hairdresser, learning to love and create, and of my having made it all possible. I was a great guy, but did a rotten job. It was an outcome that I will regret the rest of my life.

Secondarily, I had been trained to put magical belief in the patient's "self-actualizing potential," to take a term from the psychiatrist Abraham Maslow. That a person tends toward health as a plant grows toward light is a useful idea, but some patients, left to their own resources, will destroy themselves. This includes many drug addicts, alcoholics, and psychotic patients. There are times when the patient positively needs us to intervene, just as there are times when to do so would be an unforgivable insult to a person who, with trust, could have surmounted the obstacles on his own.

Coping with any crisis requires the willingness to talk unflinchingly about its worst aspects with the patient. We need courage and composure. For instance, the patient intimates wanting to get even with someone who harmed or injured him. He's planning something violent. We try to get him to talk about his urge and his actual plans. He may reply that it was just the way he felt and he has no real intention of doing anything. Still, we let him know that we understand the grievous nature of what was done to him. Or, if we don't think he has real cause—for instance, a wife he mistreated for years left him for another man, whom he now wants to kill—we can still convey to our patient that we know how hurtful it is to be abandoned.

But sometimes, although a patient suddenly withdraws his threat, we may sense that he means to go through with it. We ask him to talk more about it: "Are you really thinking of setting his house on fire?" "How serious are you about killing yourself?" Whatever he's contemplating, we may ask him why he would do it. How would particular people, his lover, his mate, his friends, we ourselves, be affected by the act? It's a bad sign if he hasn't even considered those repercussions or doesn't care. We might in some cases reassure the person that people would react to his suicide quite differently from his expectations: "Your parents will suffer terribly, and forever." However, on occasion, if I've felt the threat was essentially sadistic, I've pointed out the opposite kind of mistake. "You may be wrong. Your former husband might not be nearly as moved as you think. He'd go on the same way." Seeing that even his suicide would be unimportant may free the person from his hope of getting a reaction this way. But if our patient is serious, our predictions about the world are likely to make little difference either way.

Many therapists, who find it hard to talk about major dangers, argue that they don't want to put thoughts into the patient's mind. But our investigating, or even being the first to mention an idea explicitly, won't in itself induce a person to action. Usually the therapist who makes this excuse for avoiding the topic is rationalizing. In reality, he is hiding from knowing what the patient has in mind. He finds the patient's despair intolerable and may take it as an accusation that he himself has failed. Also his desire not to know what the patient is thinking may be a device to allow him to feel less culpable if the patient goes ahead and does the thing.

Suicide threats are, of course, our most difficult crisis, and the hardest to evaluate. Everyone at times has felt the urge to end it all. In therapy, where the patient is asked to say whatever comes to his mind, we can expect virtually everyone, at some time or other, to voice thoughts about suicide.

When we think a threat may be serious, we must enter the patient's realm. We appreciate why he feels at the end of his rope, why everything seems hopeless. We take absolutely seriously even a patient's passing impulse to act drastically. Our tone says we're with him and not flustered. Our words say that there is another way. Above all, we must never minimize how badly he feels or resort to simple reassurance that things will be all right. Maybe they will, maybe they won't. To pretend that his life surely will improve may make us feel better, but it communicates to the patient that we really don't understand how he feels—or worse yet, that we know but are afraid to get too close to him. Staying with the subject and speaking plainly is the best way to earn his trust.

In evaluating the seriousness of the threat, we may ask the patient if he's made actual plans. Has he obtained the instrument, the sleeping pills, or the gun? Has he written notes, taken out new insurance, or told loved ones where his property is? If he discusses these details with us, it may be because he wants us to exhort him not to act, but not necessarily.

The adage that barking dogs don't bite is nonsense. Many a suicide and many a murderer have proclaimed what they were going to do. At least some of these people wanted to be stopped. To disregard their threat is to incline them toward further action. Previous attempts, especially if they weren't responded to, are an even more serious sign. If the person makes even a mild effort, one that couldn't possibly succeed, we must take it seriously. He may be calling out to loved ones, asking if anyone really cares. We don't want to imply that he had better call in a louder voice next time.

While we intervene, we further evaluate the danger. Will he turn the sleeping pills over to us so that we can flush them down the toilet in front of him? Not that we can ever be sure that he's giving us all of them. We know that he can always get more. Still, the act means something. We ask him to promise that at any time of the day or night, if the impulse wells up in him and he feels in danger, he will call us at once. And if we're not going to be available, he should have someone else to call. Our part of the deal is to give him a phone number at which he can reach us in the middle of the night. Our doing this is in itself a statement. Several patients, who never actually called me, told me later that they felt very moved by my giving them my private number.

In addition, we ourselves should make a note of the patient's home address and phone number, and we should keep these with us. He may call us, perhaps confused or after taking an overdose; and we need to know right where to send an ambulance or the police. We should also be sure to secure the name and address of at least one person in his life who can be counted on in an emergency.

The suicide danger is far from over merely because the patient feels better and assures us he doesn't have the impulse anymore. Actually, the jeopardy may be greatest just as the depression begins to lift. While the person was numbed by the heavy melancholy, he found it hard to do anything, even to kill himself. Feeling slightly better, he may now have the clarity and energy to go through with it.

Therapists whose patients once toyed seriously with committing suicide are likely to keep that threat in mind throughout the course of treatment. Even after the immediate threat is gone, we should familiarize ourselves with the kinds of events that might provoke the urge. For instance, the person falls in love and fears rejection, or is told he's failing at a job. We must stay attuned to just what causes him despair, never minimizing such events. It would be better to overstate what seems to be going wrong in his life and the distress he might feel than to give empty reassurance and minimize these things.

While being alert to events that might trigger the impulse, we devote ourselves to trying to discover the underlying problems and helping the patient overcome them. Not until we do this is he truly out of danger.

For instance, many such people are brutally perfectionist. They place enormous demands on themselves, and when they fall short of the mark, hate themselves. They are haunted by a slip or a failure, often one that they see but which no one else would notice. Included among such people are some adolescents, who take romantic rejection or even poor grades as a sign that they hardly deserve to live. Also included are hardworking, usually successful middle-aged people, who prided themselves on their accomplishments and reputation. Suddenly after a business setback, or when their children grow up and leave home, they fall into deep despair. They perceive everything they've achieved as worthless. Often they mistakenly conclude that what they've learned about life and the workings of the world is the source of their sadness, as if knowledge inevitably caused it. "Sorrow is knowledge," wrote Byron. "Those who know the most must mourn the deepest o'er the fatal truths." This is no more than an illusion harbored by certain depressed people.

We can work on problems of the perfectionist, even when they bear no immediate threat of suicide. For instance, a person berates himself repeatedly in front of us for a comment he made to someone. He would give anything not to have made it. It feels to him as if he ruined the whole relationship by that one statement, which seems harmless and easily forgivable to us. The next session, he apologizes repeatedly and fervently for being a few minutes late. We point out that the thing he despised himself for yesterday now seems utterly insignificant to him, and that he torments himself over a series of minor lapses, none of which prove to be costly. Regardless of how obvious this is to us, his most recent mistake seems different to him. This one seems really catastrophic. We must go deeper, helping him see what mistakes mean to him.

Nearly all people who become suicide risks have great difficulty coping with frustration. They find it hard to see past the moment. These patients bemoan each daily discomfort, as if some divinity had singled them out to test their endurance. A driver cut them off with his automobile or someone pushed ahead of them on line at the bank. Or we ourselves were slow to grasp something they thought was obvious. When things don't immediately go their way, such patients may become unmannerly or make wild accusations. We must help them deal with their low tolerance for frustration. Progress in achieving such tolerance insulates them against rash actions—including self-destructive behavior.

Many suicidal people, and nearly all those in their teens or early twenties, are narcissistic. They are selfish. While secretly doubting their own worth, they may estrange other people by what comes across as indifference or contempt. But the problem is less that they ruin relationships than that they devalue existence and themselves by the way they act. They destroy what might give them real pleasure in life. Being overly concerned with externals, when the real problem is inside, they feel helpless to solve their problems. Getting thin won't do it, nor will sporting a new car or going to the right resort. There is no substitute for continued investment in something steady and far away. It's as if for them there won't be a journey, there is only arrival.

There is no North Star in the sky to guide us unless we put one there, and the only way to do this is by trudging north, whatever that means to each of us. Only commitment can secure a sense of purpose and the feeling that life has real value. It may be commitment to a relationship, to education, or even to a hobby. The narcissist has not made such a commitment. The sense that others depend on us, need us, and that we can come through for them is a marvelous gift to ourselves. The narcissist is without this sense.

In dealing with suicidal people, we will often confront the argument, "I've tried everything, and nothing works." Some patients actually say this, a great many more feel it. We want these patients to see that, although they may feel they've exhausted life's possibilities, they haven't. There are complex ways of acting, and experiences available to them, that they've never thought about. When working with such people, I often convey that, in Newton's words, they've only been playing on the shore "while the great ocean of truth lay undiscovered before them." What a shame it would be to conclude their existence with so much yet to be sampled! By my own example, I want them to see also that it is not naive to wonder at the novelty of small things. Life is far too short without our thinking of terminating it prematurely.

We should try, not just with suicidal patients but with all, to communicate that life is too short anyhow and that it is much to be here, that in Shakespeare's words:

> *Ere man hath power to say "Behold!"*
> *The jaws of darkness do devour it up.*

To accept this message, I think, is to embrace life to the fullest.

39

The Problem of Referrals

Most therapists are quite dedicated. I think fewer of us would change our profession if given the chance than people in practically any other field. Naturally, therapists want money and social status. But the recognition we seek above all is as confirmation for our helping our patients repair their lives. Nearly all of us, when we started in private practice, felt some embarrassment at making a living this way. We were used to helping people for nothing. It's still hard for us to raise fees when we suspect that a patient will have trouble paying. Yet therapists need income and referrals, not just to pay their debts but also for their own sense of being effective. It's always a bracing experience when someone calls up and says he wants to work with us, even if we haven't got time to see the person. Someone must have liked what we did in order to recommend us.

No one wants to solicit clientele. To the degree that we've done this, we're likely to feel needy. It's a better experience when a patient, utterly delighted with the changes in him, exhorts a friend and he calls us. Still more satisfying, I think, is the experience of having someone observe a dramatic improvement in our patient, ask him what caused it, have the patient tell him about us, and then have the person call for himself. "I'm stunned at how Peter changed. I wish you could do the same for me."

The ideal is to help people so effectively that we don't have to announce our presence. We'd like to avoid asking other professionals for referrals, or telling our patients to send us people they know. We'd like to avoid the necessity to teach classes, give speeches, or attend workshops on how to improve our practice, most of which are thinly disguised as seminars on how to motivate patients. If we teach or volunteer time in a clinic or join a country club, we should do so for its own sake, whether or not it results in new patients coming to us. Also we should avoid the numerous ploys to get dissatisfied patients to stay with us, and to have patients send their friends. Among them are exaggerating the necessity of therapy, telling people who want to quit that they are really resisting and, by implication, that a big breakthrough is imminent. It doesn't follow that someone who doubts the value of our work is necessarily resisting. Possibly he is. But maybe we're not helping him, and he really should go.

I'm not going to discourse on how to get referrals, because the ultimate way to build a practice is to inspire people—by helping them. Our patients will make sure we stay busy. Their very enthusiasm will guarantee that other people come to us. But basic to success, even more important than the right credentials, are the therapist's exuberance and values. If we're models of how people want to be, our patients will stay with us, and send other people to us. If we're not, they won't—and shouldn't. Methods of replacing patients who keep leaving are aside from the point.

However, even among well-trained and otherwise effective therapists, there are some who have great difficulty in building their practice. Their patients apparently like them but don't send other people to them. Paradoxically, although these therapists help nearly everyone who comes to them, they have much more trouble getting patients than do less effective people in the field. Close inspection reveals that the problem lies in the nature of the relationships they form with their patients. Were they to ask a patient outright why he's never sent anyone to them, the patient would answer, "I don't want to share you with anyone else." If only one patient said this, we might assume it was a problem of the transference. But where many patients say it, we are led to suspect that it stems from the therapist's way of working, and in particular, his countertransference. In most such instances, the therapist is unconsciously forming a special alliance with his patient—we two against the world.

For instance, a woman therapist sides with her female patient through the patient's divorce, and is supportive afterward when the patient has trouble with men. She doesn't help her patient see where she is herself at fault in relationships, but instead sides with her continually. She sometimes stays overtime with the patient, and virtually implies that the person is her favorite. She lets the patient owe her money when times are hard, and in other ways fosters the sense that they have a valuable bond that no one else can share. Her patient feels deep allegiance toward her. There are never any storms between them. But the patient lets her know that she would never send anyone else she knows to this therapist.

Further analysis reveals that this therapist tends to do roughly the same thing with all her patients. She secures their allegiance by gratuitously supportive acts, and doesn't confront them head-on when their behavior is harmful to others. She has truly helped certain patients this way. But none of them would refer a friend or acquaintance, and most of them admit to feeling very possessive of her. Even worse, when they improve enough to feel capable of taking criticism, some leave her in favor of a therapist who charges more and will cherish them less. She feels heartbroken when they announce this decision, and they too feel sad. But they go because they recognize that something is missing.

Lurking in this problem is the therapist's unresolved sense

of inadequacy, which makes it hard to confront his patients. The therapist fears what the patient might say if infuriated. Ironically, this fear of losing the patient's favor, which motivates the overdelicate handling of the sessions, leads to the patient's finally leaving—a self-fulfilling fear. But then patients are constantly making judgments about whether we need them, emotionally and financially. If we seem to need them, we may resemble their parents, who found it hard to let them go. The patient feels suffocated and leaves. Only if we have achieved our own independence from them do patients truly believe in us. We are not possessive and neither are they. Our patients get the sense that they can stay or go; recognizing this option frees them to stay, and there seems no loss in their sending us other people.

Nearly everyone when entering this profession has been making a living some other way. A common mistake is to give up that source of income too soon. A therapist worried about his rent is almost certain to communicate that concern. People are remarkable at detecting neediness. Bad habits can develop, in the direction of catering to patients. One is ready to enter private practice full-time only when a sense of independence can be sustained. Some people can achieve this readily, others need long years of success as therapists before they can. I have seen therapists indebt themselves financially for luxuries, and then show the strain in their practice, with the result that patients withdrew from them, putting them in real trouble. The beginning therapist who can withstand the loss of some of his practice is far less likely to lose it than the one who can't. Probably this holds for people in nearly every profession, but it is especially true in this one. To be compromised is to be weak.

Which of those patients referred to us can we work with? Aside from the usual problems of deciding about a new patient, if the referral was made by another patient, we need to evaluate whether seeing this person will interfere with the therapy of whoever sent him.

Psychotherapists vary widely in their thinking. Some would automatically refuse to treat the new patient, and would immediately offer him the name of a colleague. They maintain that even if the two people don't discuss their respective therapies, for each the knowledge that the other is going to the same therapist makes the experience less private. It promotes competition and jealousy. This reaches a peak when the people are intimately involved—for instance, a married couple. Neither knows precisely what the other said about him. The therapist says something to the first patient who may take it in good faith, but later he suspects the therapist of having gotten the idea from his mate. "Who told you that?" he asks, and feels ganged up on.

Also, sometimes there's the problem that insights based on what we see in the hour may lose some of their force. It's very convincing when we observe something about the patient that dovetails with what others have told him. We've confirmed something he's suspected. But now the patient doesn't know whether we've observed the tendency or been told about it by the other person.

For instance, we observe that a man has trouble controlling his temper. He makes every effort to be polite with us. But we can feel this tendency in him when things don't go his way—in small moments of rigidity, in his facial expression, and in the effort he needs to stay courteous. It's easy to imagine how hard to get along with he can be. Ordinarily, were we to broach the subject, he might be stunned that we could observe this tendency. People seldom realize how recurrent their traits are. But now, when we bring it up, he feels sure that his wife told us about his violent outbursts at home. Our very insight may lead him to think that he's been betrayed.

Finally, there's the problem of our patients wanting to learn about one another from us. "Do you think may wife still loves me?" "My husband's having an affair. You don't have to tell me. I can see by the way you're reacting."

Marriage counseling is a very different field from individual psychotherapy. It doesn't pursue deep personal truths so comprehensively. Its purpose is to unblock a relationship.

The opposing argument is that any of these problems can be solved, that they are only grist for the mill. The person who, without cause, feels ganged up on, or who is in therapy not for himself but to learn about someone else, can come to terms with his purposes. Many people have no idea what to expect at the outset, and learn as they go. All professionals rely on recommendations from those to whom they have proven their skills. For the therapist to refuse this source would be to become paralyzed by his own purity.

Here I've merely wanted to set down the chief considerations. Every therapist must decide for himself who to take and who to refuse, and why. Absolute purity is inconceivable. It might turn out during treatment that one patient knew another. What should the therapist do then? Obviously, we can't go so far as to refuse to see any two people in the same profession, and such people are likely to meet at any time. On the other hand, people deserve a private experience in therapy. We can't automatically work with everyone whom our patients send to us.

My own thought is that, although I might see a couple for a while, and see the members individually, lovers deserve separate therapists. As the therapist, we come to symbolize their hope for that relationship. Inevitably, they have secrets from one another, as all people do, and we will be asked not to tell one person something we know about the other. In the extreme case, one person starts an extramarital affair, and tells us. Naturally, we can't tell the other person, but if he finds out, he is likely to feel that we betrayed him. We knew all the time.

On the other hand, I wouldn't hesitate to see people who knew each other, even if they interacted. Admittedly this can get sticky, as when two roommates quarrel heatedly. But we can survive these storms by staying out of them. When I started in practice, I had the rule never to mention one person to the other. Now that seems artificial to me. Of course, I would never pass along what one patient had told me, but would say only what I might if I didn't actually know the person being talked about. "Well, Diana has a lot more money than you do. For her, going to Europe doesn't mean the same thing." I myself have been surprised that I never create trouble this way.

The mere fact that a patient refers someone he knows, however, isn't sufficient license for us to work with that friend. The patient may not really want us to work with the person, but made the referral because it seemed the noble thing to do. One woman, among my first patients, was full of self-hate and had already tried suicide. I helped her considerably and she started sending women friends to me. After a while, I saw that she envied these women, whom she perceived as more attractive and desirable than she was. I appreciated her expression of belief in me, and felt complimented.

Before long, however, I observed that she felt distressed at their seeing me. She had love fantasies about me, and wanted to know if I would betray her, preferring them. She had a dream about my marrying one of them. It came out that just before her attempted suicide, she had introduced a man to a woman friend, and he had abandoned her for that woman. My patient then went home and took sleeping pills. There was a strong triangle that seemed to retain its hold on her, and I was being used to play a part. There seemed nothing to do but discourage referrals, and when I did, she felt elated.

Often people who refer others to us will assure us they have no misgivings, when they do. The very nature of their problem is eclipsing themselves and then feeling sorry. A variation is their having no misgivings at the start, but then growing gradually angry with us and wanting to quit themselves. They may never mention, and not even know the reason for their feeling of disappointment. But we owe it to them not to play a part in their self-destructive program. We should study carefully why the referral is being made, and not accept it if there seems any chance that the person making it will suffer as a result of it. People who habitually play down the importance of their own lives are especially liable to share us when they really don't want to.

When we do see people who know each other, certain ground rules can help. One is that they not discuss us or what went on in the hours. Almost surely, they would distort what we said, and if they don't, their attributing comments to us so as to give them clout is unfair. We want our patients to speak for themselves. Any violation of this should be studied at once, and if it continues, we may have to exercise our right to stop seeing one of the parties involved. I think it is best for us to stop seeing the person recommended, rather than the patient who sent that person, as if seniority governed. We can explain this decision. The person who has known us the shorter time is, as a rule, better able to sustain the loss. There are exceptions to this—for instance, if we feel very able to help the second person and might wish to stop with the first anyhow. But I have seen patients who felt replaced by a mate whom they sent to their therapist, and the experience was stinging.

It may occur that, to our surprise, a patient mentions someone whom we also treat. It's a tough spot. If we say nothing, he goes on talking about that person, assuming that we don't know him. Someday he may discover that we knew him well, and may feel undone. How could we let him ramble on without saying anything? But we can't betray a confidence. Our patients have the right to absolute privacy. We'll explain this when the time comes, if it does, and bank on our patient's appreciating why we did it. If it's a friend or acquaintance of ours whom he mentions, we have some option. It might be uncomfortable to let the patient go on, withholding that we know the person, and running the risk that the patient will find out, when there was really no reason not to tell him. If we decide it won't inhibit the patient to tell him, "Oh yes, I use that butcher also; he's very fair," it may not be a loss to say this. But even here, it's never our responsibility to mention whom we know, and errors should be on the side of not saying anything.

Then too, there's the complication of having a patient come to us, and tell us he's currently going to another therapist who doesn't know he's made the appointment with us. Many professionals feel that it's unethical to see such a person, that the right thing to do is to have him go back to the other therapist and work out whatever difficulty exists between them. Only when the patient has officially terminated should he come to us. The rationale is that patients in the throes of resistances often run away, and we would be on the side of his neurosis if we treated him.

But it seems to me there's more to it. Although some patients do run away from therapists without giving them a chance, many truly want a second opinion. Just as we, if we needed a surgeon or lawyer, would be entitled to a second point of view, so is the patient. Granted, he would be better off if he could explore the question with the therapist he is now seeing, but often he can't. He finds it impossible to bring up his doubts, or feels that when he does, the therapist crushes him. The fact is that there are many therapists who feel personally threatened when a patient questions their value. They turn every objection back on the patient, calling it a resistance. Perhaps he's going to one of these.

I think all we have the right to do is to help the person make an evaluation. We should encourage him to tell his present therapist that he saw us. Sometimes, it turns out that he's been going to a therapist of limited competence, which becomes obvious very quickly. But nearly always, it's impossible for him to reach a conclusion in our presence. We can help him identify what seems wrong, and, above all, encourage him to bring up his most significant complaints. Until he does so, he hasn't given his therapy its best chance. We send him back with a clearer sense of purpose. But before actually going to another therapist, he owes it to his present one to explore the subject, and to terminate in person. Merely slipping away is never good for him in the long run.

Finally, there's the issue of referring a patient to someone else. There are many reasons why we might do this. We're too busy, or he can't afford us, or we don't like him, or we don't feel we can help him, or we're treating a patient too close to him, or we know him socially and don't have the distance we need for leverage. Sometimes we merely provide a name, but often we might wish first to talk to the patient briefly in person or on the phone. If we plan to do this, we should tell him at the very outset that we're going to send him to someone else. If we first go into his life in an attempt to match him with the right therapist, and then offer someone else's name, we may cause him to feel rejected. He had hoped to work with us, and now might conclude that he wasn't interesting or important enough for us to want to work with him.

Unfortunately, referrals are sometimes made for the wrong reasons in this profession as in most others. Therapists sometimes select someone in a position to repay them with a patient, or send the patient along to someone merely because he has helped them with their practice. Another wrong reason is because some therapist we know, whom we may be training, is having trouble with his practice. Sending a human being along who will pay is not a legitimate gift to the needy. We have the obligation to do our best to find the most effective therapist whom the patient can afford.

Naturally, we're going to select someone we know if possible, and very likely a person with roughly our view of treatment and of life. A gestalt therapist is likely to find another, and might

advise someone not to go to a Freudian. Most orthodox analysts
have stuck together, perceiving the many variations of technique
as like the fall of Rome. Some practitioners emphasize the choice
between a man and a woman. For instance, they would send a
woman who has troubles with men to a female therapist, where
she would be more comfortable. The counterargument is that
this patient could overcome the problem more directly by going
to a man. The question is whether the person could best profit
by insight that might lead to different emotional experiences
outside the therapy, or should seek the most therapeutic experience within the hour. I almost never decide that the therapist
should be of a certain sex, although sometimes the prospective
patient has a preference and I abide by it. Twenty years ago,
nearly everyone wanted a male therapist, but this has changed,
and often I no longer ask if the person has a preference, which
I used to do.

In distinguishing between therapists who seem equally competent, we still have many differences to consider. All therapists
have specialties. We can't be in different places at the same time.
Some have a slow tempo and seemingly infinite patience. With
a depressed patient, who takes a lot of time to formulate his
position, they can wait and not burst with impatience. A more
high-strung person would be tempted to plunge in, to fill up the
voids with his own conversation, and thus upstage the patient or
conceal the fact that the patient is waiting for the world to ar-
range itself. This would prevent the patient from appreciating
the depth of his own passivity. On the other hand, that same
therapist might be at a loss with certain fast-talking and articulate
patients who disrespect those who seem unable to keep up with
them. They need someone equally swift and articulate to confront them. So wide are the differences even among capable
therapists that perhaps every beginning therapist has a scope of
at least some patients whom he can help more effectively than
seasoned experts who, by their nature, are not equipped to work

with those particular types. In whatever time we have to spend with the prospective patient, and make the judgment, we try to take all these things into account.

At one time, I might have said that we should also look for common interests. Has the therapist lived similarly to the patient, and come from the same social class? Does he share the same hobbies, activities? Was he once in the same profession? If so, time could be saved. They might share metaphors, and communication might be easier when those commonalities were touched. But a commensurate loss is that the therapist from a wholly different environment, unfamiliar with the patient's special interests, can learn about them fresh, evaluating what the patient says in the light of what he knows from elsewhere. Patients often request a therapist conversant with their kind of life, and I comply; but this has its drawbacks as well as advantages.

When making a referral, I usually tell the person that, although I can vouch for the therapist's skill and integrity, he should be guided by his own feelings. I can't vouch for the chemistry between the two people who are to form the relationship. I remind the patient that if he doesn't like the person, or feels very uncomfortable, it may be a response to his going into therapy, but it may also be a reaction to the individual. We can talk about it on the phone, and he can decide whether to continue.

I nearly always tell the patient to call me after a session or two, to let me know his plans. Patients are very grateful for this. They're not being cut loose and abandoned. On occasion I've had a patient call objecting to something about the therapist I'd recommended, which I'd glossed over or hadn't seen. Sometimes they've made objections that seemed to me unwarranted. But, even so, I couldn't in good conscience insist that they go back and work it out. It would be different if the patient had tried a great many therapists and felt the same way. But if there's a good chance that the person would feel much better about someone else just as competent, it seems to me that it makes no sense for him to try to overcome misgivings about the therapist while trying to deal with a psychological problem.

It's a wonderful feeling, however, when the patient calls up to thank us for the excellent choice of therapist we made. This kind of call confirms our judgment, and the patient's decency, and it's always pleasant to hear praise for someone we know and respect.

40

The First Session

The first session is a showdown, a first date, a chance to exhibit one's expertise, a glorious opportunity to learn about a new person, to display genius or incompetence. It's then that the patient forms his impression of the therapist's personality; he judges the therapist by his appearance, and especially by how comfortable he is in his own skin, and how personally successful he is in his own life.

I've sometimes heard therapists say, "I'm bad at first sessions"; they're referring to the fact that patients very often decide against going to them after the first session. But the patient isn't thinking about whether the therapist is good at first sessions —say as opposed to fourth sessions or fortieth sessions. He's judging the therapist's ability to help him. The only reason he quits after the first session, instead of the fortieth, is that he doesn't wait that long. The therapist is like the conductor of a train that crashes into another. It's true that the first car gets crushed, but were it removed, whatever car then became the lead car would suffer the disaster.

The most important feature of the first session, I think, is the transaction of feelings between patient and therapist. When training therapists, I've observed that the way they answer two questions correlates highly with their success at first sessions, and as therapists generally: "What feelings did you have toward the patient during the hour?" "What different feelings did the patient have toward you?"

Therapists who do poorly may have no idea how the patient felt. The very question seems perplexing. They resort to describing the patient, giving details about the problem or about his childhood. It's a sorry substitute. Successful therapists, or those on their way to succeeding, are full of detail. They might recall moments in which the patient felt crowded by too many questions; others when he felt apologetic. "In the end, the patient liked me. I could tell from his smile, and he talked about 'us' working on a problem. And he was eager to schedule another hour."

The second half, "What feelings did you have during the hour?" is equally easy for the good therapist and perplexing to the therapist who didn't make a real connection. What the feelings were is not the determinant of success. It's that the therapist was sensitive to what they were. The beginner may be hesitant to acknowledge his reaction, but at least he has it. "When the patient talked about his house in the country, I felt very competitive and angry with him. I'm afraid I acted on that impulse, because I told him that I was going to India for a month." Such a slip won't be ruination. The important thing is that the therapist, alert to his own reactions and behavior, sees it now. He can brace himself to spot those feelings next time and not to respond the same way. He's in a much better position to help the patient than if he didn't recognize the reaction.

Through the instrument of our feelings, even in the first session, we sense how the patient feels, how he may get into trouble with others, and how he might make other people feel. We make judgments about how to work with him. For instance, an early resistance may be manifested in his contradicting us. Or if we say something cogent, he's apt to look for a fault in our grammar. We see that he hates to be told anything. On the other hand, the patient loves to be asked questions. He enjoys pontificating. So we'll work this way for a while.

Often after a patient has left my office, I've found myself with some ideas but many more feelings than I could make sense of. That night, or some time during the next few days, the feelings would tell me something. For instance, I got a deep sense of being hated, of something being hidden, or the recognition that in spite of a patient's sarcasm, he was counting on me to save his life. Those feelings could be used to formulate a much better sense of the patient when he came in next time.

As therapists, we convey few of our reactions to the patient, but we use them. If we sense we're pressuring the person by too many questions, we let up. If we sense that a dead silence is frightening the patient, we may ask a question. We feel it when the patient is appreciative and when the patient bristles because he doesn't want to talk about a certain subject. As in life, the combination of sensibility and the ability to assimilate experience without reacting impetuously will almost always assure success. The cultivation of our emotional responsiveness along with self-mastery isn't something the patient credits us with. It's not something most people can see, but the patient feels it.

Vital for getting therapy started on the right foot are three traits, which I want to discuss. The therapist must be *separate* as an individual, personally *engaged* with the patient, and *purposeful.* Therapists whose patients come back, and are right to come back, show these qualities in the very first session. If asked to identify why they did or didn't feel excited or hopeful about therapy, very few patients could identify these traits in the therapist. But a remarkably wide range of patients respond to the presence or absence of these traits.

By *separateness* as an individual, I mean that the therapist wants to help the patient, but not necessarily to please him. He conveys a strong potentiality to confront the patient where necessary. He keeps distance without disdain. He has a clear-cut point of view about how personality develops and how to treat people. He wants to understand the patient's plight, but may not accept the patient's explanations for it. He may not communicate that he agrees with his point of view or even that he likes him. But he is able to help him.

The contrary, which helps define what I mean by separateness, is to merge with the patient. Therapists who do this seem bent on showing that they understand how the patient feels and why, even before's he's told them. They seem eager to please, and may try to do so by conveying that there's nothing basically wrong with the patient, and that they too are like him. It's an attempt to show deep commiseration and loyalty, so that the patient will feel comfortable. Why should he go anywhere else? But often the patient doesn't come back, and these therapists, to their dismay, see him go off to someone who appears less well intended and who seems to understand the patient less well. The problem of merging is serious, and many patients pick it up fast and don't like it.

For one thing, they may sense it as a sign of weakness. It's as if the therapist didn't trust his own talent and was buying the patient's involvement by agreeing with whatever he said. The patient senses he won't receive an independent point of view. When he complains about other people, and the therapist instantly backs him up, the patient wonders, "How can he be sure I'm not really at fault? As far as he knows, I might be making the whole thing up."

Nearly everyone, including those who vociferously blame others, have some sense that they may be more at fault than they're letting on. They want a therapist capable of confronting them, of telling them what's wrong with them, not someone they can gull.

The therapist who merges by "understanding" everything

the patient says as soon as he says it is actually insulting the patient. He's implying that the patient must be rather shallow and obvious. The therapist's independence of mind is important because it challenges the patient to reconsider his own position. Every patient wants this; the last thing the patient needs is someone with exactly his own point of view.

Being emotionally engaged with the patient is vital in getting treatment under way. We try to get the feel of who he is, and particularly why he came and how he wants to change. To be pasty and lacking in energy is a crime, especially at the start. We must meet him squarely. We are eager to hear whatever is on his mind.

Very possibly, the patient has thought about therapy for a lifetime, considered it and toyed with the idea of going. There are key things he's wanted to talk about. Also, he may well have worried about the severity and curability of whatever seems wrong with him. For ages he's been afraid to reveal himself to an expert, who he expected might be appalled. We're not appalled. We don't shy away from what's most critical to him. In addition, we offer warmth, humor, and energy of involvement with him. If he's not being clear about something, we at least are clear that we haven't understood it and ask him to go over it again. We give him a solid contact with us.

Beginners, especially therapists trained in clinics and hospitals, tend to ask a battery of questions. "How old are you?" "How many brothers and sisters?" And so forth. As part of intake interviews, such questions had many purposes. They helped the interviewer classify the patient, decide on his diagnosis, and determine the kind of treatment that seemed most fitting. The person asking questions was in most instances not the one who would be doing the actual therapy. Also they provided a shield the therapist could hide behind. Often he didn't know what to do, and imagined that such questions would do no harm while he made up his mind.

But it is simply not true that a question is harmless. Everything we say and do sets the direction of therapy, expresses our values, has meaning to the patient. We can never just gather information from a patient without affecting him. For instance, one therapist routinely asks patients in the first session how much formal education they've had. He imagines that the answer may help him and that it can't hurt him to know. Certainly knowledge in itself can never be harmful. But the question suggests a value. Patients might sense that such a therapist stresses formal education—or is stiffly conventional. That seemingly innocuous question might deter a patient from telling the therapist about some perversion of his, which in the light of the question seems hopelessly disqualifying.

I am strongly against going down a list of demographic questions in the first session, or ever. Although they give the therapist something to do, they avoid the main issues. And they avoid the interaction, the way note-taking does. We will learn what we need to know about the patient's life as we go along. And when we need to know something relevant to what he's saying, we can ask. Asking the patient, apropos of nothing, what country his parents came from can sidetrack the person and reduce the depth of inquiry. I want to make the first session as personal as possible.

If we are keying in to what the patient is really telling us, we have more truly relevant questions than we can ever get to ask. Therapists who insist on asking their demographic battery of questions, reminiscent of those on a job application, are in many cases afraid of having to be on their own with the patient. By staying with their battery, they prevent themselves from learning how to draw the patient out, and may never learn. The therapist who takes the chance, gets the patient to talk about what is most central in his life, and asks questions only where necessary, constantly refines his techniques of getting people to talk about themselves. The difference in skill and ease widens over the years. In many instances, the insistence on going through a battery of questions in the first sessions is a subtle attempt by the therapist, not himself a medical doctor, to look like one. In other cases, it's a countertransference resistance. The therapist, in questioning the patient, is actually avoiding contact with him.

Just as a medical doctor's questions are mostly geared to pick up symptoms that might correlate with a given problem, so should the therapist's be. But the therapist will be seeing his patient regularly over a period of time and will learn demographic facts in the course of this time. In the fourth session, if the patient has been dwelling on one brother and a younger sister, the therapist might wish to ask if there are more siblings. The patient will tell him, and by then the patient's very emphasis on the two he talked about will be information. To require equal time for each sibling would make no sense at all. Our questions should be germane to our purpose.

We should have a reason for every question we ask. An Adlerian psychoanalyst might, for instance, ask a patient about his brothers and sisters, and where the patient stood in the birth order. A Jungian might ask about recent dreams. But this is quite different from seeking knowledge on the mere grounds that some day an answer may prove relevant.

The third quality that a patient reacts to, and ought to react to, is purpose. He ought to come away from the first session with a much clearer idea of what therapy is, and what it can do for him, than he came in with. Recall the chapter on motivating patients. We ought, in the very first session, to start to identify precisely how the patient wants to change. As therapy progresses, the patient may enlarge his ambitions for himself, and the very first session may begin this process. In essence, we want to place squarely in front of him the differential between who he is and who he can be.

For instance, we help a man see that he does too many things for other people, that he lives like a pack animal and then gets furious at friends and loved ones. He sensed for many years that his life was harder than it had to be. But he lacked sufficient self-love to know for sure. We articulate it for him. An aim of therapy would be for him to stop compromising so much against his better judgment. He must learn to see on the spot when he should hold his position or be sorry later. If we ask in the first session about his past life, it is to elucidate the history of this trait.

Moreover, we want him to see that he himself has been reproducing the perceptions that now haunt him—for instance, the idea that if he stops, people will be infuriated with him, and may leave him, or that they will fall apart. We want every patient to get a sense that he himself has been making crucial choices, that he is much less a victim than he thought. We can start in the very first session helping patients see not just the nature of their problem, but that they themselves have all along been perpetuating it. This is why merging, as by joining the patient in blaming other people, is such a disservice. The patient comes away with an ally, but feeling more hopeless than ever. On the other hand, as we reveal to him his own choices, not reprovingly but decisively, we inspire him with whole new potentialities—and they are real.

Among our aims in the first session should be to decide whether we ourselves should work with him; we can only reach such a decision when we know what he wants for himself. There's no need to mystify the person, or use razzle-dazzle interpretations, as if we were mountebanks with some special elixir. If we ourselves retain focus, and help him define how he wants to change, and how he is keeping himself the same, we are simultaneously revealing to him the enormous potential he has.

The variation is considerable in how therapists conduct their first session. No blueprint is possible, since we inquire into areas of special theoretical importance to us. We make contact differently, and in fact our relationship with each new patient differs, or should differ, from that with previous ones.

Although nearly everything that happens in the course of therapy can occur incipiently in the first session, there is the very special issue of ground rules. Nearly all therapists lay down at least some of their requirements toward the end of the first session. Among them are that the patient arrive on time, that he say whatever comes into his mind, and that he not talk about his sessions with anyone else. He's free to tell others ideas he discovered in his sessions, but it would be better if he didn't quote us or discuss what took place during the hour.

Most therapists announce their fee near the end of the hour, or possibly discuss it with the patient; they tell the patient at what intervals they want him to pay them. We ask him to let us know as far in advance as possible if he must cancel a session, and most therapists announce their policy concerning charging for missed sessions. Some discuss vacation times, possibly to give the patient the option to choose someone else who won't be out of town as long.

Although none of this is in itself objectionable, I think that too often a staccato presentation of ground rules can set the tone of the session. Theoretically, one could tell the patient one's every principle of treatment, saying, for instance, "I won't be talking about my personal life in here." But, it seems to me, that can wait. If the patient asks some question that it wouldn't be right to answer, the therapist can explain his policy. And to my mind, the same holds for some of the other ground rules mentioned. For instance, I no longer tell patients that I expect them to be on time for their sessions. I feel that it is implicit for them as well as for me. I wouldn't tell them that I expected myself to be on time, and it seems a bit condescending to say to another person, who has not yet been late, that I expect him to be on time. Even without laying this groundwork, I feel I have full license to ask a patient why he was late, or to discuss a cancellation and possibly interpret it as indifference or avoidance.

Also, in the first session we're very likely to be asked

questions about ourselves and how therapy works. The patient has every right to ask us our credentials, what degree we have, where we were trained, how long we've been in practice. These are very legitimate questions, although in no field do mere credentials assure competency. These are questions we ourselves might ask of a surgeon or hematologist, especially if we didn't know other people whom he had treated. We owe such questions straightforward answers.

Yet I've heard many therapists say that such questions were out of place, and I've seen therapists become ruffled by them. We have absolutely no right to shirk them or to be umbrageous about them, and certainly no right to construe them as resistance. I think that anyone who saw that his prospective therapist had trouble with such questions would be well advised to doubt his competence. There is absolutely no excuse not to answer them simply and at once. If the therapist in any way undermined the patient's right to ask, in my opinion that would be good reason for the person to look for someone else. I'm not passing judgment here on which credentials or experience qualify a therapist. But, obviously, if the therapist himself is so uncomfortable with his own qualifications that he feels he has to hide them, then his own sense of fraud is almost sure to affect his work in many other places.

Moreover, we ought to allow our patients to question everything we do. No ground rule need be a mystery. Perhaps we can't explain in full why we won't talk about ourselves, but we can give the patient an idea of how it could interfere with his best interests over the long run. There is a very occasional patient who, if he could question us about everything, would spend all his time getting us to explain ourselves. With such a patient, I might refuse to answer more than one or two questions (and those only at the end of the hour). But it's a good idea to tell patients to ask about anything that troubles them or seems a mystery, and a good time to do it may be in the first or second session. "Is there anything you want to know about therapy, or how we're going to work?" The patient may not have a question at the time, but our very asking gives him a sense of freedom and equality.

Both therapist and patient have to make a decision about whether they will work together. The patient may not be able to decide on the spot. Perhaps he wants to think over the experience of the hour, and call at a later time. He should certainly be given that opportunity. Or the therapist may have his doubts. He might tell the patient that he thinks another course would be preferable, perhaps offering to provide him another therapist's name. It may be that the two should schedule a handful of sessions to decide whether they will continue together. No arrangement should be ruled out if it seems useful for helping the patient find his best course of action. But if the therapist doesn't want to go on, he certainly should stay in touch with the patient until he has made other arrangements, the exception being if the patient wants no further contact with him.

Ideally, both therapist and patient will be glad after the first session that they have discovered one another. The therapist has found traits in the patient that he genuinely admires. The two have a shared sense of what they're going to work on, at least to start out with. There's a sense of adventure ahead for both of them.

41

Termination

Ending any relationship, or even a phase of it—like leaving a friend at the end of a day, going to sleep, winning the final point of a game, finishing a painting, or writing the last page of a book —can be exquisitely sad and difficult to do. Suddenly the beauty of what we no longer possess becomes apparent. Like parents at a child's school graduation, or later when the child rents his first apartment away from home, or during his marriage ceremony, we are struck by finality. We realize the preciousness of what we once possessed, and never will have again.

As therapists, even when termination is clearly called for, we may feel the impulse to hang on. We feel shocked when the patient tells us he's had enough. We still see much to be done. We imagine continued need for our services. A therapist can always find further problems in his patient, which therapy might help to solve. Our perfectionist zeal may mount. Also we'd like to correct our mistakes, and we suddenly see possible emendations everywhere. It's not easy to let go after we've been wholly committed to anything. Many of us have overstayed in relationships, remembering their splendid beginnings and refusing to acknowledge how much they've changed. And we may do the same as therapists.

But as with our own lives, endings will come, and I think our only defense against them is to be mindful of them, of the brevity of all that is given to us. It would help many therapists to say to themselves while they still have full access to their patient, "This person will soon be gone. What will I then wish I had said or done?" To deepen the time we have makes the letting go easier. But whether or not we have done this, our hanging on can sour an experience that might have been excellent, but must necessarily have been imperfect.

Many therapists have trouble letting go. Cynics might argue that this is because they want the money, but usually that's an insignificant part of it, if it is any part at all. Therapists are apt to have the problem even with patients who pay them much less than their usual fee, and whom they could replace in a day by someone who would pay them more. Therapy is for many of us a highly romantic experience, a form of love relationship, despite its one-sidedness. Toward the end, we see the double-image of the patient as he is now, and as he was then. We fortressed him against a world of harms, and now, because we did such a good job, he no longer needs us. We must grow up along with him, and accept his independence, and even admire the force he may have acquired under our very eyes.

We can usually sense when a patient is thinking about ending therapy, for right or wrong reasons, in a variety of ways. We may observe a lack of subject matter, or less enthusiasm than in the past. At one time, therapy was the center of his life; now it seems secondary. His wish to leave may surface in dreams—for instance, that an authority is hurt or angry with him. When we ask about the person, we recognize ourselves as the one he's afraid to displease by departing. We may get the sense that he would already have stopped were it not for his guilt.

Consider first the case in which it's truly time for the patient to go. Perhaps we've done wonders for him, and although we'll miss him, we realize that he's come to the end. He is no longer shy. He doesn't have the sexual problem he began with. He is no longer in pain when alone, and is much freer with other people. He is able to love, and never thought he could. He *is* in love, and we're happy for him. There are always more things a person can do for himself, but he can do them without us.

The idea of stopping may come from him or from us. Perhaps we observe him wandering in the sessions. He's appreciative and warm but isn't sure what to work on. On occasion he may ask us. There was a time when he had so much to say that the sessions seemed much too short. Now certain basic problems are solved; there are other battles to be won, and we talk about them. But he seems unmotivated. He feels he's done enough in therapy, and tells us.

The time has come to help him prepare to leave. For the first time we talk explicitly about his leaving, what it will mean to him. We review his accomplishments, and talk about the pitfalls still ahead. We discuss how he feels about leaving, and about us in particular. We ask him to talk about the whole experience of therapy and what it meant to him. In fact, if there is anything that he may wish in the future that he had said to us, and didn't say, we want him to say it.

An important way we can make the ending easier for him is by talking about ourselves. In many cases, our very secrecy about our private life has created its own mystique. It has imbued the sessions with a magic, which was helpful but now stands in the way. Not knowing us, he feels he may never meet anyone else like us. No one else will have our aura. If we talk about ourselves more, giving him some carefully chosen facts that we withheld for the sake of the transference, we start to reduce this magical hold on the patient. We're flesh and blood. It's not that he thinks less of us now that he knows we're married and where we send our children to camp, or other facts about how we live. But as we become specific individuals to him, the mystique dissipates. Leaving seems more feasible.

Finally, we set a date for the last session. It could be a few months away, or more. It should not be less than a month. As the time draws closer, we talk about termination and what it will mean. I think we should touch the subject in virtually every session as therapy draws to a close.

The last session is special. No matter how many times we've gone over it, I think in that session we owe the patient a clear statement of what he's accomplished. We might also talk with him about the challenges ahead. We may talk too, in that last session, about his personal strengths and weaknesses, and perhaps mention one last time what tendencies in himself he should watch out for, and underscore his personal greatness. We make it clear that though we will no longer be seeing him at the regular time, his personal evolution will continue in exactly the same way.

Especially in that last session, we should not hold back delight at his achievements. Naturally, we feel sorry to lose touch with him. But we must stay aware of whatever misgivings we have, and not do anything to inhibit his departure. Often I tell the person that I would be eager to hear from him, a phone call or a brief note letting me know how things are going. And, of course, if he wants to schedule some further sessions, I will be available. Nearly always, the person thanks us, and we will remind him for the last time that we identified problems but the real accomplishments were his.

The patient who wishes to terminate prematurely presents a very different picture. He has fought us off from some region of his life, or perhaps completely. In many cases he has been artificial with us, or downright fraudulent. He has let us know he won't commit himself—by cancelling hours, forgetting to pay us, or by spending his time bragging about his life and accomplishments. It's a deadly sign when a patient assures us that he has no problems, that all is going well. Healthy people are full of unresolved areas in their lives. Whether or not they wish to continue in therapy with us, they are greedy to understand themselves better and to take more as they go along. More often than not, the patient who has problems but doesn't want to work on them becomes angry with us. He sees us as threatening his repressive devices. He wants to leave but for a time doesn't know how. Such people may finally make the break by simply not returning, and either not calling us or offering us the slimmest of pretexts as to why they don't want to continue.

Many of these people never believed in therapy to begin with. They came because someone demanded it of them, or because they were in acute pain and there seemed nothing to lose. Even then, they felt a strong desire to defeat us, to disprove the validity of therapy. Or they saw therapy as a battle of wits, and sought to prove that they were smarter than any therapist. Common is the situation in which a person started in therapy when things were bad, and wants to quit as soon as they get better, even if the improvement was purely circumstantial.

For instance, a very narcissistic man entered therapy saying that he couldn't form a lasting relationship. He went back and forth between disparaging women and professing to be at fault. "Somehow I must be to blame, though I don't see how." It turned out that a woman had just walked out on him, and he had gone for help because he wanted to get her back. He talked about his pain, but what he really wanted was strategy. He never actually examined why she left him or would consider what might be wrong with him. The therapist struggled hard to motivate him, trying to help him see that this had happened before and would keep happening unless he worked on himself. He sought to utilize the patient's pain over rejection to get him to examine his own personality. However, the woman, who was herself rather shaky, responded to this patient's late-night call, and the two of them got together again. The patient quit therapy the next day saying there was nothing more to work on.

We can't talk such a person into continuing, and we

shouldn't try. But we do owe him a clear statement of how we see him. He has problems that will, very likely, worsen his life. He ought to work on them. We spell out what they are, and recommend that he continue therapy with us, or see someone else. He may even agree with us in words, but we sense that he wants to get away as fast as possible. Being expedient himself, he may ascribe to us only self-serving motives in wanting him to continue. However, we have done our best.

Such people may cause us pain because, although they don't care about their inner lives, we do. There's always a feeling with them that we've failed. We scour our performance, wondering how we might have been more effective. It's important not to let such people turn us against ourselves. Narcissists especially get others to engage in self-recriminations.

It's very important with these people not to make complete fools of ourselves during the last session. Some therapists plead their case with a person who has already decided to leave. They sense while doing this that they look beggarly to the patient, but find it hard to stop. Either we recognized all along that he wasn't committed or we're just finding it out. Either way, it's too late. Our words are feeble once he's told us he's going. If he's testing us, we should let him go, and he will have his answer: We don't need him, but were willing to work with him for his sake. If he's not testing us, then our pleas are nothing more than attempts to assuage our own sense of narcissistic injury. We had ample time to use whatever techniques we could to help him see the truth.

I've also seen therapists in anger make dire predictions about the patient. "If you leave now, you'll never have what you want," or use hideous diagnoses to scare the person into staying. The psychiatrist Lawrence Kubie told Tennessee Williams that if he didn't give up his homosexuality he would never achieve greatness as a playwright. Such predictions and diagnoses are like a lover's angry phone call when he's been rejected. Dignity at the end befits us, and if there's any small chance that the person will try therapy again, with us or someone else, we've preserved it.

Between the ideal termination and the premature one are the great majority of endings. Most patients are conflicted about stopping. Therapy may take violent turns just as it seems to be ending smoothly, or, at the other extreme, there are patients who clutch on and refuse to consider that an end should ever come.

That we've been associated with a person's success is enough to create uncertainty over how necessary we are. He's experiencing a different universe than he did before we came into the picture. It remains to be proven that he can do the same when we're gone. Besides, there's real loss. He could count on us as a repository of knowledge about him, and perhaps the sessions brought tremendous pleasure. It is understandable that many patients, deliberately or not, act in ways that suggest that maybe they shouldn't stop.

Sudden regressions are common. Real problems, which seemed to have been solved back in the past, rear up. Suddenly the patient reports being afraid to go on trains; his fits of temper come back, or his fear of being alone. Naturally, we want to hear about these incidents. We may even learn to expect them, and don't dismiss them. However, we recognize their function, and know that these symptoms will probably be short-lived. In other instances, the patient unexpectedly reveals things about himself that he had withheld throughout the course of treatment. He lets us know that he's having an extramarital affair or tells us some childhood incident that still troubles him. These may be more than attempts to prolong treatment. The patient, aware that therapy is drawing to a close, may realize that if he continues to withhold some important truth, he will have cheated himself. He always intended to talk about it, but kept postponing the day. Now he realizes that the day will never come unless he creates it.

Whether the patient has relapsed or told us some new and important truths about himself, if he wants to continue for a while, we may accede to his wishes. Even if the recrudescence of symptoms is an attempt to test us, I think we should go along with him. We are still aiming toward the end of treatment, but we are open to changing our schedule with him.

Especially with patients who seem conflicted, it's important to keep asking the person how he feels about us. Perhaps he'll tell us that in certain respects we failed; we never understood him as he had hoped we would. He may be right, or it may be that he yearned for an ease of communication that is impossible. The infant, who doesn't know how his mother can infer so much about his feelings, imagines that she can read his mind. Our patient may still harbor this infantile hope, and we have disappointed him. Either way, the important thing is to listen and not to defend ourselves. We don't want to end the last session with an argument, and very likely, we can't be absolutely certain of the truth, any more than he can.

It might help to taper off, perhaps scheduling a few monthly sessions before the end. But I usually prefer to finish distinctly and tell the patient he can call and schedule hours if he wants them. This relieves him of the necessity to return when he may not be in the mood. Some patients get busy with their own lives and are then sorry they made the appointment. Why should we burden them? Those same people might want to consult with us even years later over something big that comes up, such as a job opportunity or some other major decision. When the person does come in, even if much sooner, it's because he chose to do so. It feels different to him. He has a sense that his therapy is over. Some do this as a way of reconfirming our presence. Then they're gone for good, knowing that we're available, but knowing too that they can do quite well without us. We certainly don't want our patients imagining that every petty psychological problem calls for a consultation with us.

For some therapists the hardest problems are presented by patients who make an addiction out of therapy. They hang on, making clear that they'd feel utterly devastated if the therapist even suggested that he'd done all he could for them. Complicating the problem is that these people may really be getting something positive. But then there is always a possibility of improvement for all of us, and we could better use our time helping others.

Many of these people are isolates. They enjoy the undivided attention we give them, and which they may find nowhere else. Others are engaged in life but feel it is too much for them. They seem always to be facing some emergency that they need to discuss with us. Whatever time we contemplated stopping would seem the very moment they needed us most. They find the sessions gratifying beyond anything else in their lives.

Nearly always, the difficulty resides with the patient and also with the therapist's way of working. Dependent patients are likely to transfer their excessive needs onto us. Our task is to help them appreciate the real choices they are making—in particular to see how they are opting for dependency. We help them to discover the history of their fear, and to understand precisely what they are afraid of. We oversee their efforts as they gradually depart from this pattern, and as they take new chances. We study with them the fears that mount, and we help them develop the strength to make mistakes.

Once again, the warning about doing the work for the patient becomes important. To the extent that we take on the burden, making fancy interpretations, giving constant support as if the patient would collapse without it, we nurture his dependency on us. Our theory and practice must both be robust. We thus start our incursions against overdependency very early in treatment. Problems of termination are in large part a measure of how well we've done, just as a young adult's independence measures how well the parent has given him space and opportunity.

The mark of a successful therapist is not that his patients stay forever, but that they leave with what they came to acquire.

Index

Index